OS X Yosemite

CHRIS KENNEDY

Questing Vole Press

OS X Yosemite
by Chris Kennedy

Editor: Bill Gregory
Proofreader: Pat Kissell
Compositor: Birgitte Lund
Cover: Questing Vole Press

Contents

1 OS X Basics 1

About This Book 1

What's New 2

Installing Yosemite 7

Startup 8

User Accounts 9

Logins & Logouts 12

The Keyboard 16

The Mouse 19

The Trackpad & Multitouch Gestures 21

Menus 22

Toolbars 24

Icons 25

Windows 26

Scrolling 27

Dialog Boxes & Controls 28

Get Info 28

Transferring Content 29

Getting Help 31

System Information 31

Preferences 32

2 The Desktop 33

The Dock 34

Stacks 37

Exposé 38

Spaces 40

Dashboard & Widgets 42

Full-Screen Apps 44

Mission Control 45

Hiding Programs 46

Organizing Desktop Icons 46

Notification Center 47

3 System Preferences **51**

System Preferences 51
Accessibility 53
App Store 54
Bluetooth 54
CDs & DVDs 54
Date & Time 55
Desktop & Screen Saver 56
Dictation & Speech 58
Displays 62
Dock 63
Energy Saver 64
Extensions 66
General 67
iCloud 68
Internet Accounts 71
Keyboard 71
Language & Region 72
Mission Control 72
Mouse 72
Network 72
Notifications 72
Parental Controls 72
Printers & Scanners 72
Security & Privacy 72
Sharing 72
Sound 73
Spotlight 74
Startup Disk 74
Time Machine 74
Trackpad 74
Users & Groups 74

4 Files, Folders & Drives **75**

System Folders 76
Home Folder 76
Finder 78
Folder Views 82
Quick Look 85
Managing Files & Folders 86
Spotlight 93
Smart Folders 97
Burning CDs & DVDs 98
Drives 99

5   **Programs & Documents**.. **101**

Installing & Removing Programs... 102

Opening, Switching & Quitting Programs 104

Running Older Programs... 106

Saving Documents... 107

Opening Documents... 109

Associating Documents with Programs............................. 109

Applications & Utilities... 111

Services.. 130

6   **Printing, Faxing & Fonts** **133**

Setting Up a Printer.. 134

Printing Documents.. 136

Controlling Printouts.. 138

Sharing a Printer.. 139

Faxing... 139

Fonts... 140

7   **Networks & Sharing** **143**

Types of Networks... 144

File Sharing... 146

The Shared Folder.. 149

Screen Sharing.. 150

CD & DVD Sharing.. 151

Bluetooth Sharing.. 151

Share Sheets.. 152

Twitter Integration.. 152

Facebook Integration... 153

AirPlay Mirroring.. 153

Continuity & Handoff.. 154

8   **Online Connections**.. **155**

Connection Order.. 156

Broadband Connections.. 157

Ad-hoc Networks... 158

Dial-up Connections... 158

Network Locations... 159

Internet Sharing... 159

VPN Connections... 160

9   **Security & Privacy**... **161**

Firewall.. 162

FileVault.. 163

Keychain Access... 164

Parental Controls... 166

Password Assistant.. 167

Secure Virtual Memory.. 167

Privacy Settings.. 168

10 Maintenance & Backups **169**

    Software Updates 170

    Power Nap 171

    Time Machine 172

    Target Disk Mode 174

11 Switching from Windows **175**

12 Keyboard Shortcuts **179**

    Accessibility 180

    Apple Menu 180

    Dashboard 181

    Dialog Boxes 181

    Dock 182

    Finder 182

    Folder Navigation & Icons 184

    Frozen Programs 186

    Menus 186

    Mouse Keys 186

    Programs, Exposé, Spaces & Launchpad 187

    Screenshots 187

    Spotlight 188

    Startup 188

    Trash 189

    Windows 189

Index **191**

OS X Basics

On your Apple Mac computer, OS X 10.10—better known as Yosemite—is the software that controls:

The user interface
OS X manages the appearance, behavior, and interaction of the windows, buttons, icons, folders, cursors, menus, pointers, and other visual elements on your screen, either directly or indirectly through another program.

Storage
OS X's file system allocates space for and gives access to files—programs and documents—stored on drives or in memory.

Other software
OS X is a launching platform for programs. Word, iTunes, The Sims, and all Mac programs rely on the services and building blocks that OS X provides for basic operations such as drawing a user interface, saving files, and sharing hardware.

Peripheral devices
OS X controls or syncs with peripheral hardware such as your mouse, keyboard, trackpad, display, printer, scanner, external drives, digital camera, ereader, smartphone, iPhone, iPad, and iPod.

Networks and security
OS X controls the interaction of a group of computers and peripheral devices connected by a communications link such as Ethernet or wireless. OS X also protects your system and data from harm or loss.

System resources
OS X handles the allocation and use of your computer's low-level hardware resources such as memory (RAM) and central processing unit (CPU) time.

Task scheduling
OS X acts like a traffic cop, setting priorities and allocating time slices to the processes running on your machine.

Tip: OS stands for "operating system" and the X is pronounced "ten".

About This Book

This book is for you if you're new to OS X, you're upgrading from an earlier version of OS X, or you need a quick reference at hand. It's organized, linked, and cross-referenced to help you find things fast.

Conventions

A shorthand instruction to navigate to a nested folder or to choose a command looks like this:

Choose > System Preferences > Dock > Position on Screen > Left.

Each name between the > symbols refers to an icon, folder, window, dialog box, menu, button, checkbox, option, link, or pane; just look on the screen for a matching label. The refers to the Apple menu (page 23), in the top-left corner of the desktop.

Keyboard shortcuts (Chapter 12) are given in the form "Shift+Command+N".

Default Settings

OS X's **defaults** are Apple-defined settings shipped with the product. In some cases, someone else—an administrator or whoever set up your computer—will have changed some defaults, so your initial setup might look or behave a little differently than I describe.

Paths

A **path** specifies the unique location of a file or folder on a drive or network. A slash (/) separates folder and file names. A path that begins with a slash starts from the **root** (topmost) level of the drive. The path to Disk Utility, for example, is /Applications/Utilities/Disk Utility. A tilde (~) denotes your home folder. For a user named tom, for example, the paths ~/Library/Fonts and /Users/tom/Library/Fonts are equivalent.

What's New

Yosemite's big-ticket new features include:

Design
OS X gets an iOS-style makeover. The redesigned user interface includes new icons, blurred translucency effects, subtle animations, clean lines, and flat colors. The system font is now Helvetica Neue (replacing Lucida Grande). Traditional title bars have disappeared from Maps, Safari, Contacts, and other apps. The dock is now a 2D translucent rectangle (instead of a 3D shelf). You can darken the menu bar and dock (sometimes handy for working with photos and videos).

Family Sharing (page 68)
Family Sharing lets up to six people in a family share each other's iTunes, iBooks, and App Store purchases without sharing Apple ID accounts. All family purchases are made with the same credit card, and adults can remotely approve childrens' spending. Families also share photo albums, calendars, reminders, and location information.

iCloud Drive (page 68)
Store any file in iCloud and access it from your Mac, Windows PC, iPhone, iPad, or iPod touch. Your files are synchronized across all devices. Any changes that you make to a file while offline are synced automatically as soon as your Mac is back online. iCloud Drive appears in the Finder sidebar and Go menu like any other system folder.

Continuity (page 154)
Continuity lets you move seamlessly between your Mac, iPhone, iPad, and iPod touch, or use them together. You can start an email or document on your iPhone, for example, and then pick up where you left off on your Mac. You can use your Mac to make and receive phone calls through your iPhone.

Extensions (page 66)
Extensions are small, functional add-ons that enhance and customize OS X. You can choose which extensions appear in Action menus, Share menus, and Notification Center's Today view. Third-party developers can also provide extensions that add functionality to OS X.

Notification Center (page 47)
Notification Center now mimics its iPad counterpart with Notifications view and Today view. You can customize Today view with widgets.

Spotlight (page 93)
Spotlight search results and previews now appear in a large window in the center of the screen. Search results now include Wikipedia articles, map locations, Bing.com search results, unit conversions, local movie showtimes, digital

media from the iTunes and iBooks stores, and software from the Mac App Store.

Full-screen apps (page 44)

The green button ⬤ now takes an app full screen. The dedicated full-screen button in the toolbar is gone. (To use the old zoom behavior, Option-click the green button.)

Apple menu (page 23)

The Software Update menu item is gone, and the App Store item has assumed its duties. The Dock menu item is gone.

Game Center (page 117)

Game Center now looks and acts like its iPad counterpart. Abstract colored spheres have replaced wood grain and green felt textures.

FaceTime (page 116)

Answer FaceTime calls on the lock screen without having to enter your password. Put your current conversation on hold to answer another incoming call (call waiting). Set custom ringtones to identify callers.

Photos (page 124)

The new Photos photo-management application replaces iPhoto and Aperture.

Script Editor (page 128)

AppleScript Editor is now called Script Editor, and supports JavaScript for Automation.

Dictation Commands (page 53)

Dictation Commands (formerly called Speakable Items) has been updated and merged with Dictation (page 58).

Batch-rename files (page 86)

You can quickly rename a set of selected files or folders in Finder, and add custom text and numbers to each filename.

Tags (page 89)

Drag a tag from the Finder sidebar to the dock for quick access to all the files with that tag.

Default web browser (page 67)

You can now set the default browser in the General panel in System Preferences.

New features from Mavericks

Yosemite inherits the following new features from Mavericks (OS X 10.9):

Free

Upgrading to the current version of OS X from OS X Snow Leopard or later costs nothing.

Finder tabs

Finder tabs let you declutter your desktop by consolidating multiple Finder windows into a single, tabbed window (similar to web browsers, where each webpage appears as a separate tab in the same window). Each tab behaves like its own Finder window, so you can change the view of each one independently. You can open folders in new tabs, switch among them, move them, close them, drag files between them, and more.

Tags

Assign meaningful words and phrases to files to make them easy to sort and find—tag a batch of photos with *san francisco* and *2015*, for example. OS X comes with some sample tags, and you can create your own to describe and organize your files. You can tag files in apps or in Finder, and use the Finder sidebar to quickly show all files with specific tags.

Multiple displays

Each display has its own menu bar. The dock is available on all screens. Each display can independently show the desktop or a full-screen app. Use Mission Control to get an overview of what's running on each display. With AirPlay and an Apple TV, you can use an HDTV as a full-fledged display, complete with dock and menu bar.

iBooks

OS X gets Apple's ebook reader from iOS. Shop for books in Apple's iBooks Store and read them in iBooks. Store purchases are downloaded to all your Macs and iDevices automatically. Open multiple books in separate windows. Read books in one-page or two-page view. Go full-screen to focus on the words without distraction. Turn pages by clicking, flicking, or using keyboard shortcuts. Bookmarks, highlights, notes, and reading progress are synced across all your devices.

Maps

Apple's iOS mapping and navigation app comes to OS X. Open multiple maps in separate windows. Find a business or other point of interest and get its address, phone number, and other info. Mark spots on a map. Find your current location. Get travel directions (walking or driving). Plan a trip on your Mac and then send the map to your iPhone. Show real-time traffic conditions. Show 3D views and photo-realistic Flyover views. Zoom, pan, tilt, or rotate the map. Bookmark your favorite places. Switch to satellite view. Share locations with friends. Print a map or export it as a PDF file.

iCloud Keychain

iCloud Keychain encrypts and stores your website user names and passwords on the devices that you've approved (Macs or iDevices), and syncs them wirelessly and automatically across those devices. When you need to create a new password for a website, Password Generator suggests a strong password and saves it to your iCloud Keychain. Passwords and user names are filled in automatically when you need them, so you don't have to remember or type them. iCloud Keychain can also store and sync encrypted credit-card details for online shopping.

Notification Center

Respond to email, message, or FaceTime notifications without leaving the app you're in. Sign up with websites to receive news headlines, sports scores, auction (eBay) alerts, and more as notifications, even when Safari isn't running. View notifications when your Mac is locked. Silence notifications with Do Not Disturb.

Redesigned apps

Calendar, Contacts, and Notes all get an iOS-style makeover (clean lines, flat colors, lightweight fonts, and no fake leather or textures) and now resemble their iPad counterparts. Activity Monitor has been redesigned and has a new Energy tab that lists power-hogging apps (now also listed in the battery status menu).

Safari

Redesigned Top Sites. New sidebar. Shared Links shows you links from people you follow on Twitter and LinkedIn.

Preferences

Bigger icons. Software Update is now App Store. Mail, Contacts & Calendars is now Internet Accounts. Print & Scan is now Printers & Scanners. Language & Text is now Language & Region. The Text and Input Sources panes have moved from Language & Region to Keyboard. Accessibility lets you set the fonts and formatting of video language tracks, subtitles, and closed captions. Dictation lets you dictate offline. App Store permits automatic updates.

Removed or replaced in Mavericks

Tags replace colored labels in Finder. iTunes DJ is gone.

New features from Mountain Lion

Yosemite inherits the following new features from Mountain Lion (OS X 10.8):

Notification Center

Collate alerts and reminders from various apps and display them on your desktop.

Dictation

Talk anywhere that you can type, and Dictation converts your words into text (internet connection required).

Gatekeeper

Restrict which downloaded apps can be installed, protecting your Mac from viruses, spyware, and other malware.

Game Center

Play games on Apple's online multiplayer social gaming network.

Messages

Send iMessages and SMS/MMS messages, chat with video or audio, and exchange files.

Notes
Type notes on a virtual pad of scratch paper.

Reminders
Create and manage to-do lists.

Share sheets
Share text, documents, links, photos, contacts, locations, videos, and more from apps that have a Share button Share button or Share menu.

Twitter integration
Tweet text, links, and photos directly from Safari, Photo Booth, Photos, and other apps.

Facebook integration
Post photos, links, comments, or locations via share sheets; add Facebook friends to Contacts; get Facebook notifications in Notification Center; or update your status.

AirPlay Mirroring
Wirelessly mirror (duplicate) whatever is on your Mac's screen to a high-definition TV (HDTV) via Apple TV.

Power Nap
When your Mac is sleeping, silently and automatically download updates, make backups, and more.

Widget browser
Dashboard now has a full-screen widget browser instead of a widget bar.

Screen-saver slideshows
Screen Saver now offers slideshows as well as traditional screen savers.

Launchpad search box
Launchpad now has a search box that helps you find and launch apps quickly.

Deeper iCloud integration
iWork apps (Pages, Numbers, and Keynote) let you save or open online documents in iCloud for synced access across Macs, iPads, iPhones, and iPod touches. Preview and TextEdit let you move documents to the cloud. Third-party developers are also free to tap into iCloud.

Software updates via App Store
Updates for OS X and other Apple software are now released through the Mac App Store rather than through the dedicated Software Update app (which has been dropped from OS X).

Features for China
New features for Chinese speakers include a Chinese dictionary; Baidu search in Safari; QQ Mail, 163, and 126 services in Internet Accounts; new Chinese fonts; Sina Weibo, Youku, and Tudou share sheets; and improved Chinese keyboards and text input.

Apps renamed or replaced
iChat is now Messages. Address Book is now Contacts. iCal is now Calendar. Universal Access is now Accessibility. Speech is now Dictation & Speech.

Removed from Mountain Lion
iCloud replaces MobileMe. App Store replaces Software Update. RSS support has been removed from Safari and Mail. Notes has been removed from Mail (Notes is now a separate app). Java and X11 are now on-demand downloads.

New features from Lion

Yosemite inherits the following new features from Lion (OS X 10.7):

Multitouch gestures
Tap, drag, flick, pinch, spread, and rotate your fingers on a trackpad to control what's on your screen.

Full-Screen Apps
Expand certain applications to fill your screen edge-to-edge, hiding the dock and other windows.

Mission Control
Display a bird's-eye view of what's open on your computer.

iCloud
iCloud stores your content online and syncs it wirelessly and automatically across your Mac, Windows PC, iPhone, iPad, and iPod touch.

Launchpad

Show a full-screen grid of application icons to open, switch, or delete apps.

Resume

When you open an app, it starts where you left off the last time you ran it, with the same windows open in the same positions. When you log in or restart, all the apps that you were using automatically relaunch with the same open windows.

Auto Save and Versions

Certain applications save your documents automatically in the background as you work (you don't even have to save before you quit the app). You can create, browse, and revert to past versions of documents by using a Time Machine-like interface.

Mac App Store

Buy, download, install, and update OS X applications directly from Apple's online store.

AirDrop

Quickly and wirelessly send files to other nearby AirDrop users, without any setup, passwords, special settings, or base stations.

Removed from Lion

Front Row. iSync. iDisk. Native faxing. FTP services. To-do lists in Mail. PowerPC app support. People Finder, Business, and iTunes dashboard widgets. Boot Camp support for Windows Vista and XP (Boot Camp supports Windows 7 and later).

Installing Yosemite

Unlike early (pre-Lion) versions of OS X, you can't get a copy of Yosemite on a DVD. Instead, you download Yosemite from the Mac App Store (> App Store > Updates pane). Yosemite is a large download (>5 GB); if you don't have a fast or reliable network connection, you can take your Mac to an Apple retail store to get help installing Yosemite. You can install it on any Mac that meets Apple's system requirements. The general requirements are:

- OS X 10.6.8 or later (that is, Snow Leopard, Lion, Mountain Lion, or Mavericks)

- 2 GB of memory

- 8 GB of available space

- iMac (Mid 2007 or newer)

- MacBook (Late 2008 Aluminum, or Early 2009 or newer)

- MacBook Pro (Mid/Late 2007 or newer)

- MacBook Air (Late 2008 or newer)

- Mac mini (Early 2009 or newer)

- Mac Pro (Early 2008 or newer)

- Xserve (Early 2009)

Tip: If you're running OS X 10.5 (Leopard) or earlier, you must upgrade to OS X 10.6 (Snow Leopard) and *then* upgrade to Yosemite. You can buy Snow Leopard from the Apple Store.

Some features, such as Continuity (page 154), require recent (2012 or newer) models. To determine whether your Mac qualifies, choose > About This Mac. The Overview pane shows your model, release date, and memory (click Storage to check free space). You can install Yosemite on all your Macs, without serial numbers or copy protection.

Tip: In Terminal, you can use the command **uname -a** to print technical details about your hardware and operating system.

Reinstalling Yosemite

Should the need arise, you can reinstall Yosemite without using a DVD or disk image. When you first install Yosemite, the installer silently creates a new partition on your hard drive that you can use to reinstall Yosemite. (Your existing data are safely preserved during repartition.) This stealth partition, named Recovery HD (or Recovery-10.10), is invisible in Finder and Disk Utility, but you can see it by using the `diskutil list` command in Terminal. To recover Yosemite, hold down the Option key during startup and then choose Recovery HD when the list of startup partitions appears. Alternatively, hold down Command+R during startup to boot directly to Recovery HD. For details, read the Apple support article "OS X: About OS X Recovery" at *support.apple.com/HT201314*. To create a bootable OS X installer on a USB flash drive, read "Creating a bootable OS X installer" at *support.apple.com/HT201372*. You can also boot to Recovery HD from a locally connected Time Machine backup drive.

Tip: If FileVault (page 163) is turned on, Recovery HD won't appear when you hold down the Option key during startup, but you can still hold down Command+R to boot directly to it.

Startup

Pressing the Power button ⏻ starts (**boots**) the Mac normally. OS X also offers startup options for special situations. See also "Drives" on page 99.

To start normally: Press ⏻.

To start from a bootable CD/DVD: Hold down C when you press ⏻.

To start from the first drive/partition: Hold down D when you press ⏻.

To reset the laptop display: Hold down R when you press ⏻.

To start from a network (NetBoot) server: Hold down N when you press ⏻.

To start in target disk mode: Hold down T when you press ⏻. Target disk mode (page 174) lets one FireWire/Thunderbolt-equipped Mac act as an external hard drive on another Mac.

To start from an external drive/disc: Hold down Shift+Option+Command+Delete when you press ⏻.

To start in 64-bit mode: Hold down 6 and 4 when you press ⏻.

To prevent automatic login: Press ⏻ and then hold down the left Shift key when the spinning progress indicator appears. See also "Logging In" on page 12.

To suppress Login Items and Finder windows at login: Hold down Shift after clicking the Log In button in the login window.

To select a startup drive/partition: Hold down Option when you press ⏻. Boot Camp (page 112) users can use this feature to start Windows.

To force-boot OS X even if another OS is the default: Hold down Command+X when you press ⏻.

To eject a CD/DVD at startup: Hold down the left mouse button when you press ⏻.

To start in safe mode (safe boot): Hold down Shift when you press ⏻ and then release Shift when the login screen indicates a safe boot. For details about safe mode, see "Try safe mode if your Mac doesn't finish starting up" at *support.apple.com/HT201262*.

To troubleshoot at startup: When you press ⏻, hold down Command+S (single-user, Unix command-line mode), Command+V (verbose mode showing Unix console messages), or Option+Command+P+R (resets NVRAM/Parameter RAM—wait for the second chime).

To reinstall (recover) OS X: Hold down Command+R when you press ⏻.

To start, wake, sleep, or shut down automatically at a specified time: Choose > System Preferences > Energy Saver > Schedule.

To designate the startup drive for future startups: Choose > System Preferences > Startup Disk.

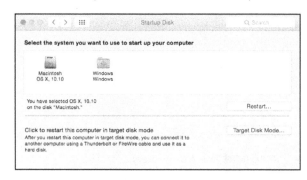

Tip: To select the current startup drive, in Finder, hold down the Shift key and then choose Go > Select Startup Disk on Desktop.

User Accounts

OS X lets many people use the same computer without being able to see or change each other's files and settings. **User accounts** identify who has permission to log in to a particular computer (or network).

To start an OS X session, you log in to your user account, which gives you personalized access to the system. You, like each user, have your own files and settings, including:

- Login items
- Application preferences
- Desktop setup
- System preferences
- Email and internet accounts
- Screen saver
- Apple ID
- iCloud account
- System language
- Files and folders
- Documents
- Internet settings (including bookmarks, home page, history, cookies, and cached webpages)
- User (personal) fonts
- Sharing permissions
- Network connections

Your private files, folders, and preferences generally are stored on the OS X drive in /Users/*user_name*—your home folder (page 76)—which lets OS X personalize your desktop each time that you log in.

On a new computer or during a clean installation, you create the first user account when you set up OS X. If you upgraded from an earlier version of OS X, your existing accounts migrated to the new installation and appear in the login window. If you're on a large network, ask your network administrator how to log in.

To create an account: Choose > System Preferences > Users & Groups > Add button (+) (click if the settings are dimmed).

Complete the following account settings:

New Account
    Select one of the following account types from the New Account pop-up menu:

    Administrator. An administrator has sweeping systemwide rights to create, edit, and delete user accounts and passwords; open, edit, move, and delete everyone's files and folders; install programs, fonts, and hardware; change preferences; use Disk Utility; and bypass FileVault.

    Standard. This account has access only to its own home folder and to shared folders. Standard users can change settings related to only their own accounts (picture, password, and desktop preferences, for example) and install programs for only their own use.

    Managed with Parental Controls. This account is the same as a standard user but with additional usage limits set by an administrator using Parental Controls (page 166).

    Sharing Only. This account can access the computer only remotely (over a network) to share files. It has no home folder and can't change settings or log in via the login window.

Group. A group contains the names of one or more other accounts and is used to set sharing privileges for multiple users at the same time. In the Membership box that appears, select the accounts of the group members.

Full Name

The full name typically is the name of a person (first, last, or both names) but can be any word(s). You can change the full name after creating the account.

Account Name

OS X proposes a **short name** but you can change it to any word without spaces or punctuation. The login window lets you use your full or short name, but network and dial-up connections require a short name. The user's home folder is labeled with the short name. You can't (easily) change this name after creating the account.

Password

Choose whether to log in to OS X by using the same password as an iCloud account (so you have to remember only one password), or by using a separate, independent password. If you choose "Use iCloud password", then an internet connection is required to authenticate the iCloud password the first time that the user logs in. See also "iCloud" on page 68.

Tip: Use an **Apple ID** (*appleid.apple.com*) for your iCloud Account. Your Apple ID identifies you uniquely for Apple.com store transactions, iTunes Store, App Store, iBooks Store, Messages, AirDrop, iCloud, Apple retail store reservations, and Apple.com support. An Apple ID requires a valid email address to register. Use a personal address that you anticipate having for a long time (such as a Gmail or Yahoo email address); don't use your work or school email address.

---

iCloud ID (if "Use iCloud password" is selected)

Type the email address used for the user's iCloud ID.

Required, Verify (if "Use separate password" is selected)

Type and then retype the user's password, or leave both fields empty for a passwordless account. To get password advice, click 🔑.

Hint (if "Use separate password" is selected)

Type an (optional) memory-jogging hint for the password. (All users can see this hint.) The login window shows hints only if they're enabled in Login Options (page 12).

Click the "Create User" button and then complete the following options in the Password pane. The available options depend on your account type (administrator, standard, and so on) and whether you're changing your own account or someone else's.

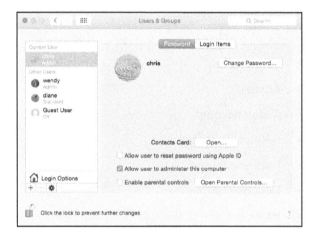

Picture

Accept the sample picture or click it to choose another or take a snapshot by using a built-in camera. You can also drag a picture from a folder onto the sample picture.

Change Password/Reset Password

Change the user's login password and password hint.

Contacts Card

View or edit the user's Contacts entry.

Allow user to reset password using Apple ID

Lets the user reset a forgotten password after entering an Apple ID.

Allow user to administer this computer
Gives a standard or managed user administrative rights.

Enable parental controls
Adds Parental Controls restrictions to Standard accounts.

Login Items
Click Login Items to specify any programs, documents, drives, network servers, files, or folders to open automatically at log in. To add a program to this list quickly, right-click (or click-and-hold) its dock icon and then choose Options > Open at Login.

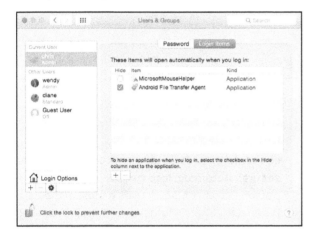

To edit an account: Choose > System Preferences > Users & Groups > select the account (click if the settings are dimmed). Nonadministrators can change only some settings. You can't edit another user who's logged in via fast user switching (page 13).

To delete an account: Choose > System Preferences > Users & Groups > select the account (click if the settings are dimmed) > Delete button (–). You can archive the former user's home folder, leave it undisturbed, or delete it. You can't delete another user who's logged in via fast user switching.

To enable the Guest account for temporary, passwordless logins: Choose > System Preferences > Users & Groups > select Guest User (click if the settings are dimmed) > select "Allow guests to log in to this computer". You can also apply parental controls and prevent guests from using shared folders. When the guest logs out, the account is reset and all its files, email, browser history, and settings are erased.

To set an administrative master password (to access encrypted home folders): Choose > System Preferences > Users & Groups > Gear button (click if the settings are dimmed) > Set Master Password.

Logins & Logouts

Logging in starts your session in OS X. **Logging out** ends the session and prevents others from accessing your files and settings. **Fast user switching** maintains your session in the background when others are logged in. When you're finished using your computer, you can put it to sleep or shut it down.

Logging In

After startup, you'll see the **login window**. Logging in identifies you uniquely so that OS X can load your personal settings, grant you certain permissions, and take you to the desktop.

To log in: In the login window, click your name (or type it if there's no list), type your password if prompted, and then press Return or click the arrow icon in the password box. In a long list, use the arrow keys to scroll to your name or type its first few letters.

To suppress Login Items and Finder windows at login: Hold down Shift while logging in.

To correct a mistyped password: The password box shakes when you type the wrong password: correct it or click the question mark in the password box to show your password hint (if you've set one in Users & Groups). Passwords are case-sensitive; ⇧ appears in the password box if Caps Lock is on. By default, you can mistype your password an unlimited number of times.

To log in automatically at startup: Choose > System Preferences > Users & Groups > Login Options (click if the settings are dimmed) > "Automatic login" pop-up menu. Other users still can use their accounts via fast user switching or when you log out. This option is convenient but insecure because anyone can log in just by turning on the computer.

To prevent automatic login at startup: Press ⏻ and then hold down the left Shift key when the progress indicator appears.

To require logins for all users: Choose > System Preferences > Security & Privacy > General pane >

select "Disable automatic login" (click if the settings are dimmed).

To set up the login process: Choose > System Preferences > Users & Groups > Login Options (click if the settings are dimmed).

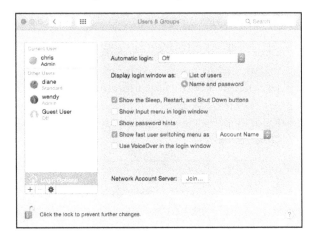

Set the following options:

Automatic login
Enable automatic login for a specific user (more convenient) or force all users to log in (more secure). Automatic login works best if only one person uses the Mac, or uses it most of the time. When auto-login is turned on, startup bypasses the login window and shows the specified user's desktop automatically. Other users still can use their accounts via fast user switching or when the user logs out (> Log Out). This option is convenient but insecure because anyone can log in just by turning on the computer.

Display login window as
The "List of users" option (more convenient) shows a list of user names and pictures in the login window. The "Name and password" option (more secure) hides the pictures and makes every user type a name and password.

Show the Sleep, Restart, and Shut Down buttons
Choose whether to show these buttons in the login window (more convenient) or hide them (more secure). A technically savvy enemy can circumvent OS X security by bypassing the login window during a restart (restarting at the Unix Terminal or in target disk mode, for example).

Turning off this option adds a modest layer of security, but for strong security, use FileVault (page 163).

Show Input menu in login window
Choose whether to let users select a keyboard language in the login window. Turn on this option if the Mac's various account holders speak different languages or use different keyboard layouts and alphabets.

Show password hints
Choose whether to let users see their password hints set in Users & Groups. OS X displays a password hint on the login window at the user's request. If this option is turned off, then hints don't appear (which adds a layer of security, depending on how obvious the hints are).

Show fast user switching menu as
Choose whether simultaneous logins are allowed.

Use VoiceOver in the login window
Choose whether to have VoiceOver speak the parts of the login window (for blind users).

Network Account Server
If you're on a large network, your network administrator will tell you how to connect to an open directory server, active directory domain, or OS X Server.

Tip: For more login options, choose > System Preferences > Security & Privacy > General pane.

Forgotten Passwords

You forgot your login password.

If you're not an administrator (or if you are one but there's another administrator account), then the administrator can choose > System Preferences > Users & Groups, click your account name, and then click Reset Password.

If you're the only administrator, you have several options, provided you turned them on in advance:

- **Password hint.** Show the password hint that you set in > Preferences > Users & Groups. The login window shows hints only if they're enabled in Login Options.

- **Apple ID.** If "Allow user to reset password using Apple ID" was previously turned on in > System Preferences > Users & Groups, then you can click the question mark in the password box when you're logging in. A message appears: "If you forgot your password, you can reset it using your Apple ID". Click → to open the Reset Password dialog box. Enter your Apple ID and password and then click Reset Password. A message appears telling you that changing your account password creates a new keychain (page 164). (The old keychain remains and can be unlocked if you remember your the old password.) Click OK. Enter a new password (twice) and password hint, and then click Reset Password. Click Continue Log In to log in with your new password.

- **FileVault recovery key.** If FileVault (page 163) is turned on, then you can use your recovery key (an emergency master password) to log in. (If you opted to store the recovery key with Apple, then call Apple tech support; they'll give it to you.) Restart the Mac. On the login window, click your name, click the question mark, and then click "Reset it using your Recovery Key", and then type your recovery key.

Switching Users

Fast user switching lets multiple users stay logged in at the same time. You can leave your programs running and documents open securely and invisibly in the background while someone else logs in. When you switch back to your account, OS X resumes your session where you left off. Fast user switching is handy when you're logged in, and someone else wants to use the computer for a moment to check email or a calendar. Depending on how many programs are open and how much memory your Mac has, switching accounts may cause small delays and increased drive activity.

To enable fast user switching: Choose > System Preferences > Users & Groups > Login Options (click if the settings are dimmed) > select "Show fast user switching menu as". Use the pop-up menu to show the accounts menu as a user name or a compact icon .

To switch users: Choose another user name from the accounts menu on the right side of the menu bar. This menu appears only when fast user switching is turned on and shows a check mark next to the name of each logged-in user. To be safe, save all work before switching (in case another logged-in user shuts down or restarts the computer).

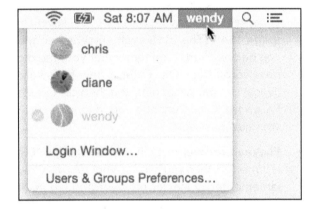

If you try to shut the Mac down or restart it while other people are logged in, a dialog box tells you, "There are currently logged in users who may lose unsaved changes if you shut down this computer". You can click Cancel or you can type an administrator password and then click Shut Down (shutting down all accounts open in the background and their open documents, possibly making enemies of the other users).

Tip: You can't make changes to accounts (in System Preferences) that are still logged in. You also can't turn off fast user switching or turn on FileVault (page 163) while other people are logged in.

Logging Out

When you log out, OS X disconnects your online connections and prevents others from using your user account to access your files or network. Programs that don't use Auto Save (page 107) prompt you to save any unsaved work. Your computer remains turned on and OS X shows the login window to let the next person log in.

To log out after a cancelable delay: Choose > Log Out *user_name* (Shift+Command+Q) > Log Out (Return).

To log out immediately: Hold down the Option key and then choose > Log Out *user_name* (Shift+Option+Command+Q).

To log out automatically after an idle period: Choose > System Preferences > Security & Privacy > Advanced button (click if the settings are dimmed) > select "Log out after _ minutes of inactivity".

Sleeping, Locking, Restarting, and Shutting Down

When you're not using your computer, you can put it to sleep, lock its screen, or shut it down. **Sleep** blanks the screen but maintains your session; your computer stays on but draws little power and awakens quickly. **Locking** keeps you logged in but hides and password-locks your screen, though administrators can unlock it and any user can shut down and restart. You can **restart** your computer to troubleshoot or complete a software update. **Shutting down** powers off the computer (if you have a laptop, wait for it to shut down completely before closing the lid). If you restart or shut down, OS X prompts you to save any unsaved work.

Tip: You can create an "If found, contact…" message that always appears in the login window: choose > System Preferences > Security & Privacy > General (click if the settings are dimmed). Turn on "Show a message when the screen is locked", click Set Lock Message, and then type your message (press Option+Return to create a new paragraph).

To sleep: Do any of the following:

- Choose > Sleep.
- Press Option+Command+Eject ⏏.
- Close the laptop lid.
- Press Ctrl+Eject ⏏ > Sleep (S).
- On an Apple Remote, press-and-hold the Play button.

To sleep automatically after an idle period: Choose > System Preferences > Energy Saver > Computer Sleep slider.

To sleep by moving the pointer to a screen corner: Choose > System Preferences > Mission Control > Hot Corners > Active Screen Corners menus > Put Display to Sleep (holding modifier key(s), if desired).

To wake a sleeping computer: Press a key, click the mouse, tap the trackpad, or open the laptop lid.

To disable sleep: Choose > System Preferences > Energy Saver > Computer Sleep slider > Never.

To disable sleep for a fixed time period: In Terminal, type the command `caffeinate -t timeout`, where *timeout* is the number of seconds to prevent your Mac from sleeping. To prevent sleep for an hour, for example, type `caffeinate -t 3600`.

To configure sleep: Choose > System Preferences > Energy Saver and > System Preferences > Bluetooth > Advanced > "Allow Bluetooth devices to wake this computer".

To lock (password-protect) the screen: Choose > System Preferences > Security & Privacy > General pane > select "Require password after sleep or screen saver begins". If fast user switching is enabled, the password dialog box lets you choose a user when you unlock.

To restart after a cancelable delay: Choose > Restart.

To restart immediately: Do any of the following:

- Hold down the Option key and then choose > Restart.
- Press Ctrl+Command+Eject ⏏.
- Press Ctrl+Eject ⏏ > Restart (R).
- Press ⏻ > Restart (R).

To force restart (last resort): Press Ctrl+Command+⏻.

To shut down after a cancelable delay: Choose > Shut Down.

To shut down immediately: Do any of the following:

- Hold down the Option key and then choose > Shut Down.
- Press Ctrl+Option+Command+Eject ⏏.
- Press Ctrl+Eject ⏏ > Shut Down (Return).
- Press ⏻ > Shut Down (Return).

To force shut down (last resort): Press-and-hold ⏻.

To shut down/sleep/wake/restart automatically at a specified time: Choose > System Preferences > Energy Saver > Schedule.

The Keyboard

Apple has changed its keyboards and keyboard layouts over the years. This book covers the thin aluminum keyboards and newer laptop keyboards.

Keyboard Shortcuts

Keyboard shortcuts save you from moving your hand from keyboard to mouse repeatedly. These shortcuts involve the **modifier keys** that sit in the bottom corners of the keyboard's main section. Press these keys—**Shift** ⇧, **Control** ⌃ (Ctrl), **Option** ⌥ (equivalent to the Alt key in Windows), **Command** ⌘, and **Fn**—together with other keys to change the action. The C key pressed by itself types a lowercase c; pressed along with the Shift key, it types an uppercase C; and pressed along with the Command key, it issues the Copy command.

In this book, modifier keys are joined to other keys with a plus sign. Command+C, for example, means "Press the Command key, hold it down while you press the C key, and then release both keys". A three-key combination such as Shift+Command+N means "Hold down the first two keys while you press the third one and then release all three keys". The modifiers are always listed first.

Shortcuts change over time. This book gives the current ones. The F3 key, for example, invokes Mission Control and is labeled 🖥 on newer keyboards (F3 used to invoke the Copy command).

Special Keys

Function and Fn

The **function keys** (F1, F2, F3, and so on) invoke Mac-specific features. F1 ☼ and F2 ☀, for example, change screen brightness; F4 ⊞ displays Launchpad; and F10 ◀, F11 ◀, and F12 ◀ change the speaker volume. To invoke program-specific functions, hold down the **Fn key** and press a function key. Fn+F1 undoes the last action in Microsoft Word, for example. You can configure the keyboard to reverse Fn-key behavior.

Navigation

The **navigation keys** move things around and scroll windows. The four **arrow keys** ←→↑↓ scroll in that direction, move the insertion point or selected item(s), or select the adjacent item. **Home** (Fn+←) and **End** (Fn+→) jump to the start or end of whatever is active: a webpage or document, a list of files in Finder, the frames of a movie, a series of photos, a line of text, the cells of a table row, and so on. **Page Up** (Fn+↑) and **Page Down** (Fn+↓) scroll up or down one page or windowful.

Return and Enter

The **Return key** and the **Enter key** usually do the same thing (typically, insert a paragraph break, complete an entry, or confirm a dialog box).

Delete

The **Delete key** (or **backspace key**), labeled "delete" or ⌫, deletes the character or selection *before* the insertion point. The **Forward Delete key**, labeled "del" or "delete" or ⌦, deletes *after* the insertion point; if your keyboard lacks this key, Fn+Delete mimics it.

Eject

Press-and-hold the **Eject key** ⏏ to eject a CD or DVD.

Tab

The **Tab key** advances to the next tab stop in a line of text, cycles through dialog-box and webpage fields, jumps to the next cell in a spreadsheet, or moves to the next item in a series. Shift+Tab jumps backward. Its behavior depends on the context and active program.

Escape

The **Escape key**, in the keyboard's upper-left corner, means "Never mind" or "Stop". Press it to close dialog boxes, cancel commands, interrupt long processes, close menus, change modes, or dismiss message boxes. Sometimes Escape does nothing. Its behavior depends on the context and active program.

Configuring the Keyboard

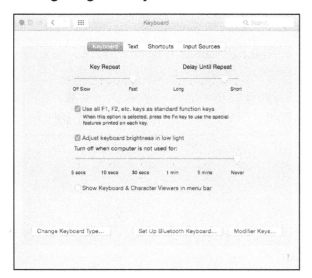

To change how fast characters repeat when you hold down a key: Choose > System Preferences > Keyboard > Keyboard pane. Drag "Delay Until Repeat" to set the wait before a character starts to repeat and then drag "Key Repeat" to set how fast it repeats.

To change Fn+Function Key behavior: Choose > System Preferences > Keyboard > Keyboard pane. To use unmodified function keys for Mac-specific functions (volume, brightness, Mission Control, and so on) and Fn+function keys for program-specific functions, select "Use all F1, F2, etc. keys as standard function keys". To reverse this behavior, clear this checkbox.

To get a list of keyboard shortcuts: In Finder, choose Help > Mac Help and then search for *keyboard shortcuts* by using the Search box. See also Chapter 12.

To change keyboard shortcuts: Choose > System Preferences > Keyboard > Shortcuts pane. Click a category in the list on the left. In the list on the right, use the checkboxes to toggle shortcuts. To assign or change keyboard shortcuts, click a shortcut's name and then press Return (or click to the right of a shortcut's name), and then type the new keystroke. To return the shortcuts to their original settings, click Restore Defaults.

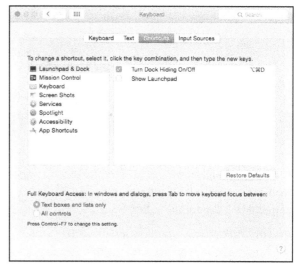

To change the modifier and Caps Lock keys: Choose > System Preferences > Keyboard > Keyboard pane > Modifier Keys. You may find it convenient to remap Caps Lock as either Control or Command.

To set up a Bluetooth keyboard: Turn on the keyboard. Choose > System Preferences > Keyboard > Keyboard pane > Set Up Bluetooth Keyboard.

To toggle keyboard backlighting: Choose > System Preferences > Keyboard > Keyboard pane. Select "Adjust keyboard brightness in low light". To save power by dimming an idle keyboard, drag the slider away from "Never".

To make the keyboard easier to use if you're disabled: Choose > System Preferences > Accessibility > Keyboard.

To use an unrecognized keyboard: Choose > System Preferences > Keyboard > Keyboard pane > Change Keyboard Type.

Spelling, Text Substitutions, and Smart Quotes

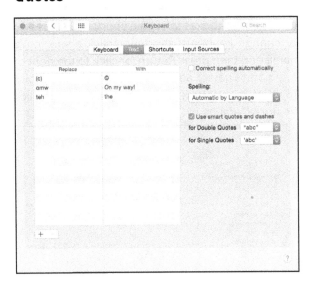

The settings in the Text pane in the Keyboard panel work systemwide in Apple programs (TextEdit, Messages, Mail, Calendar, Safari, Stickies, and so on).

Replace/With (text substitutions)
> Automatically replaces text with other text (like AutoCorrect in Microsoft Word). Autoreplace *jqp* with *John Q. Public*, for example. To add or remove substitutions, click (+) or (–). To use this feature, choose Edit > Substitutions > Text Replacement in each target application (such as TextEdit).

Correct spelling automatically
> Determines whether automatic spelling correction is turned on in applications that support it.

Spelling
> Choose the language(s) that you want to use to check your spelling as you type.

Use smart quotes and dashes
> Determines the type of quotes—"curly" or "straight", for example—inserted automatically when you type single or double quotation marks. To use this feature, choose Edit > Substitutions > Smart Quotes in each target application.

International Keyboards

If you communicate in more than one language, the Input Sources pane in the Keyboard panel lets you add keyboards for other languages. You can switch keyboards at any time.

To type in a different language: Choose > System Preferences > Keyboard > Input Sources pane.

Click (+) and then select the desired language(s). Select "Show Input menu in menu bar". On the right side of the menu bar, choose a keyboard from the Input menu (a flag icon or similar symbol) and then start typing in the selected language. To show the Input menu in the login window, see "Logging In" on page 12. To remove a language, select it and then click (–). See also "Language & Region" on page 72.

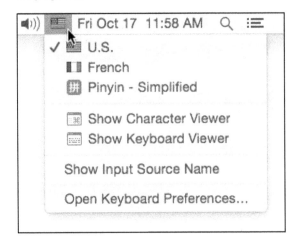

To view the onscreen keyboard or type special characters: Choose > System Preferences > Keyboard > Input Sources pane > select "Show Input menu in menu bar". Click the Keyboard pane and then select "Show Keyboard & Character Viewers in menu bar". On the right side of the menu bar, choose Show Keyboard Viewer from the Input menu. To see or type special characters, hold down modifier keys in Keyboard Viewer or choose Input menu > Show Character Viewer. To change the Input-menu keyboard shortcuts, choose > System Preferences > Keyboard > Shortcuts pane > Keyboard. To resize Keyboard Viewer, click its zoom button or drag its corner.

The Mouse

Most mice have a left and a right button; the left button is used for most actions but frequent use of the right button, which opens a shortcut menu, is a key to working quickly.

Mouse Gestures

Clicking and dragging

To **point**, move the tip of the **pointer** over the target item to which you want to point. To **click**, point to an item and then press and release the left mouse button without moving the mouse. To **double-click**, point to an item and then click the left mouse button twice quickly without moving the mouse (if you click too slowly, OS X interprets it as two single clicks). To **right-click**, point to an item and then click the right mouse button without moving the mouse. (To "right-click" with a one-button mouse, hold down the Ctrl key and then click normally.) To **drag**, point to an item, press-and-hold the left mouse button while you move the pointer to a new location, and then release the button (press Esc during a drag to cancel the drag). The normal pointer ▶ may change depending on what you're dragging or pointing to.

Scrolling

If your mouse has a wheel, ball, or multitouch surface, you can use it to scroll documents, webpages, and more. By default, content moves in a direction *opposite* that of scrolled content in Windows and older (pre-Lion) OS X versions. This default behavior mimics that of touchscreen devices (such as the iPad and iPhone); if you find this to be disorienting, you can revert to the traditional scrolling behavior by using Mouse preferences.

Modifiers

Modifier keys work with the mouse gestures. To **Command-click**, hold down Command and then click before releasing the key. To **Command-drag**, hold down Command and then drag and drop before releasing the key. To **Command-scroll**, hold down Command while spinning the mouse wheel. Clicks, drags, and scrolls can be similarly modified with the Shift, Control, and Option keys.

Insertion point

In text documents, don't confuse the **insertion point** (also called the **cursor**), a steadily blinking vertical bar I, with the pointer, a nonblinking I-beam I. The insertion point indicates where text or graphics will be inserted when you type or paste.

Configuring the Mouse

To reverse the scrolling direction: Choose > System Preferences > Mouse > "Scroll direction: natural". To use the traditional (Windows and pre-Lion) scrolling behavior, clear this checkbox.

To change mouse sensitivity: Choose > System Preferences > Mouse. "Tracking Speed" sets the pointer's acceleration (which moves the pointer farther onscreen than you move the mouse on your desk). Fast settings are useful if you have multiple monitors. "Double-Click Speed" sets the tiny time interval that distinguishes a double-click from two single clicks. "Scrolling Speed" affects the response to the scroll wheel or ball. "Primary mouse button" swaps the functions of the left and right buttons. For an Apple Magic Mouse, more options appear. Settings for non-Apple mice may appear elsewhere in Preferences.

To zoom by using the mouse (if available): Choose > System Preferences > Mouse. Select "Zoom using scroll wheel while holding". Select a modifier key from the pop-up menu or press multiple modifier keys. To set how the zoomed image moves with the pointer, click Options. This feature is useful for examining photos closely and reading small type; it's not available if your mouse lacks a ball, wheel, or multitouch surface. See also "Accessibility" on page 53.

To set up a Bluetooth mouse: Turn on the mouse. Choose > System Preferences > Mouse > Set Up Bluetooth Mouse.

To resize the pointer: Choose > System Preferences > Accessibility > Display > Cursor Size.

To make the mouse easier to use if you're disabled: Choose > System Preferences > Accessibility > Mouse & Trackpad.

The Trackpad & Multitouch Gestures

If you have a built-in laptop trackpad, an Apple Magic Trackpad, or an Apple Magic Mouse, then you can interact with OS X by using your fingertips to do multitouch gestures. *Multitouch* refers to a touch-sensing surface's ability to recognize the presence of two or more points of contact (fingertips) with the surface.

Multitouch Gestures

OS X's multitouch gestures are the same as those for iPad and iPhone.

- To **tap**, gently tap the trackpad with one finger.

- To **double-tap**, tap twice quickly (if you tap too slowly, OS X interprets it as two single taps).

- To **touch and hold**, touch the trackpad with your finger and maintain contact with the surface.

- To **drag**, touch and hold a point on the trackpad and then slide your finger across the surface.

- To **flick** (or **swipe**), fluidly whip your finger across the trackpad.

- To **pinch**, touch your thumb and index finger to the trackpad and then pinch them together or spread them apart.

- To **rotate**, spread your thumb and index finger, touch them to the trackpad, and then rotate them clockwise or counterclockwise.

Tip: Modifier keys work with the trackpad; you can hold down Shift, Control, Option, or Command during a gesture.

Common Multitouch Tasks

The effect of a multitouch gesture depends on which application you're using. Gestures are usually accompanied by animations that clarify the effect. Common gestures include:

Click
Tap one finger to simulate a mouse click.

Right-click
Tap two fingers to right-click.

Define a word
Tap a word with three fingers to look it up in the built-in dictionary.

Scroll
Drag two fingers to scroll documents, webpages, and more. You can choose whether scrolled content moves in the same or opposite direction in which you move your fingers.

Zoom
Spread two fingers apart or pinch them together to zoom in or out of documents, webpages, photos, and more.

Smart zoom
Double-tap two fingers to magnify a particular image or block of text.

Navigate pages
Drag two fingers left or right to flip through documents, webpages, and more.

Move among screens
Flick three fingers left or right to move among spaces, full-screen apps, and the dashboard.

Show Mission Control
Flick three fingers up to see a miniature image of every open window.

Exposé view
Flick three fingers down to see a miniature image of every open window for the current application.

Preview in Quick Look
Select one or more files in Finder and then tap three fingers to see a pop-up thumbnail image of the files.

Show Launchpad
Pinch three fingers and your thumb to show Launchpad.

Show the desktop
> Spread three fingers and your thumb to move all open windows off the screen, revealing the desktop.

Open Notification Center
> Flick two fingers leftward from the right edge of the trackpad.

Configuring the Trackpad

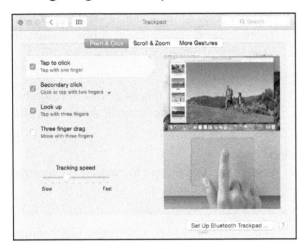

To reverse the scrolling direction: Choose > System Preferences > Trackpad > Scroll & Zoom pane > "Scroll direction: natural". To use the traditional (Windows and pre-Lion) scrolling behavior, clear this checkbox.

To change trackpad sensitivity and toggle gestures: Choose > System Preferences > Trackpad > Point & Click pane. The "Tracking speed" slider sets the pointer's acceleration (which moves the pointer farther onscreen than you drag your fingers on the trackpad). In the different panes, use the checkboxes and drop-down menus to toggle or fine-tune individual gestures. Hover the pointer over a particular gesture to trigger a tutorial video.

To make the trackpad easier to use if you're disabled: Choose > System Preferences > Accessibility > Mouse & Trackpad.

Menus

OS X has one **menu bar** that runs along the top of the screen (unlike Microsoft Windows, where each window has its own menu bar). The **pull-down** menus in the bar list commands in groups. A command with a ▶ next to it has additional choices listed in a **submenu**. A **checked command** √ represents an on/off option or mutually exclusive choice. An **inactive command** is dimmed if it's unavailable in the current context (the Copy command is unavailable if nothing is selected, for example) or you lack the administrative privileges to invoke that command.

Most commands take effect as soon as you choose them. A command followed by an ellipsis (Ellipsis) opens a dialog box because it needs more information to complete. The Find command, for example, has an ellipsis because it needs to know what to find.

Menus show keyboard shortcuts for commonly used commands. The modifier keys and their symbols are:

- Shift ⇧
- Control ⌃
- Option ⌥
- Command ⌘
- Arrow keys ←→↑↓
- Home ↖
- End ↘
- Page Up ⇞
- Page ⇟

- Return ↵

- Enter ⌤

- Delete (Backspace) ⌫

- Forward Delete ⌦

- Eject ⏏

- Tab ⇥

- Escape ⎋

- Power ⏻

Apple Menu

The leftmost menu is the **Apple menu** , which contains common OS X-specific commands that are always available regardless of which application is active. You can't customize the Apple menu, but you can press and hold the Option key or the Shift key to use command variants. To choose which items appear in the Recent Items submenu, choose > System Preferences > General > "Recent items".

Application Menus

Next to the menu are the **application menus**, which change depending on the active window. The name of the active application (Finder, iTunes, or Photoshop, for example) appears first, in bold, followed by other application-specific menus. The File, Edit, Window, and Help menus are fairly consistent across programs. The File menu usually has the commands New, Open, Save, Save As, and Print. Edit has Undo, Cut, Copy, and Paste.

Menu Extras

The right side of the menu bar holds status menus, represented by icons, for various OS X system preferences and programs. (Menu extras are the equivalent of the icons found in the Windows taskbar system tray.)

To add or remove a menu, look in a program's preferences. The ◀)) menu, for example, shows the speaker-volume slider and is toggled with > System Preferences > Sound > "Show volume in menu bar". Option-clicking a status menu usually reveals extra commands or information.

Shortcut Menus

A **shortcut menu** is a context-sensitive menu that appears when you right-click (or Ctrl-click) an item. Shortcut menus offer common commands quickly and OS X provides them for almost everything: icons, files, folders, drives, desktop, dock, and so on. Commands apply only to the item (or group of items) to which you point. Applications have custom shortcut menus: right-click a link in Safari, selected text in TextEdit, or a picture in Photos, for example.

Tip: If a program adds its own commands to shortcut menus with or without your permission, you can usually remove those commands via the program's Preferences dialog box (Command+,) or by turning off the program's Services keyboard shortcuts (> System Preferences > Keyboard > Shortcuts pane > Services).

Menu Tasks

To choose a menu command by using the keyboard: Press Ctrl+F2 (or Fn+Ctrl+F2) to highlight the menu or Ctrl+F8 (or Fn+Ctrl+F8) to highlight menu extras. Use the arrow keys ←→↑↓ to navigate to a menu command (or type a command name in the selected menu), and then press Return. To close a menu without choosing a command, press Esc or click outside the menu.

To change the color of selected menu items: Choose > System Preferences > General > Appearance pop-up menu.

To rearrange menu-extras icons: Hold down the Command key and then drag the icons left or right. To remove an icon, Command-drag it out of the menu bar. (You can't rearrange or remove the or application menus.)

To change the menu language: See "Configuring the Keyboard" on page 17.

To darken the menu bar (and dock): Choose > System Preferences > General > select "Use dark menu bar and Dock". If the menu bar is not dark, then the desktop wallpaper colors will show blurrily under the menu bar.

Toolbars

A **toolbar** is a block of buttons and controls that runs along the top of windows in Finder, Preview, Mail, Safari, and many other programs. Hover the pointer over a control for a pop-up tip. Toolbars provide quick access to common menu commands. Toolbar commands vary by application; some of the following commands apply to only Finder toolbars.

To show or hide a toolbar: Choose View > Hide/Show Toolbar (Option+Command+T).

To rearrange toolbar icons: Hold down the Command key and then drag the icons. To remove an icon, Command-drag it off the toolbar. You can also Command-drag the spacers between icons.

To customize a toolbar: Choose View > Customize Toolbar, or right-click the toolbar and then choose a command. If a window is too narrow to show all its toolbar icons, click Chevron right on the right edge of the toolbar.

To use a toolbar via the keyboard: Press Ctrl+F5 (or Fn+Ctrl+F5) to move to the toolbar; press ←, →, or Tab to select an icon; press Return to "click" the selected icon.

Icons

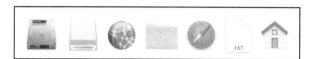

An **icon** is a small picture that represents an item you can manipulate. OS X uses icons on the desktop and in folders to represent folders, files, drives, documents, programs, the Trash, and hardware devices.

You select (highlight) an icon or group of icons to perform an action. Left-click to select; right-click to open the shortcut menu; or drag to move.

What happens when you open (double-click) an icon depends on the icon's type. A folder, drive, removable-storage, or portable-device icon opens in a Finder window. A document, picture, video, or music icon opens in its associated program, launching that program if it's not already open. An application icon launches the program. A smart-folder icon searches your computer and lists all files that match what you're looking for. The Trash icon shows the items to be deleted when you empty it.

To select an icon: Do any of the following:

- Click it.

- Press the arrow keys until the icon is selected.

- Press the first letter of the icon's name. If the correct icon isn't selected, press Tab, Shift+Tab, or the arrow keys to select it.

To select multiple icons: Do any of the following:

- Command-click each icon to select it.

- Drag a selection rectangle diagonally around the icons.

- In a list or column view, click the first icon that you want to select, and then Shift-click the last icon (all icons in between are selected automatically).

- In a list or column view, click an empty area in a row and then drag up or down.

To extend a previous selection: Normally, selecting icons deselects any previously selected icons. To keep these icons selected, press Command or Shift when you make a new selection.

To select all icons: Choose Edit > Select All (Command+A). To select *almost* all icons, select them all, and then Command-click each icon that you *don't* want.

To deselect icons: To deselect all icons, click anywhere in the window or desktop other than a selected icon (or press Option+Command+A). To deselect a specific icon in a multiple selection, Command-click it.

To change an icon's picture: Copy the new picture to the clipboard, typically by opening it in Preview and then choosing Edit > Copy (Command+C). Select the file or folder whose icon you want to replace, choose File > Get Info (Command+I), and then, at the top of the Info window, click the icon picture and then choose Edit > Paste (Command+V).

To change the color of a selected icon's name: Choose > System Preferences > General > "Highlight color" pop-up menu.

Windows

OS X lets you work with multiple overlapping windows. You identify the window by its **title bar**, which runs along the top of the window and gives the title of the window's folder, application, document, or device. Each window has its own boundaries and can present different views of its contents. Some applications—including Maps, Safari, Notes, Reminders, and Contacts—lack a traditional title bar.

When multiple windows are open, only one is active at any time. The **active window**, identified by its darker title bar, is the one that receives your keystrokes (text entry, navigational movements, or commands). An inactive window can be hidden behind other windows and remains inactive until you bring it to the foreground.

The buttons ⊗ ⊖ ⊚ in the window's upper-left corner let you **close** a window, **minimize** it to an icon in the dock, or expand it to **full screen**. You can also resize a window freely. To manage multiple windows, see Chapter 2.

To activate a window: Do any of the following:

- Click anywhere in the window.

- Click its icon in the dock.

- Right-click (or click-and-hold) the application icon in the dock and then choose the window when the menu appears.

- Command+Tab to the desired application or window.

- Press F3 (or Fn+F3) to open Mission Control and then click the desired window.

To move a window: Drag its title bar or, if present, the status bar running along the bottom edge of the window. If the window lacks a traditional title bar, drag an empty area in the space at the top of the window where the title bar would normally appear (be careful not to click a button or other control when you're hunting for valid draggable area).

To move a window without activating it: Command-drag its title bar or status bar.

To close a window: Click the red Close button (×) or choose File > Close (Command+W). In some applications, a centered dot instead of × in the Close button denotes a window with unsaved work. In Finder, Safari, Terminal, and other applications that use tabbed windows, choose File > Close Window (Shift+Command+W) or File > Close Tab (Command+W).

Tip: In OS X (unlike Windows), closing an application's only open window doesn't usually quit the application. To quit, choose File > Quit (Command+Q).

To minimize a window to the dock: Click the yellow Minimize button (–) or double-click the title bar. In Finder, Command+M works too. (To toggle double-click minimizing, choose > System Preferences > Dock > "Double-click a window's title bar to minimize".)

To expand a window to full screen: Click the green Full-Screen button ⊚. To restore the window to its previous size, move the pointer to the top edge of the screen and then, when the menu bar appears, click the green button ⊚; alternatively, press Ctrl+Command+F or (for some programs) press Esc once or twice. If the application doesn't support full-screen view, then the window will enlarge but not to full screen. For details, see "Full-Screen Apps" on page 44.

To enlarge a window without making it full screen: Hold down the Option key and then click the green button ⊕. To restore the window to its previous size, hold down the Option key and then click the green button again. Some applications also have a Window > Zoom command. (This type of window zooming was the normal behavior for the green button in older (pre-Yosemite) versions of OS X.)

To apply the same action to all a program's windows: Hold down Option during the action. To minimize all Finder windows, for example, Option-double-click a folder's title bar, or press Option+Command+W to close them all.

To resize a window: Drag any window edge or corner. The pointer becomes a double-headed arrow near a window's border.

Scrolling

A window that's too small to show all its contents displays scrollbars. A **scrollbar** is a vertical or horizontal bar at the side or bottom of a window used to slide that window's contents around. Drag the **scroll box** to move to an arbitrary location, or click an empty area in the scrollbar **shaft** (the long, narrow background in which the scroll box travels) to jump by one windowful at a time. Old-style scrollbars have **scroll arrows** at the ends for moving contents incrementally.

The size of a scroll box is proportional to the fraction of the window contents displayed, so the scroll box indicates visually how much you *can't* see, as well as showing you where you are.

Many programs scroll automatically in common situations. Dragging or extending a selection of text or graphics near a window's edge autoscrolls in the direction of the drag, often at a speed proportional

to how far past the edge you drag. Tabbing to a text box or typing in a partially hidden text box auto-scrolls a form to reveal the whole box. Using Find, Go To, or a similar command autoscrolls to show the matching selection or new cursor location.

You can replicate most scroll-bar actions by using the mouse wheel, navigation keys, or multitouch gestures.

To configure scrollbars: Choose > System Preferences > General. The "Show scroll bars" options determine whether scrollbars fade away when not in use. The "Jump to the spot that's clicked" option scrolls to the spot where you click on the scroll-bar shaft instead of scrolling by one windowful ("Jump to the next page"). Option-clicking in the shaft swaps between the two methods temporarily. To reverse the scrolling direction, use Mouse and Trackpad preferences.

To toggle smooth scrolling: OS X uses **smooth scrolling**, which slides content rapidly when you press Page Up or Page Down (rather than changing the view instantaneously). Older (pre-Mountain Lion) versions of OS X let you turn off smooth scrolling easily, but you can still disable it if it draws your eye too much. In Terminal, type the commands:

```
defaults write -g \
NSScrollAnimationEnabled -bool NO
killall Dock
```

To return to smooth scrolling, retype the commands, but change NO to YES.

Dialog Boxes & Controls

A **dialog box** is a small temporary window that a program opens to respond to a command or event. **Controls** let you enter new content or view or change existing settings. The common controls in dialog boxes and other parts of the user interface include:

- *Radio buttons* choose one of several mutually exclusive options.

- *Checkboxes* turn options on or off.

- *Pop-up menus* Small select one option from a list.

- *Sliders* set a value in a restricted range.

- *Buttons* OK are labeled by actions (pressing Return "clicks" the darker, pulsing button).

- Clicking a menu item or button with an *ellipsis* (...) Options... makes a dialog box appear.

- *Text boxes* 15 contain typed or pasted (input) text.

- *Tabs* Desktop Screen Saver show individual panes within a dialog box.

When a control is dimmed, it's unavailable in the current context or you lack the administrative privileges to use it.

To use the keyboard to navigate in a dialog box: Choose > System Preferences > Keyboard > Shortcuts pane > "All controls" (at the bottom). With this option turned on, Tab and Shift+Tab move forward and backward through controls; the arrow keys and letter keys choose items in lists and open pop-up menus; and Spacebar "clicks" the active control. Keyboard shortcut to toggle this setting: Ctrl+F7 (or Fn+Ctrl+F7).

Get Info

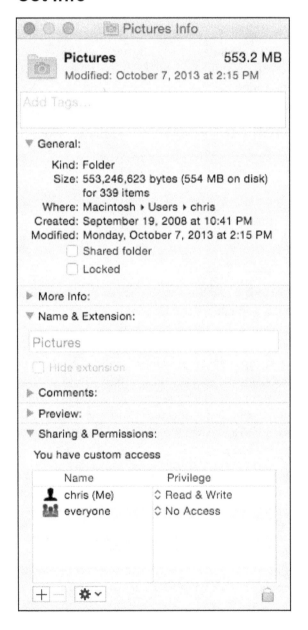

Almost every item (icon) has an Info window full of information, called **metadata**, about its contents and settings. The attributes shown are appropriate for the item selected. The Info window for a drive shows capacity statistics, for example; for a file or folder, it shows creation and modification dates. You can summon separate Info windows for each selected item or a single summary window, called an Inspector window, for multiple items.

To open separate Info windows for each item: Select an item, or group of items, and then choose File > Get Info (Command+I), or right-click any selected item and then choose Get Info.

To open a summary Info window for multiple items: Select the items, and then choose Ctrl+File > Get Summary Info (Ctrl+Command+I), or Ctrl-click any selected item and then choose Get Summary Info.

To open a window that shows information about the current selection: Select any item, and then choose Option+File > Show Inspector (Option+Command+I), or Option-click any item and then choose Show Inspector. The contents of the Inspector window change to reflect whatever is selected.

To show or hide a panel in an Info window: Click ▶ or ▼ in the panel.

Tip: The Info window also lets you add tags (page 89) to files and folders.

Transferring Content

OS X gives you a few ways to move data around: copy webpage text to an email message, embed charts and graphics in reports and slides, move paragraphs around in a document, and so on.

Cut, Copy, and Paste

Cut, copy, and paste are used to organize documents, folders, and drives. **Cut-and-paste** removes (cuts) content and places it on the clipboard so that it can be moved (pasted) elsewhere. Cutting deletes the content from its original location. **Copy-and-paste** copies content to the clipboard so that it can be duplicated (pasted) elsewhere. Copying leaves the original content intact (nothing visible happens when you copy).

The **clipboard** (in Finder, choose Edit > Show Clipboard) is the invisible area of memory where OS X stores cut or copied content, where it remains until it's overwritten when you cut or copy something else. This scheme lets you paste the same thing multiple times in different places. You can transfer content from one program to another provided that the second program can read content generated by the first. A little experimenting shows that you often can combine dissimilar content; you can paste text from TextEdit into Photoshop, for example. You can't paste something that you've **deleted** or **cleared** (as opposed to cut), because OS X doesn't place the deleted item on the clipboard.

The Cut, Copy, and Paste commands are in a program's Edit menu, but each program may handle these operations differently. In Finder, for example, you can copy files and folders from one drive or folder to another. In Mail, you can copy or move text or graphics to another part of a message or to a different message. In Safari, you can only copy material from webpages, not cut it.

To cut: Select (highlight) the content to remove, and then choose Edit > Cut (Command+X), or right-click the selection and then choose Cut.

To copy: Select (highlight) the content to copy, and then choose Edit > Copy (Command+C), or right-click the selection and then choose Copy.

To paste: Click the mouse (or move the cursor to) where you want the content to appear, and then choose Edit > Paste (Command+V), or right-click and then choose Paste.

To undo a cut or paste: Immediately choose Edit > Undo (Command+Z).

Tip: You can also copy and paste text to the clipboard by using the **pbcopy** and **pbpaste** commands in Terminal.

Drag-and-Drop

TextEdit, Mail, iWork, Microsoft Office, and many other programs let you drag-and-drop as a faster alternative to cut-and-paste: click in the middle of some highlighted content and then drag it elsewhere within the same document or to a different window or program. (This technique doesn't involve the clipboard and won't change its contents.) You can often press a modifier key, such as Ctrl or Option, as you drag to copy, rather than move, the content. Dragging text to the desktop creates a "scrap" or "clipping" file for later reuse.

Intermediate Formats

Another way to exchange data between programs is to save it in a format that both the source and target programs can read and write. To read a list of addresses into a mailing-list program from a spreadsheet or database, for example, save the addresses in a CSV-format file (a text file of comma-separated values), and then open it in the mailing-list program. The source program's Save As dialog box lists the format types that you can save. The target program usually autoconverts the CSV file when you open it with File > Open, but you may have to step through an "interview" to organize the incoming data. Image-editing programs such as Photoshop can exchange files in JPEG, GIF, TIFF, PNG and other popular graphic formats.

Import/Export

Use import and export tools to transfer large amounts of data or data in incompatible formats. Most address-book, browser, email, office-suite, and database programs have Import and Export commands, typically in the File menu. The commands vary by program (they're not part of OS X), so read the documentation for both the source and target programs. Import/export operations can be routine—most database and accounting programs can skip the CSV step and export to the native Excel format directly, for example—but they're superlative when no standard exchange-format exists. If you want to try new email and browser programs, then import/export is the only practical way to transfer all your addresses, messages, bookmarks, cookies, and other content. Choosing File > Import Bookmarks in Safari, for example, lets you import browser bookmarks from Mozilla Firefox.

Getting Help

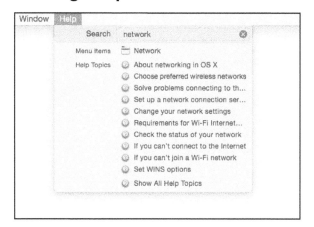

OS X's Help system lets you use web-style links and searches to access standard documentation, animated tutorials, and troubleshooting guides. Each program has its own set of help files, accessed from its Help menu. OS X-specific help is available when Finder is active. The Mac Help window floats atop other windows; minimize or resize it if it's in the way.

Tip: OS X help files are stored in /Library/Documentation/Help.

To get help by searching: Choose Help (Shift+Command+?) and then type or paste a search phrase (one or more keywords) in the Search box. Help shows relevant topics as you type. Click any link in the results list or click Show All Help Topics for a complete list. Pointing to a Menu Items link opens the relevant menu.

To get help by browsing: Choose Help > Mac Help (if this command isn't visible, click × in the Search box). Use the Search box or click a linked topic to open it. Use the toolbar buttons to revisit help topics, show or hide the table of contents, or save, share, or print help topics.

To find text within a help topic: Press Command+F.

System Information

System information is useful when diagnosing problems, getting technical support, or installing new hardware.

To get general system information: Choose > About This Mac.

To get detailed system information: Click the System Report button in the About This Mac window or choose Applications > Utilities (Shift+Command+U) > System Information.

Preferences

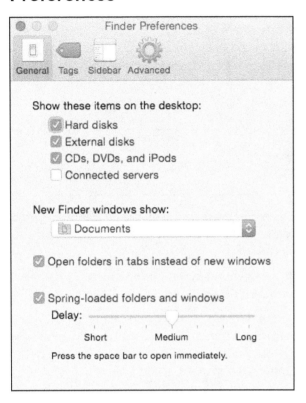

Most applications have a Preferences dialog box that sets programwide options. Preferences is one of the first places to look at when you're new to a program. In general, any changes that you make to preferences apply to only your user account.

To open Preferences: Open or activate the desired program and then choose Preferences from the application menu or press Command+, (comma). Some programs have a similar dialog box, named Options, available in the program's application menu or Tools menu.

The Desktop

After you log in, OS X shows the **desktop**, which is the backdrop of your working environment and lets you organize your computer's resources. This chapter covers the main desktop-management tools:

- The dock lets you access often-used files, folders, and programs.

- Stacks expands the contents of docked folders and drives.

- Exposé declutters a screenful of windows.

- Spaces organizes windows into groups.

- Dashboard gives you instant access to specialized miniprograms called widgets.

- Full-screen apps can fill your screen edge-to-edge, hiding the dock and other windows.

- Mission Control unites OS X's window-management features to give you a bird's-eye view of all your open spaces, widgets, programs, documents, and folders.

- Notification Center collates alerts from various apps and displays them on the desktop.

The other parts of the desktop, covered elsewhere, are the menu bar, Finder, and the Trash. You can also use various System Preferences (Chapter 3) panels to personalize your desktop.

The Dock

The **dock** comes with (removable) Apple-installed icons, and you can add shortcuts to your own files, folders, drives, programs, documents, and internet bookmarks. An icon in the dock is only a pointer; removing it doesn't delete the file to which it's linked, nor does dragging an icon to the dock move the original file, though you can drag icons (or Command-drag them freeze the dock icons for better accuracy) directly into docked folders and their spring-loaded (page 88) subfolders.

Each dock icon has its own shortcut menu, available via right-clicking (or Ctrl-clicking).

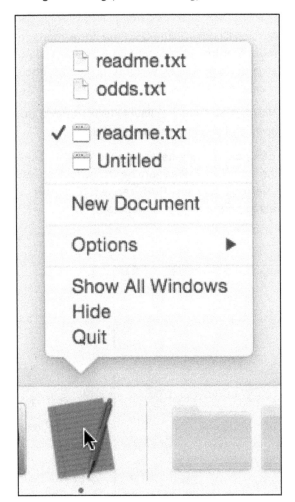

The dock itself has its own shortcut menu for customizing the dock (right-click the dock divider).

Hovering the pointer over an icon shows its name. Clicking an application or document icon opens it, or activates it if it's already open. Clicking a folder or drive icon shows its contents in a stack. To make a small dot appear next to the dock icon of every open application, choose > System Preferences > Dock > select "Show indicators for open applications". All open applications appear in the dock. All minimized windows appear in the dock as thumbnails or are accessed by right-clicking the dock icons of their parent programs.

Some apps try to get your attention by displaying an **alert badge**—a number in a little red circle superimposed on the app's dock icon. The number is the count of new, unread, or unattended items for that app. Mail shows the number of incoming mail messages, for example; App Store shows the number of updates available.

A divider separates application icons from all other types of icons. Application icons sit to the left of the divider. Everything else (documents, folders, the Trash, and so on) sits to the right.

Some application icons show "live" information. The icon for Mail, for example, shows the number of unread messages; the icon for Activity Monitor can show a real-time graph of CPU usage and statistics.

To open or activate a dock item: Click its dock icon.

To open a document by using the dock: Drag the document from the desktop or a folder window onto a compatible dock application. To force-open, Option-Command-drag (some apps can't be forced).

To see an item's shortcut menu: Right-click (or click-and-hold) its icon in the dock.

To see the dock's shortcut menu: Right-click the dock divider.

To add items to the dock: Drag an icon (or group of icons) from the desktop or a folder window to the dock, or drag a proxy icon (page 81) from a window's title bar to the dock. Drag applications to the left of the dock divider, and files, folders, and drives to the right.

To add an open program to the dock: Right-click (or click-and-hold) its icon in the dock and then choose Options > Keep in Dock.

To reorder items: Drag dock icons to reorder them.

To remove an item: Drag it out of the dock, or right-click it and then choose Options > Remove from Dock. You can't remove icons for Finder, the Trash, and minimized documents. If you remove the icon of an open program, it vanishes from the dock after you quit that program.

To see an item in Finder: Command-click its dock icon, or right-click its dock icon and then choose Options > Show in Finder.

To switch to another program and hide the active one: Option-click the dock icon of the program that you want to activate.

To hide all programs but one: Option-Command-click the dock icon of the program that you want to activate.

To quit an open program: Right-click (or click-and-hold) its dock icon and then choose Quit.

To force-quit a frozen program: Hold down Option, right-click (or click-and-hold) its dock icon, and then choose Force Quit.

To navigate the dock by using the keyboard: Press Control+F3 (or Fn+Control+F3) to activate the dock. Press ← or → to select an icon; press Return to open an icon; or press ↑ or ↓ to open or close an icon's shortcut menu. To cancel without choosing a command, press Esc.

To view or change dock-related keyboard shortcuts: Choose > System Preferences > Keyboard > Shortcuts pane > Launchpad & Dock.

To configure the dock: Choose > System Preferences > Dock. For quick access to a subset of dock preferences, right-click (or Ctrl-click) the dock divider and then use the dock's shortcut menu.

To minimize windows easily: Choose > System Preferences > Dock > select "Double-click a window's title bar to minimize". When this option is selected, a window minimizes to an icon in the dock when you double-click its title bar.

To determine how windows behave when you minimize them: Choose > System Preferences > Dock > "Minimize windows into application icon". When this option is turned off, windows minimize to thumbnails in the dock (often leading to a crowded dock). When this option is turned on, windows minimize invisibly into the dock icons of their parent applications. To open a minimized window, right-click (or click-and-hold) its parent application's dock icon and then click the document name in the shortcut menu (a check next to the name denotes the active document; a diamond denotes a minimized document).

To autohide the dock when you're not using it: Choose > System Preferences > Dock > "Automatically hide and show the Dock". When this option is turned on, the dock disappears when the pointer moves away from the dock and reappears when it moves toward it. To toggle this feature on and off quickly, press Option+Command+D.

To show small indicators (dots) next to the dock icons of open applications: Choose > System Preferences > Dock > "Show indicators for open applications". Older (pre-Lion) versions of OS X showed these indicators by default. Keeping too many applications open at the same time makes OS X juggle memory (RAM), possibly draining battery power quickly.

To magnify the dock by using the keyboard: Hold down Shift+Control as the pointer approaches the dock.

To reposition the dock by using the mouse: Shift-drag the dock's divider to an edge of the screen.

To reset the dock: In /Users/*user_name*/Library/Preferences, delete the file com.apple.dock.plist, and then relogin. (If you don't see the Library folder in Finder, hold down Option and then choose Go > Library.) Resetting the dock reverts it to its factory settings. A reset is useful if you accidentally drag a large number of files *onto* the dock instead of *into* a folder in the dock (deleting many dock icons one at a time would take ages).

To add a folder of recently used or favorite items to the dock: In Terminal, type the commands:

```
defaults write com.apple.dock \
persistent-others -array-add \
'{ "tile-data" = \
{ "list-type" = 1; }; \
"tile-type" = "recents-tile"; }'
killall Dock
```

When the stack appears in the dock, right-click it to choose which items to show.

To increase the dock's maximum size: In Terminal, type the commands:

```
defaults write com.apple.dock \
tilesize -int 256
killall Dock
```

Don't exceed 256. To change the dock's size, choose > System Preferences > Dock > Size slider.

To increase the dock's maximum magnification: In Terminal, type the commands:

```
defaults write com.apple.dock \
largesize -int 512
killall Dock
```

Don't exceed 512. To change the dock's magnification, choose > System Preferences > Dock > Magnification slider.

Stacks

A **stack** is a folder or drive shortcut in the dock. Clicking a stack springs open its contents in an arced fan of icons (for few items), a grid of icons (for many items), or a list of names (for a compact view). The dock comes with (removable) Apple-installed stacks, and you can add your own. It's common practice to create a stack folder named, say, Favorites and fill it with aliases (page 88) of often-used programs, files, and folders. Clicking an item in a stack opens that item, or activates it if it's already open, and then closes the stack.

To add a stack to the dock: Drag a folder or drive icon from the desktop or a folder window to the dock (to the right of the dock divider).

To remove a stack from the dock: Drag it out of the dock, or right-click it and then choose Options > Remove from Dock.

To open a stack: Click a folder or drive icon in the dock. To open it in slow motion, Shift-click.

To open an item in a stack: Open the stack and then do any of the following:

- Click the item.

- Use the arrow keys to highlight it and then press Return.

- Type the first few letters of the item's name to highlight it and then press Return.

- Scroll the mouse wheel to highlight the item and then click.

- Drag on the trackpad to highlight the item and then tap.

Tip: In grid and list views, scrollbars appear in crowded stacks. In grid view, clicking a subfolder opens it within the stack. To return to the parent folder, click ‹ in the stack's top-left corner.

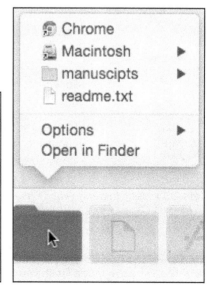

To show a stack item in a Finder window: Open the stack and then Command-click the item.

To move an item by using a stack: Open the stack and then drag the item out of the stack to the desktop or a folder window.

To copy an item by using a stack: Open the stack and then Option-drag the item out of the stack to the desktop or a folder window.

To alias an item by using a stack: Open the stack and then Option-Command-drag the item out of the stack to the desktop or a folder window.

To open multiple items without closing a stack (fan and grid views): Open the stack and then hold down Option while you click items.

To close a stack without opening an item: Press Esc, click off the stack, or click the stack's dock icon (which changes to ▼ when the stack is open).

To open a stack's shortcut menu: Right-click the stack's dock icon.

To change a stack's sort order: Right-click the stack icon and then choose an option under "Sort by".

To change a stack's dock icon: Right-click the stack icon and then choose an option under "Display as". The option Stack shows a pile of the icons contained in the stack. The option Folder shows an ordinary folder or drive icon.

To force a particular stack view: Right-click the stack icon and then choose an option under "View content as". The option Automatic lets OS X determine the view based on your screen size. The option Fan isn't available if the dock is positioned on the screen's left or right edge.

To bypass a stack view: Right-click the stack icon and then choose Open "*item_name*".

Exposé

Exposé shrinks and tiles all open windows on your screen so you can find a particular window on a crowded desktop. By using keyboard shortcuts or multitouch gestures, you can tile all windows (grouped by program), tile only a certain program's windows, or hide all windows (revealing the desktop). If you press-and-hold an Exposé keyboard shortcut, the windows return to their original size when you release the keys. If you tap the keys quickly, Exposé stays activated until you dismiss it or choose a window.

The need to press the Fn modifier key for keyboard shortcuts depends on your keyboard type (standard, portable, or old) and your setting for > System Preferences > Keyboard > Keyboard pane > "Use all F1, F2, etc. keys as standard function keys". Multitouch gestures depend on your settings in > System Preferences > Trackpad > More Gestures pane.

To see all open windows: Press the Mission Control key F3 (or Fn+F3) or press Control+↑ or flick three fingers up. To activate a window, click it, tap it, or point to it and press the keyboard shortcut again. To dismiss Exposé without activating a window, press the keyboard shortcut again (without pointing to a window), repeat the multitouch gesture, or press Esc.

To see all open windows for the current program: Press Control+↓ or flick three fingers down. Alternatively, right-click (or click-and-hold) a program's icon in the dock and then choose Show All Windows. The window-activation commands described above also apply here.

To hide all windows and show the desktop: Press F11 (or Fn+F11) or spread three fingers and your thumb. The dock, Finder, menu bar, icons, Eject, and other parts of desktop operate normally in this desktop view. To dismiss desktop view, press the keyboard shortcut again, repeat the multitouch gesture, click a screen edge or window edge, or double-click an icon. See also "Hiding Programs" on page 46.

To cycle through Exposé windows or program windows: With Exposé active, press Tab or Command+Tab. Add the Shift key to cycle backward.

To switch among Exposé's views: Use the keyboard shortcut or multitouch gesture for the desired view, even when in another view.

To run Exposé in slow motion: Hold down Shift when you activate Exposé.

To activate Exposé by moving the pointer to a screen corner: Choose > System Preferences > Mission Control > Hot Corners > Active Screen Corners pop-up menus (holding down modifier key(s), if desired).

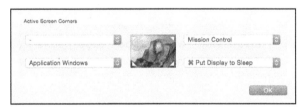

To change how windows are grouped in Exposé view: Choose > System Preferences > Mission Control > "Group windows by application". When this option is turned on, windows are grouped in piles, one pile per application. When this option is turned off, windows maintain their relative desktop positions (the resulting arrangement is a bit haphazard, but shows more of each window's content).

To change the Exposé keyboard shortcuts: Choose > System Preferences > Mission Control and then use the pop-up menus in the Keyboard and Mouse Shortcuts section. Alternatively, choose > System Preferences > Keyboard > Shortcuts pane > Mission Control (this pane lets you restore the default shortcuts).

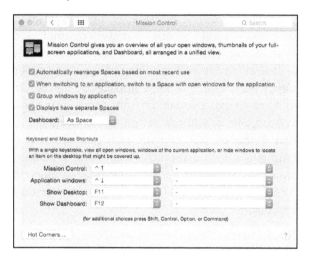

To attach a file to an email message by using Exposé: Start dragging the file and then trigger Exposé to show all windows (F3 or Control+↑). Drag the file over the target email window, press F3 or Control+↑ again and then drop the file in the message. You can use the same technique, but pressing Control+↓, to copy or drag text or graphics between only a particular program's windows.

To move or copy an item to the desktop by using Exposé: Start dragging the item and then trigger Exposé to show the desktop (F11). To move the item, drop it on the desktop. To copy it, hold down Option before dropping. To make an alias, hold down Option+Command before dropping. You can also drag an item onto a program's dock icon and hover until Exposé displays the program's windows; hover again over the target window until it activates and then drop the item.

Spaces

Spaces organizes windows into user-defined groups called **spaces**. Each space is a virtual screen containing only the windows assigned to that space. You typically define a space by logically related tasks (an "internet" space for browsing, email, and chat, for example) or by specific projects or events (a "travel" space with itinerary, photos, and emergency numbers). The same application can run in multiple spaces but with different documents open in each one, or you can assign applications to particular spaces. You can see only one space at a time and switch among them by using keyboard shortcuts or multitouch gestures. Spaces pays off nicely after some initial fine tuning, memorization, and disorientation.

To add spaces: Press the Mission Control key F3 (or Fn+F3) or press Control+↑ or flick three fingers up. Move the pointer (or drag a window) to the top-right corner of the screen and then click the Add button (+). You can add up to 16 spaces. When you're done adding spaces, press the keyboard shortcut again (without pointing to a window), repeat the multitouch gesture, or press Esc.

To set Spaces keyboard shortcuts and multitouch gestures: For keystrokes, choose > System Preferences > Keyboard > Shortcuts pane > Mission Control. For gestures, choose > System Preferences > Trackpad > More Gestures pane. The default Control+arrow-key shortcuts scroll left or right through spaces. The default Control+1 shortcut jumps directly to Desktop 1. You can press any combination of modifier keys (Shift, Control, Option, or Command) when you assign a custom keyboard shortcut.

To switch spaces: Do any of the following:

- Open Mission Control (F3 or Control+↑) and then click the target space at the top of the screen.

- Press a Spaces keyboard shortcut (Control+→ or Control+1, for example).

- Flick three fingers left or right.

To move a window from one space to another: Do any of the following:

- Drag the window to a screen edge, pause until the adjacent space slides into view, and then drop the window in the new space.

- Click-and-hold anywhere in the window and then press the arrow-key or number-key keyboard shortcut of the target space.

- Switch to the space that contains the window that you want to move, open Mission Control (F3 or Control+↑), and then drag the window up to the target space at the top of the screen.

To assign an application to particular spaces: If the application's icon isn't visible in the dock, then open the application. Right-click (or click-and-hold) the application's icon in the dock, point to Options, and then choose This Desktop (to make the app open in only the current space), All Desktops (to make the app open in every space), or None (to make the app open in whatever space you're currently using).

To reorder spaces: Open Mission Control (F3 or Control+↑) and then, at the top of the screen, drag the thumbnails for the spaces (or full-screen apps) left or right.

To delete a space: Open Mission Control (F3 or Control+↑), point over the target space, and then click the Delete button ⊗ when it appears (after a slight delay) on the space. If the deleted space contains windows, the windows are moved to another space.

To configure Spaces: Choose > System Preferences > Mission Control.

Set the following options:

Automatically rearrange Spaces based on most recent use
> Determines whether spaces are sorted dynamically so that you can access recently used ones quickly. Turning on this option makes Mission Control keep the desktops that you're using most often next to each other, making back-and-forth switching easier.

When switching to an application, switch to a Space with open windows for the application
> Determines whether the desktop autoscrolls to the space containing the open windows of an application that you open or switch to. For example, if you have Safari open in Desktop 3 while you're working in TextEdit in Desktop 1, and you then switch to Safari by pressing Command+Tab, you'll jump to Desktop 3. Turning off this option prevents the jump (you'll activate Safari but stay in Desktop 1).

Displays have separate Spaces
> Determines whether you can set up separate spaces for each display, if you're using multiple displays.

Dashboard
> Choose "As Space" to make the dashboard appear when you open Mission Control (F3 or Control+↑) or switch spaces. Choose "As Overlay" to make the dashboard appear as a semi-transparent overlay over the desktop or any space. Choose "Off" to disable the dashboard and widgets.

Dashboard & Widgets

Dashboard displays a host of widgets in a separate screen or space. Widgets are single-purpose mini-programs grouped on a dark or semi-transparent background that can be summoned or dismissed at any time. OS X comes with starter widgets (weather, stock ticker, and so on) stored in the widget browser, and you can get more online.

To show or hide the dashboard and widgets: Do any of the following:

- Click the Dashboard icon in the dock.

- Press F12 (or Fn+F12). On older Macs, press F4 ⊚ (or Fn+F4).

- Open Mission Control (F3 or Control+↑) and then click the dashboard thumbnail image at the top of the screen. (This method works if the dashboard is configured to appear as a space.)

    To hide the dashboard, press the keyboard shortcut again, press Esc, use a Spaces keystroke or gesture (page 40), click the arrow in the dashboard's bottom-right corner, or click an empty area on the dashboard overlay.

To configure the dashboard: Choose > System Preferences > Mission Control. Select the dashboard type from the "Dashboard" pop-up menu, set the Show Dashboard keyboard shortcut, or click Hot Corners to show the dashboard by moving the pointer to a screen corner. For shortcuts to common dashboard tasks, right-click (or click-and-hold) the Dashboard icon in the dock.

To open or close the widget browser: To open the widget browser, show the dashboard and then click ⊕ in the dashboard's lower-left corner. To find specific widgets, type in the search box at the top of the widget browser. To close the widget browser, press Esc or click an empty area on the screen.

To add a widget to the dashboard: Click it in the widget browser. You can add multiple copies of the same widget. For example, add multiple World Clock or Weather widgets for different cities.

To move a widget: Drag it around the dashboard or the widget browser.

To close a widget: In the dashboard, hold down Option or click ⊖, move the pointer over the target widget, and then click ⊗.

To customize a widget: In the dashboard, move the pointer over the widget and then click the small Info button *i* that appears in one corner. Features vary by widget (widgets that can't be customized don't have an *i* button).

To update a widget's data from the internet: Click the widget and then press Command+R (for "refresh" or "reload").

To download and install widgets: Open the widget browser and then click More Widgets in the lower-left corner. The Dashboard Widgets website opens in your default browser (on the desktop, not in the dashboard). Locate a widget and then click its Download button. When the Widget Installer opens, click Install. If the installer doesn't open automatically, go to the downloaded file and open it; if the filename has the extension .zip, double-click it to unzip it and then open the .wdgt file. The new widget is added to the widget browser.

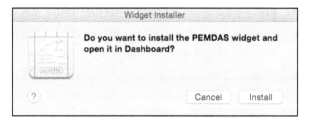

To group widgets into folders in the widget browser: To create a folder, drag one widget's icon over another, and then drag other widgets to add to the folder. To change a folder's name, click the folder to open it, click the current name, and then type the new name. To move a widget out of a folder, click the folder to open it, and then drag the widget out of the folder.

To delete a widget: Open the widget browser, hold down Option or click ⊖, and then click ⊗ on the target widget. (A widget with no ⊗ is an Apple-installed widget.) Your personal widgets are stored in /Users/*user_name*/Library/Widgets.

To delete an Apple-installed widget: In Finder or Terminal, go to /Library/Widgets and then delete the widget's .wdgt file. (Apple-installed widgets can't be easily reinstalled after they're deleted.)

To show an auto-updating portion of a webpage (Web Clip) on the dashboard: Open Safari and then go to the desired webpage. In the Safari toolbar, click ⌧ , point to highlight the desired portion of the page, and then click. If necessary, drag the highlight box to reposition it or drag its edge handles to resize it. Click Add. To customize the widget, move the pointer over it and then click its Info button *i*. If ⌧ isn't visible on the toolbar, choose View > Customize Toolbar.

Full-Screen Apps

You can expand certain applications to fill your screen edge-to-edge, hiding the dock, the menu bar, and other windows. Apps that can go full-screen include Finder, Maps, iBooks, iTunes, Mail, Messages, Calendar, Safari, Notes, Photo Booth, FaceTime, Preview, Photos, iMovie, GarageBand, QuickTime Player, Game Center, Chess, Keynote, Pages, and Numbers. Not all apps can expand to full screen (full-screen Calculator, for example, makes little sense). You can have multiple full-screen apps open at the same time and move among them easily. If you're using multiple displays, you can run an app full screen on each display.

To expand an application to full screen: Do any of the following:

- Click the green button 🟢 in the top-left corner of the application window. (If the app can't go full screen, then the window will enlarge, but not to full screen.)

- Choose View > Enter Full Screen.

- Press Ctrl+Command+F.

Tip: To enlarge a window without making it full screen, hold down the Option key and then click the green button 🟢. To restore the window to its previous size, hold down the Option key and then click the green button again. This type of window zooming was the normal behavior for the green button in older (pre-Yosemite) versions of OS X.

To see the menu bar of a full screen app: Move the pointer to the top edge of the screen.

To move from window to window in full-screen view: Do any of the following:

- Flick three fingers left or right.

- Press a Spaces keyboard shortcut (page 40).

- Open Mission Control (F3 or Control+↑) and then click the target window at the top of the screen.

Tip: Full-screen apps stay full-screen even when you switch to another app or to the desktop.

To reorder full-screen apps: Open Mission Control (F3 or Control+↑) and then, at the top of the screen, drag the thumbnails for the full-screen apps (or spaces) left or right.

To return to standard view: Do any of the following:

- Move the pointer to the top edge of the screen. When the menu bar appears, click 🟢 in the top-left corner of an application window or choose View > Exit Full Screen.

- Press Ctrl+Command+F.

- Press Esc once or twice (for some programs).

To set the full-screen multitouch gesture: Choose > System Preferences > Trackpad > More Gestures pane.

Mission Control

Mission Control unites Exposé, Spaces, Dashboard, Full-Screen Apps, and multiple displays into a comprehensive view of what's open on your computer. Open windows are grouped by application in Exposé view. Spaces, full-screen windows, and the dashboard are shown as separate thumbnails at the top of the screen.

To open Mission Control: Press the Mission Control key F3 (or Fn+F3) or press Control+↑ or flick three fingers up. To activate a window (or space), click it, tap it, or point to it and press the keyboard shortcut again. To dismiss Mission Control without activating a window, press the keyboard shortcut again (without pointing to a window), repeat the multitouch gesture, or press Esc.

To configure Mission Control: Do any of the following:

- To set general preferences, choose > System Preferences > Mission Control.

- To set keyboard shortcuts, choose > System Preferences > Keyboard > Shortcuts pane > Mission Control.

- To set multitouch gestures, choose > System Preferences > Trackpad > More Gestures pane.

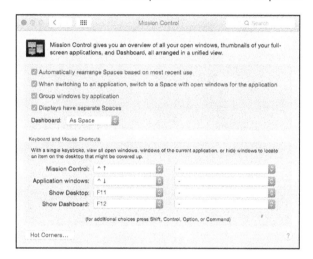

Hiding Programs

Program-hiding is a quick alternative to Exposé for getting programs out of your way. Hiding a program causes all its windows and panels to vanish. They return when you unhide it. The bold application menu (next to the menu) has the Hide commands.

To hide the current program: Choose the Hide command (Command+H) from the program's application menu, or Option-click any visible spot on the desktop.

To hide the current program and open another: Option-click the other program's icon in the dock or any visible part of the other program's windows.

To hide any open program: Command+Tab to the program's icon, release the Tab key, and then press H. (If the program is already hidden, it unhides.)

To hide all programs but the current one: Choose Hide Others (Option+Command+H) from the program's application menu.

To open a program and hide all others: Option-Command-click the program's icon in the dock.

To unhide a program: Command+Tab to it, click its dock icon, or choose Show All from any application menu.

Organizing Desktop Icons

OS X provides clean-up tools for desktop icons.

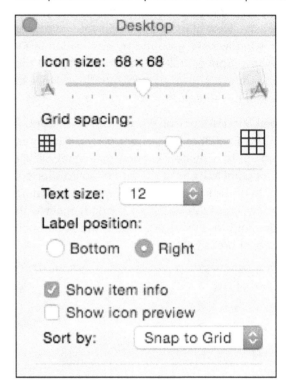

To set the size, spacing, labels, and arrangement of desktop icons: Right-click an empty area on the desktop and then choose Show View Options.

To choose which items appear on the desktop: Click an empty area on the desktop to activate Finder, choose Finder > Preferences > General pane, and then select the desired desktop items.

To snap desktop icons to an invisible grid: Right-click an empty area on the desktop and then choose Clean Up or Clean Up By.

To change the sort order of desktop icons: Right-click an empty area on the desktop and then choose Sort By.

Notification Center

Notifications Center provides you with timely alerts and reminders from applications (Notifications view) and an overview of your day's events (Today view). Notification Center for OS X works like its counterpart feature on iOS devices (iPad, iPhone, and iPod touch).

Notifications View

Certain applications can push notifications to your Mac, even when you're not actively using the program. Notification Center is the central list of all the apps that are trying to get your attention. Apps that can send notifications include:

- Calendar for events and invitations.

- Reminders for reminders coming due.

- Game Center for friend requests and game invitations.

- Mac App Store for software updates.

- Mail for incoming email from all senders, only contacts, or only VIP senders.

- Messages for new messages.

- Safari for website alerts. You can sign up with websites to receive news headlines, sports scores, auction (eBay) alerts, and more as notifications, even when Safari isn't running.

- FaceTime for missed calls.

- Twitter for direct messages and mentions (you can also tweet right to Twitter from Notification Center).

- Facebook for Facebook notifications (you can also post right to Facebook from Notification Center).

- Third-party apps whose developers tap into Notification Center.

When you receive a notification, a small floating window appears in the top-right corner of the screen, containing the notification. Notifications come in two forms: banners and alerts. A **banner** slides into view and then disappears after 5 seconds. An **alert** remains visible until you acknowledge it by clicking Close, OK, Dismiss, Options, Read, Snooze, or whatever. Clicking a banner opens the corresponding application to show the related item. Some notifications are interactive—if you receive an email, message, or FaceTime call, for example, you can respond without leaving the app you're in.

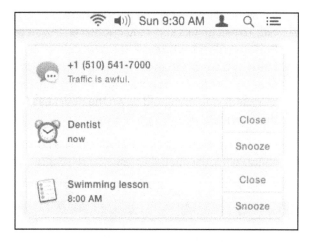

If a banner notification disappears before you can get to it, you can open Notification Center at any time (even from a full-screen app) to see a list of recent notifications.

When you open Notification Center, an overlay shifts leftward to reveal all current notifications in a sorted list along the right edge of your screen.

Tip: Some notifications will appear even if the associated application is closed, whereas others will appear only if the underlying application is open (whether it's active or in the background). Notifications for new messages, for example, appear even if the Messages app is closed, whereas new-mail notifications appear only if the Mail app is open. An open program will have a small dot next to its icon in the dock.

To open Notification Center: Do any of the following:

- Click the Notification Center icon ≣ near the right edge of the menu bar. (You can't hide this icon.)

- Flick two fingers from the right edge of the track-pad into the center (as if you were pulling something away from the right side of the screen). Accuracy counts: you must start to flick from the right edge. To toggle this gesture, choose > System Preferences > Trackpad > More Gestures.

- Press the Notification Center keyboard short-cut. To assign this shortcut, choose > System Preferences > Keyboard > Shortcuts pane, click Mission Control (on the left), select Show Notification Center (or double-click it if it's already selected), and then hold down the new keys for the shortcut.

To read notifications: Click the Notifications button at the top of Notification Center.

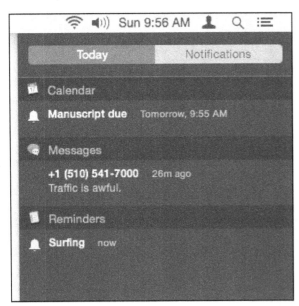

To close Notification Center without responding to a notification: Do any of the following:

- Click ≣ in the menu bar.

- Flick two fingers to the right.

- Click anywhere off Notification Center.

To hide alerts and banners temporarily (Do Not Disturb): Do any of the following:

- Hold down the Option key and then click ≣ in the menu bar.

- Open Notification Center, click the Today button, scroll to the top of the pane, and then turn on "Do Not Disturb".

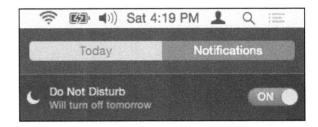

Only pop-up alerts and banners are hidden. Notifications still appear when you open Notification Center. To fine-tune Do Not Disturb to fit your schedule, choose > System Preferences > Notifications > Do Not Disturb.

Tip: Alerts and banners are hidden automatically when you're presenting in Keynote, when your Mac is connected to a projector, or (optionally) when your display is sleeping or mirrored on an external display.

To configure Notification Center: Choose > System Preferences > Notifications, or open Notification Center and then click the gear icon in the bottom-right corner.

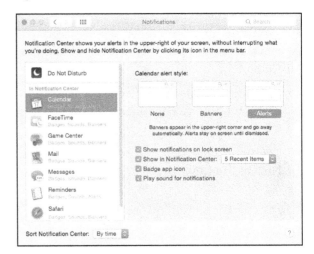

Apps that can send notifications are listed on the left. Click an app to change its settings.

For each app, you can set:

- Whether an app sends notifications.

- Whether you receive banner or alert notifications (or none at all).

- The order in which notifications are listed (for manual sorting, drag apps up or down to reorder the list).

- How many recent notifications appear in Notification Center.

- Whether to display an alert badge (a number in a little red circle) on the notifying app's dock icon.

- Whether the notification appears when your Mac is locked.

- Whether to play a sound as part of the notification.

- Whether to display a short preview of a message or email.

Some applications let you set additional notification and alert options within the app itself (typically in the Preferences dialog box). In Mail, for example, choose Mail > Preferences > General pane > "New message notifications". In Safari, choose Safari > Preferences > Notifications pane.

Today View

Today view summarizes the day's events, reminders, upcoming birthdays, weather, and so on, and previews tomorrow's schedule. The current day and date always appear at the top of Today view, and you can customize the rest of the view by adding, removing, or reordering **widgets**—small, single-purpose panels that display up-to-date information. OS X comes with a handful of widgets (Calendar, Weather, Reminders, and so on), and you can find more from third-party developers in the Mac App Store (page 111).

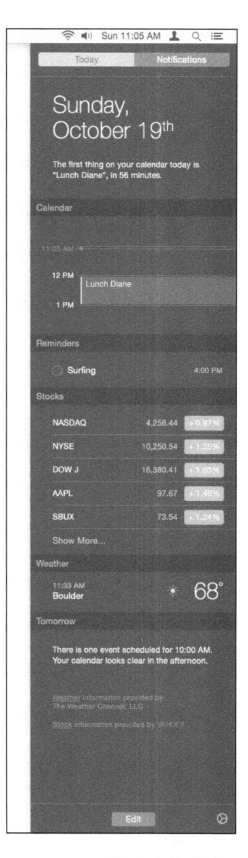

To add or remove widgets: Click the Today button at the top of Notification Center and then click Edit at the bottom of the view. The widget drawer opens. To add or remove widgets, click the green (+) or red (–) buttons, or drag widgets to or from the view or widget drawer. When you're finished, click Done.

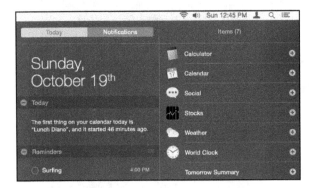

To reorder widgets: In Today view, drag widgets up or down. The Today Summary and Tomorrow Summary widgets are anchored at the top and bottom of the view, respectively—they can be added or removed, but not reordered.

To configure an individual widget: In Today view, point to the widget and then click the circled i that appears in the widget's upper-right corner. Not all widgets can be configured individually—you can configure Stocks and Weather, for example, but not Calendar and Reminders.

Tip: You can also select and reorder widgets by using the Extensions panel (page 66) in System Preferences.

System Preferences

You can change OS X's factory settings to suit your own preferences and abilities. The hundreds of customizable settings range from superficial to meaningful. Changes to graphics, colors, and animation are usually cosmetic, whereas some other settings—the language used or features for disabled users—change the way that you work with OS X.

System Preferences

 Use **System Preferences** panels to change personal and systemwide settings. Changes that affect everyone who uses the computer, rather than only your user account, require

administrator access. The controls for administrator settings are dimmed and locked, click 🔒 (in the panel's lower-left corner) to unlock them with an administrator password.

You can list panel icons in functional categories (hardware, internet, and so on) or alphabetically (preferred by experienced users who have memorized the icon names). You can open System Preferences showing icon shortcuts to all panels or jump straight to a specific panel.

To open System Preferences: Do any of the following:

- Click the System Preferences icon in the dock.

- Choose > System Preferences.

- Press Command+Spacebar to open Spotlight search, type *sys*, and then press Return when System Preferences is highlighted.

To show or hide specific icons: In System Preferences, choose View > Customize, toggle the checkboxes next to each icon, and then click Done.

To view all icons (return to the main Preferences panel): In System Preferences, choose View > Show All Preferences (Command+L) or click the ⊞ button. (The Show All command doesn't unhide hidden icons.)

To change how icons are organized: In System Preferences, choose View > Organize by Categories or View > Organize Alphabetically.

To open a specific panel: With System Preferences open, do any of the following:

- Click the panel's icon.

- Choose the panel from the View menu.

- Click-and-hold the ⠿ button and then choose the panel from the pop-up menu.

- Right-click (or click-and-hold) the System Preferences icon in the dock and then choose the panel from the pop-up menu (you may have to hold down the Control key when you click the dock icon).

- In the search box (Command+F), start typing the panel name or setting name (*brightness*, for example) and then click the relevant highlighted icon.

To open System Preferences in a specific panel: Do any of the following:

- Click a menu-extras icon on the right side of the menu bar and look for a Preferences command (the Wi-Fi menu 🛜, for example, has the command Open Network Preferences.)

- Hold down Option and press a Function key (press Option+F3, for example, to open the Mission Control panel). You may have to hold down the Fn key too.

- Press Command+Spacebar to open Spotlight search, start typing the panel name or setting name (*network*, for example) and then choose the relevant panel when it appears in the results list under System Preferences.

To require an administrator to unlock each System Preferences panel individually: Normally, only administrators can change System Preferences that affect the entire computer and everyone who uses it (Date & Time, Users & Groups, Network, and Security & Privacy, for example). A nonadministrator can change these secure preferences only if an administrator clicks 🔒 and enters a name and password to approve the changes. Unlocking any *one* System Preferences panel, however, unlocks them *all*, and the user can keep making changes without the administrator's knowledge. To require an administrator to unlock each System Preferences panel individually, choose > System Preferences > Security & Privacy > Advanced button (click 🔒 if the settings are dimmed) > select "Require an administrator password to access system-wide preferences".

Accessibility

Use the Accessibility panel to toggle and configure features for disabled users with poor eyesight, hearing, or mobility. Keyboard shortcut: Option+Command+F5.

Display

Use high-contrast or grayscale color schemes, or enlarge the pointer. Keyboard shortcuts: Ctrl+Option+Command+8 (white-on-black), Ctrl+Option+Command+comma (reduce contrast), and Ctrl+Option+Command+dot (increase contrast). See also "Displays" on page 62.

Zoom

Enlarge all or part of the onscreen image. Keyboard shortcuts: Option+Command+8 (on/off), Option+Command+= (zoom in), and Option+Command+- (zoom out).

VoiceOver

VoiceOver describes aloud what appears onscreen and speaks the text in documents and windows. To read and listen to a VoiceOver tutorial, click Open VoiceOver Training. To set up VoiceOver, click Open VoiceOver Utility. VoiceOver also supports braille displays. On/off keyboard shortcut: Command+F5 (or Fn+Command+F5).

Descriptions

Listen to a description of the visual content in movies, TV episodes, and other video, if available.

Captions

Set the fonts and formatting of video language tracks, subtitles, and closed captions.

Audio

Add a widescreen flash to alerts or convert multichannel sound to single-channel sound (useful if you have hearing loss in one ear). See also "Sound" on page 73.

Keyboard

Set additional options for the keyboard. Sticky Keys lets you press keyboard combinations, such as Ctrl+Option+Command, one key at a time, or show pressed keys onscreen (on/off keyboard shortcut: tap Shift five times). Slow Keys lets you increase the amount of time that OS X takes to recognize that a key is being pressed.

Mouse & Trackpad

Set additional options for the mouse and trackpad. Mouse Keys lets you move the pointer around the screen by using the numeric keypad. On/off keyboard shortcut: tap Option five times.

Switch Control

Enable access for assistive devices.

Dictation

Control OS X by speaking commands that edit or format text, quit or switch applications, open or save documents, and so on. OS X comes with basic dictation commands, and you can create more. See also "Dictation & Speech" on page 58.

App Store

Updates OS X software (page 170).

Bluetooth

Use the Bluetooth panel to set up Bluetooth devices. This panel appears only on Macs with a built-in or USB Bluetooth transmitter. **Bluetooth** is a wireless technology that provides short-range (about 30 feet/10 meters) radio links among computers, phones, mice, keyboards, earpieces, iPads, and other Bluetooth-equipped devices. It doesn't need a line-of-sight connection and eliminates cable clutter while simplifying communications, sharing, and data synchronization between computers and devices. For two Bluetooth gadgets to talk to each other, they must both be made **discoverable** and then be **paired**. Bluetooth is turned off by default to save battery power. See also "Bluetooth File Exchange" (page 112) and "Bluetooth Sharing" (page 151).

To set up a Bluetooth device: Choose > System Preferences > Bluetooth. Click Turn Bluetooth On. If OS X doesn't detect your Bluetooth device automatically, click Advanced, launch the Bluetooth Setup Assistant, and then follow the onscreen instructions. When the list of discoverable, in-range Bluetooth devices appears, choose the one that you want to pair. If you're pairing a secure device such as a keyboard or mobile phone, then note or set the passcode used for pairing. You may be prompted for other settings, such as syncing. After setup, the device is listed on the Bluetooth panel.

To delete a Bluetooth device: In the Bluetooth panel, select the device and then click ×.

To quickly view Bluetooth connection information: Hold down the Option key and then click the Bluetooth menu in the menu bar. (To show the Bluetooth menu, choose > System Preferences > Bluetooth > select "Show Bluetooth in menu bar".)

To configure Bluetooth: In the Bluetooth panel, click Advanced and then set the following options:

Open Bluetooth Setup Assistant at startup if no keyboard/mouse/trackpad is detected
Determines whether the Bluetooth Setup Assistant opens automatically when your Mac can't find a particular input device at startup.

Allow Bluetooth devices to wake this computer
Determines whether a sleeping Mac wakes when you press a key or click a button on a paired Bluetooth device.

CDs & DVDs

Use the CDs & DVDs panel to set the Mac's default action when you insert a blank, music, photo, or movie CD or DVD. (See also "Burning CDs & DVDs" on page 98.)

Ask what to do
Asks you what to do with the disc.

Open [application]
Opens the specified program automatically. Choose "Open other application" to specify an unlisted program.

Run script
Runs the specified script (page 128).

Ignore
Shows the disc icon on the desktop and does nothing.

Date & Time

Use the Date & Time panel to set system date, time, and time zone, and configure the menu-bar clock. OS X uses the system time to time-stamp files and email, schedule tasks, and record events.

Date & Time Pane

Set date and time automatically
Determines whether you set the time manually or OS X sets it automatically off an internet time server, accounting for daylight savings time where applicable. Turn on this option if you have an always-on internet connection. If you connect via dial-up modem, turn it off to suppress autodialing.

Calendar and clock
Sets the date and time manually if automatic updating is turned off. To change a number, click it, and then type a new number, press the up and down arrow keys, or click the arrow buttons. Press Tab to highlight the next number. You can also click a date in the calendar or drag the hands of the clock.

Open Language & Region
Opens the Language & Region panel (page 72). Use this panel's Formats pane to format the date and time.

Time Zone Pane

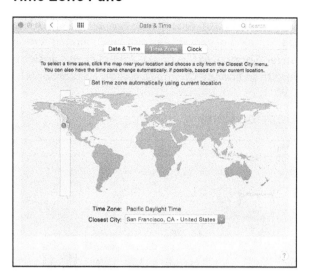

Set time zone automatically using current location
Sets the time zone automatically and drops a pin on the map to show your current location. A wireless or internet connection is required to locate you. To disable autolocation, choose > System Preferences > Security & Privacy > Privacy pane > Location Services > clear Enable Location Services (click if the settings are dimmed).

Map
To set the time zone manually, click the point on the map closest to you, and then select or type the name of the closest town or city in your time zone.

Clock Pane

Show date and time in menu bar
Determines whether the current date and time appear on the right side of the menu bar. Choose a digital (5:58 PM) or analog ⌧ clock face and set the other options. "Use a 24-hour clock" (19:18 instead of 7:18 PM) affects only the menu-bar clock. You can click the clock on the menu bar to show the day and date, toggle analog/digital display, or open the Date & Time panel.

Announce the time
Makes the Mac speak the current time at specified intervals ("It's seven forty-five").

Desktop & Screen Saver

Use the Desktop & Screen Saver panel to set the background of your screen and the (optional) screen saver. Shortcut to this panel: right-click the desktop and then choose Change Desktop Background.

Desktop Pane

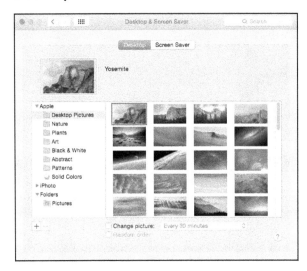

You can change the image (**wallpaper**) that appears under the icons on your desktop to a solid color, pattern, or photo (your own or the ones that come with OS X).

To set up the desktop background: Click an image category in the list on the left, and then click a specific image in the sample box on the right. "Photos" show photos that you've imported to the Photos application. "Folders" shows any JPEG, PICT, and TIFF images in your Pictures folder. When you choose an imported image, a pop-up menu appears above the sample box to help you fit the image on your desktop. High-resolution (≥1024 × 768 pixels) photos look best.

To use images from a folder other than Pictures, click (+) to add it to the list. To remove an added folder, select it and then click (–). To autochange images at a specified interval, select "Change picture". To view the images in random order rather than alphabetically by file name, select "Random order".

Tip: To make the menu bar, dock, and other screen elements opaque, choose > System Preferences > Accessibility > Display > "Reduce transparency".

Screen Saver Pane

A screen saver blanks the screen or shows images after a specified time passes without keyboard, mouse, or trackpad activity. Pressing a key, moving the mouse, or tapping the trackpad deactivates the screen saver. OS X offers two type of screen savers: slideshows and traditional screen savers. An animated slideshow cycles through a collection of pictures (either a built-in collection or a folder containing your own pictures). A traditional screen saver shows dancing patterns of light, artwork, or text.

To set up the screen saver: Click a slideshow or a screen saver in the list on the left (scroll the list to see all the choices). If you choose a slideshow, click the Source pop-up menu under the sample box and then choose a built-in picture collection or a folder containing your own pictures. High-resolution (≥1024 × 768 pixels) photos look best. If you choose a screen saver, click the Screen Saver Options button (if available) under the sample box to fine-tune the display.

To change the screen saver every time that it activates, select the "Random" screen saver. To show the time on the screen saver, select "Show with clock". To see a full-screen preview, hover the pointer over the image in the sample box and then click Preview. To set the idle time before the screen saver starts, click the "Start after" pop-up menu ("Never" disables the screen saver). To start or disable the screen saver by moving the pointer to a specified corner of the screen, click Hot Corners and then choose "Start Screen Saver" or "Disable Screen Saver" from any of the pop-up menus. To password-lock a screen saver, choose > System Preferences > Security & Privacy > General pane > select "Require password after sleep or screen saver begins". See also "Energy Saver" on page 64.

Tip: You can use a Terminal command to specify any time interval (not only the preset menu choices) that must pass before the screen-saver password requirement kicks in: `defaults -currentHost write com.apple.screensaver askForPasswordDelay -int` *interval*, where *interval* specifies the number of seconds to wait before a password is required.

Dictation & Speech

Use the Dictation & Speech panel to make OS X type spoken words or read text aloud in a synthesized voice.

Dictation Pane

You can dictate text instead of typing on the keyboard. Dictation works with text areas in any OS X app, without special setup or voice training (for third-party apps, no additional third-party developer support is required). To dictate, you must be connected to the internet (unless you select Use Enhanced Dictation). When you dictate text, what you say is sent to Apple to convert it to text. Other personal information (such as contact names) may be sent too. For details, click About Dictation and Privacy in the Dictation pane. Dictation supports parental controls.

To set up dictation:

1 Choose > System Preferences > Dictation & Speech > Dictation pane.

2 In the Dictation pane, turn on Dictation.

3 Choose your language and dialect from the Language pop-up menu.

4 If you like, use the Shortcut pop-up menu to change the keyboard shortcut that triggers dictation.

   To create a shortcut that's not in the list, choose Customize and then press two or more keys you want to use.

5 To dictate by using a specific microphone, click the pop-up menu below the microphone icon.

To dictate text:

1 Place the insertion point where you want the dictated text to appear.

   You can dictate text anywhere that you can type it.

2 Press the Fn key twice or choose Edit > Start Dictation.

3 When the microphone icon appears, speak your text calmly at a normal pace.

   The icon glows to show your speaking volume.

4 When you're done, press the Fn key or click the Done button.

   Your spoken text appears.

To practice, try dictating a note in Notes (page 123).

To enter punctuation, say the punctuation mark. Suppose that you want to dictate "Let's eat, grandma." Say this:

Let's eat comma grandma period

The more you use Dictation, the better it understands you. Unclear text is underlined in blue. If the text is wrong, click it and then select an alternate, or type or dictate the correct text. Make sure that the mic is unobstructed by hands, clothing, or other objects. If you dictate in a noisy or echo-prone place, it may help to use a headset microphone. If you use an external mic, set its input volume high enough to respond to your voice (choose > System Preferences > Sound > Input pane).

Tip: Dictation is integrated with Contacts. Say a contact's name, and Dictation knows who you mean and spells it correctly.

Line break

To insert a line break (like pressing the Return key once), say "new line".

New paragraph

To start a new paragraph (like press the Return key twice), say "new paragraph".

Punctuation

"period" or "full stop" types . (followed by a space and an uppercase letter)

"dot" or "point" types . (without a trailing space)

"comma" types ,

"semicolon" types ;

"colon" types :

"question mark" types ?

"exclamation point" types !

"inverted question mark" types ¿

"inverted exclamation point" types ¡

"hyphen" types - (without surrounding spaces)

"dash" types – (with surrounding spaces)

"em dash" types — (with surrounding spaces)

"quote" types "

"unquote" or "end quote" or "close quote" types " (with a trailing space)

"open single quote" types ' (without a trailing space)

"close single quote" types ' (with a trailing space)

"backquote" types ´ (with a trailing space)

"ampersand" types &

"slash" types /

"asterisk" types *

"at sign" types @

"underscore" types _

"ellipsis" or "dot dot dot" types ...

"section sign" types §

"tilde" types ~

"vertical bar" types |

"pound sign" types #

"open parenthesis" or "open paren" types (

"close parenthesis" or "close paren" types)

"open bracket" types [

"close bracket" types]

"open brace" types {

"close brace" types }

Capitalization

"cap" or "capital" capitalizes the next word

"caps on" or "caps off" toggles capitalization for the first letter of every word

"all caps" makes the next word all uppercase

"all caps on" or "all caps off" toggles all uppercase

"no caps" makes the next word all lowercase

"no caps on" or "no caps off" toggles all lowercase

Tip: The first new word after a period, question mark, or exclamation point is capitalized automatically (you don't need to say "cap").

Spacing

"spacebar" inserts a space instead of a hyphen in a normally hyphenated word; for example, "first spacebar class hotel" types *first class hotel*

"no space" prevents a space between words

"no space on" or "no space off" toggles spaces between words

Tip: Speak each of the capitalization and spacing on/off commands as a separate utterance, with a small pause before and after.

Numbers

To type *5* rather than *five*, say "numeral five". Saying more than one digit in a row also produces numerals: saying "four five" types *45*, not *four five*. Say "point" or "dot" to insert a decimal point: "six point five" types *6.5*.

Mathematical symbols and operators

"plus sign" types +

"minus sign" types -

"asterisk" types *

"slash" types /

"caret" types ^

"percent sign" types %

"greater-than sign" types >

"less-than sign" types <

"degree sign" types °

"equals sign" types =

Currency

"dollar sign" types $

"cent sign" types ¢

"euro sign" types €

"yen sign" types ¥

"pounds sterling sign" types £

Tip: Currency amounts are recognized automatically. "fourteen dollars and twenty five cents" types *$14.25*. "five hundred yen" types *¥500*. "six point five euros" types *€6.5*.

Dates

Dates are recognized automatically. "july twenty seventh twenty twelve at six thirty AM" types *July 27, 2012 at 6:30 AM*.

Emoticons (smileys)

"smiley" or "smiley face" or "smile face" types :-)

"frowny" or "frowny face" or "frown face" types :-(

"winky" or "winky face" or "wink face" types ;-)

Web and email addresses

You can say "dub dub dub" to type the "www" part of a web address (URL). Say "dub dub dub dot apple dot com", for example, to type *www.apple.com*.

Dictation recognizes email addresses by listening for the central "at sign". Say "john underscore smith at sign gmail dot com", for example, to type *john_smith@gmail.com*.

Trademarks and copyrights

"copyright sign" types ©

"registered sign" types ®

"trademark sign" types ™

Alphabet letters

To type *A B C D* and so on, say "a bee cee dee" and so on. (This method typically isn't very accurate.)

Tip: You can say letters to voice-type words rather than inserting punctuation or symbols. For example, to voice-type the word "dot" (rather than insert a dot or period symbol), say "no space on, no caps on, dee, oh, tee, no space off, no caps off". Typing with your fingers is usually easier in cases like these.

Text to Speech Pane

Text to Speech uses a synthesized voice to read aloud alert messages (including text in dialog boxes) or text that you highlight. See also VoiceOver (page 53).

To set up the synthesized voice: In the Text to Speech pane, choose the default system voice and then set the speed at which it speaks. To hear a sample sentence using the current settings, click Play.

To hear alert messages: In the Text to Speech pane, select "Announce when alerts are displayed", and then click Set Alert Options to override the system voice, set a preamble phrase for the spoken alert, or set the number of seconds that OS X waits before it speaks the message.

To hear selected text: In the Text to Speech pane, select "Speak selected text when the key is pressed", hold down one or more modifier keys (Shift, Control, Option, or Command), and then press another key to set the keyboard shortcut to hear selected text. To hear selected text spoken, select it, and then press the keyboard shortcut.

Tip: You can also convert text to speech by using the **say** command in Terminal.

Displays

Use the Displays panel to adjust your monitor(s). Shortcut to this panel: Option+F1/F2 (or Fn+Option+F1/F2). The panes and options that appear in this panel depend on your monitor setup.

Display Pane

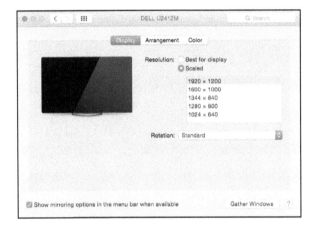

Resolution
> Sets the fineness of detail of your screen's image, expressed in pixels wide by pixels high. (A **pixel** is the smallest building block—"dot"—of the display.) Higher resolutions make screen text and objects smaller but show a greater area. For LED, LCD, laptop, and Retina displays, choose "Best for display" to use **native resolution**. To use a different resolution, choose Scaled. A non-native resolution may blur your screen image.

Brightness
> Adjusts the screen luminosity. Keyboard shortcuts: F1 and F2 (or Fn+F1/F2).

Rotation (swivel displays only)
> Rotates the screen image in 90-degree increments.

Gather Windows (multiple displays only)
> Moves all open Displays preferences windows (one per display) to the same screen.

Show mirroring options in the menu bar when available
> When multiple displays are being used, this option shows or hides the mirroring menu on the right side of the menu bar. See also "AirPlay Mirroring" on page 153.

Automatically adjust brightness
> Determines whether the light sensor dims the screen and backlit keyboard automatically in dark rooms.

Colors (CRT displays only)
> Sets the number of colors (typically, Millions) that the screen can show simultaneously.

Refresh Rate (CRT displays only)
> Sets the frequency at which the screen is redrawn to maintain a steady image. Higher refresh rates yield less flicker and eyestrain.

Using Multiple Displays

If your Mac is connected to multiple displays:

- You can set up the displays as an extended, continuous desktop, or show the same image on all screens (**mirroring**).

- Each display has its own menu bar.

- The dock is available on all screens (there's no primary or secondary display). If the dock isn't visible on a display, move the pointer to the screen edge where the dock normally appears (typically the bottom edge) to make the dock slide into view.

- Each display can independently show the desktop (with multiple open windows) or show a full-screen app.

- Open Mission Control (F3 or Control+↑) to get an overview of what's running on each display. You can drag app thumbnails between displays to customize the view.

- With AirPlay and an Apple TV (page 153), you can use an HDTV as a full-fledged display, complete with dock and menu bar.

Tip: To allow a single window to span multiple displays, choose > System Preferences > Mission Control, and then clear "Displays have separate Spaces".

Color Pane

Use this pane to create a ColorSync profile (page 114) when you calibrate your display to show colors accurately. You can switch among multiple color profiles or, if you have multiple displays, assign a different profile to each display. To create a profile, click Calibrate, and then follow the onscreen instructions.

Dock

Configures the dock (page 34).

Energy Saver

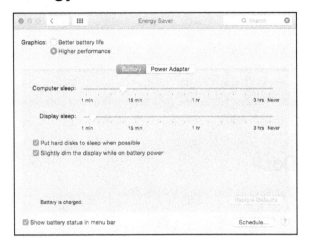

Use the Energy Saver panel to configure hardware features that reduce power consumption and extend the life of computer parts by switching them to a low-power state. This panel's options vary by Mac model (laptop, desktop, old, new, and so on). See also "Activity Monitor" on page 111.

Graphics
Adjusts the tradeoff between better battery life (for writers and shoppers) and higher graphics performance (for gamers and film editors). Re-login to effect the change.

Battery/Power Adapter panes
A desktop has only one set of sliders and options. A laptop has two sets: Battery applies when running on battery power and Power Adapter applies when plugged into a power source.

Computer/Display sleep sliders
Sets the computer, or only the display, to sleep automatically after it's idle for the specified time period ("Never" disables sleep). Put only the display to sleep if your computer is in the middle of a task that you want to finish.

Put the hard disks to sleep when possible
Determines whether to stop an idle hard drive's disks from spinning.

Slightly dim the display while on battery power
Determines whether laptop screen brightness is dimmed when on battery power.

Enable Power Nap while on battery power
Toggles Power Nap (page 171), which lets App Store updates, iCloud synchronization, and other updates and backups occur while your Mac sleeps, draining little power.

Wake for network access
Determines whether you can access a sleeping Mac's shared resources (printers or iTunes, for example) over a wireless or wired network.

Start up automatically after a power failure
Determines whether the Mac restarts automatically after a power interruption.

Allow power button to put the computer to sleep
On desktop Macs, determines whether pressing ⏻ shuts down or sleeps the Mac.

Automatically reduce brightness before display goes to sleep
Determines whether the screen brightness dims (typically as a warning to move the mouse) before the display fully sleeps.

Show battery status in the menu bar

Shows the battery menu on the right side of the menu bar. The battery's icon indicates its status: draining (shrinking progress bar), charging (lightning bolt), fully charged (full battery), or something's wrong (×). This menu also lists power-hogging apps and shows the estimated time remaining until the battery dies or, if plugged in, is fully charged. Choose Show Percentage to display the remaining battery charge on the menu bar. Option-click this menu to see the battery condition.

Schedule

Sets a daily schedule for putting your computer to sleep or turning it off and on.

Extensions

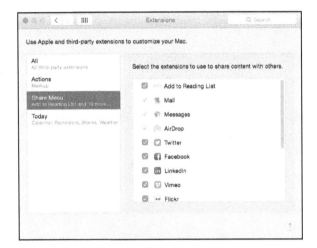

Extensions are small, functional add-ons that enhance and customize OS X. You can use the Extensions panel to choose which extensions appear in Action menus ⚙, Share menus ⬆, and Notification Center's Today view (page 49).

Third-party developers can also provide extensions that add functionality to OS X. Extensions come bundled with applications; they can't be purchased or installed separately. A single application can provide multiple extensions.

You can't launch extensions directly. Instead, OS X finds extensions automatically and launches them in response to your actions. OS X can launch an extension even when its containing application isn't running. Extension processes are short lived—OS X kills them quickly when they're no longer needed.

The same privacy settings that apply to an application also apply to its extensions. If you let an application access your Contacts data, for example, then all that app's extensions can also access Contacts data.

The Extensions panel lists four types of extensions:

- **All** extensions are provided by third-party applications (that is, extensions other than OS X's Apple-provided native extensions).

- **Actions** extensions alter content within an application. The Markup feature in Mail, for example, is an action extension.

- **Share Menu** extensions appear in OS X's ubiquitous Share menus ⬆.

- **Today** extensions, called widgets, appear in Notification Center's Today view.

General

Use the General panel to make minor alterations to the look of windows, menus, buttons, scrollbars, and fonts.

Appearance
Blue is the standard OS X color for default buttons, menu highlighting, progress bars, window-sizing buttons, and other odds and ends. Graphite mutes the color scheme to grayscale.

Use dark menu bar and Dock
Use dark backgrounds and light text for the menu bar and dock (sometimes handy for working with photos and videos). Darkened elements are still translucent, not opaque.

Tip: To make the menu bar, dock, and other screen elements opaque, choose > System Preferences > Accessibility > Display > "Reduce transparency".

Highlight color
Choose the highlight color of selected text. This color also outlines windows that you drag icons into.

Sidebar icon size
Changes the size of icons in the sidebar of Finder windows.

Show scroll bars/Click in the scroll bar to
Changes the appearance and behavior of scrollbars.

Default web browser
Choose the web browser that opens when you click a link in email, messages, documents, and so on.

Ask to keep changes when closing documents
Determines whether unsaved changes are saved automatically when you close documents. To be prompted to save changes, turn on this option. See also "Auto Save and Versions" on page 107.

Close windows when quitting an app
Determines whether document windows open to their previous size and position when you relaunch an app. If you want to launch apps with a clean slate, turn on this option. See also "Resume" on page 106.

Recent items
Sets how many of your recently opened programs, documents, and servers appear in the Recent Items submenu in the Apple menu .

Use LCD font smoothing when available
Determines whether onscreen (but not printed) text is smoothed (**antialiased**). The smoothing effect may be subtle, so experiment with various small and large type sizes to see which setting you prefer. After you change this setting, close then reopen a program to see the change; for Finder, you must log out and then log in again.

iCloud

iCloud is an online storage and computing service that uploads (copies) your content to Apple's remote data center and pushes it wirelessly to your Mac, Windows PC, and iOS devices (iPhone, iPad, and iPod touch). Your music, photos, documents, and more are available on-demand across all your computers and iDevices. iCloud is integrated with your programs and works in the background silently and automatically (without manual syncing or sending). You can also view and manage your content and settings at *icloud.com* in a modern browser. Some iCloud features work across OS X, Windows, and iOS, whereas others are iOS-only.

A few iCloud tips:

- The minimal system requirements for iCloud are at "System requirements for iCloud" at *support. apple.com/HT204230*.

- iCloud provides unlimited free storage for purchased music, TV shows, iOS apps, and books. It also includes 5 GB of free storage for mail, documents, and backups. Higher storage capacities are available for an annual fee (*support. apple.com/HT201318*). You can manage your storage by controlling backups and choosing which documents to store in the cloud (*support. apple.com/HT204247*).

- iCloud identifies you by your Apple ID (*support. apple.com/HT204053*).

- iCloud stores your data securely. For details, read "iCloud security and privacy overview" at *support.apple.com/HT202303*.

To set up iCloud (OS X): Choose > System Preferences > iCloud, enter your Apple ID and password (if prompted), and then select the services that you'd like to enable. The following services are available:

Family Sharing

Family Sharing (also available on iOS 8 and later) lets purchases be shared among members of a single household while still allowing everyone to have their own Apple ID. Each family has one organizer who can invite up to five additional members. Invitees receive an email, and once they accept, become members of the family group.

All purchases by family members use a single payment method controlled by the organizer. Family members get immediate access to each other's purchased music, movies, TV shows, books, and apps on their Mac. The family organizer and (optionally) other adult family members can remotely approve purchases made by children in the iTunes Store, iBooks Store, and App Store. Being part of a family also includes shared photo albums, calendars, reminders, and location information.

To set up Family Sharing, choose > System Preferences > iCloud > Set Up Family, and then follow the onscreen instructions. For details and restrictions, read the Apple support article "Family Sharing" at *support.apple.com/ HT201060*.

iCloud Drive

iCloud Drive lets you securely store your documents, presentations, spreadsheets, PDFs, images, and any other kind of file in iCloud and access them from your iPhone, iPad, iPod touch, Mac, or Windows PC. To upload files to iCloud, drag them into the iCloud Drive folder on your Mac or Windows PC. Or start a new document by using an iCloud-enabled app on your iOS device. Then you can access the latest version of these files from all your devices. You can start creating a presentation on your Mac at home, for example, and then make final edits and present it at work by using your iPad. All the changes that you make along the way appear automatically on all your devices.

iCloud Drive requires OS X Yosemite (OS X 10.10) or later on a Mac, Windows 7 or later on a PC, and iOS 8 or later on an iPhone, iPad, or iPod touch. iCloud Drive completely replaces "Documents & Data" storage (see below) found in older (pre-Yosemite) versions of OS X. Upgrading to iCloud Drive is an optional, irreversible, one-time process. You'll be prompted to upgrade during the account setup process. If you decline, you can upgrade later by turning on iCloud Drive in the iCloud panel in System Preferences.

In OS X, iCloud Drive appears in the Finder sidebar and Go menu like any other system folder (its specific location is /Users/*user_name*/Library/Mobile Documents). Deleting or moving a file stored in iCloud Drive is accompanied by a warning to remind you that such an operation has far-reaching effects and isn't just a normal file manipulation. Progress bars in Finder indicate the synchronization status of files in iCloud Drive. Files in iCloud Drive are available on your Mac even when you're not connected to the internet. Any changes that you make to a file while offline are synced automatically as soon as your Mac is back online. For details, read "iCloud Drive FAQ" at *support.apple.com/HT201104*.

Documents & Data

Transfer Pages, Keynote, and Numbers documents between your computer and your iOS devices. Sign in to *icloud.com* in a modern browser, and all your iWork for iOS and iWork for iCloud documents will be there, complete with your most recent edits. You can also drag an iWork for Mac or Microsoft Office document (Word, PowerPoint, or Excel) from your computer to one of the iWork apps on *icloud.com*; it will appear automatically on all your iOS devices for viewing and editing. Third-party developers can make their apps work with iCloud, too. If you

can't update or upload documents to iCloud, read "iCloud: Troubleshooting Documents in the Cloud" at *support.apple.com/HT203517*. You can also move documents to the cloud from Preview (page 125) and TextEdit (page 129).

Tip: Documents & Data storage has been superseded by iCloud Drive (see above) in OS X Yosemite (OS X 10.10) and later.

Photos

When **My Photo Stream** is turned on (click Options), photos imported to your Mac or Windows PC are pushed to iCloud automatically, as are photos taken on iOS devices. On your Mac, you can view the photos in the Photos application (page 124). For details, read the Apple support article "My Photo Stream FAQ" at *support. apple.com/HT201317*. You can also use My Photo Stream photos as a screen saver. iCloud Photo Library and iCloud Photo Sharing work with the Photos app (page 124).

Mail

iCloud includes an *icloud.com* (formerly *me.com*) email account that keeps your mail and folders up-to-date across all your devices. For details, read "iCloud: Set up iCloud Mail on your devices" at *support.apple.com/kb/PH2621*.

Contacts

Changes to your contacts in Contacts, iOS Contacts, and Microsoft Outlook 2007 or later are pushed automatically to iCloud across all your devices.

Calendars

Changes to your calendars in Calendar, iOS Calendar, and Microsoft Outlook 2007 or later are pushed automatically to iCloud across all your devices. You can share your calendars with other iCloud users.

Reminders

Changes to your reminders in Reminders, iOS Reminders, and Microsoft Outlook 2007 or later are pushed automatically to iCloud across all your devices.

Safari

Your Safari bookmarks, Reading List, and open tabs are pushed automatically to iCloud. In Windows, Safari and Internet Explorer bookmarks are pushed. To view synced tabs in Safari, click the iCloud button ☁ in the Safari toolbar.

Notes

Changes to your notes in Notes and iOS Notes are pushed automatically to iCloud across all your devices.

Keychain

iCloud Keychain encrypts and stores your website user names and passwords on the devices that you've approved (Macs or iDevices), and syncs them wirelessly and automatically across those devices. When you need to create a new password for a website, Password Generator suggests a strong password and saves it to your iCloud Keychain. Passwords and user names are filled in automatically when you need them, so you don't have to remember or type them. iCloud Keychain can also store and sync encrypted credit-card details for online shopping. See also "Keychain Access" on page 164.

Back to My Mac

Provides remote access to your Mac from another Mac anywhere on the internet. For details, read "Set up and use Back to My Mac" at *support.apple.com/HT204618*.

Find My Mac

Helps locate a missing Mac. Sign in at *icloud. com* to see your missing Mac on a map. You can send a message, lock the Mac, or securely erase all its data.

To set up iCloud (Windows): Download and install the iCloud Control Panel from Apple at *icloud. com/icloudcontrolpanel*. On the Windows desktop, choose Start > Control Panel > Network and Internet > iCloud, enter your Apple ID and password (if prompted), and then select the desired services.

To set up iCloud (iOS): On the Home screen of your iPad, iPhone, or iPod touch, tap Settings > iCloud, enter your Apple ID and password (if prompted), and then turn on the desired services.

Other iCloud Services

Other iCloud services, not specific to OS X, include:

iTunes in the Cloud

Automatically downloads newly purchased iTunes music, movies, TV shows, iOS apps, and books to all your iOS devices wirelessly over a wi-fi or cellular signal (previous purchases are downloaded at no charge). To enable automatic downloads, open iTunes on your Mac, and then choose iTunes > Preferences > Store pane > Automatic Downloads. In iTunes for Windows, choose Edit > Preferences (Control+,) > Store pane > Automatic Downloads. In iOS, on the Home screen, tap Settings > iTunes & App Store > Automatic Downloads.

iTunes Match

A fee-based service that gives the benefits of iTunes in the Cloud for music that you didn't buy from iTunes, including pirated music and music ripped from CDs. iTunes Match is built into iTunes on your Mac or Windows PC and the Music app on your iOS devices. You can download your entire music library from iCloud at any time.

Backup

iCloud automatically backs up important data on your iOS devices daily over wi-fi. Backups include purchased music, TV shows, apps, and books; photos and video in the Camera Roll; device settings; app data; home screen and app organization; messages (iMessage, SMS, and MMS); and ringtones. To restore a backup on your device (or set up a new device), connect the device to wi-fi, and then enter your Apple ID and password. Your backed-up data will appear on your device. For details, read "Archive or make copies of your iCloud data" at *support. apple.com/HT204055*.

Find My iPhone/iPad

Works like Find My Mac, but for iOS devices. To see your missing device on a map, sign in at *icloud.com* or use the Find My iPhone app (available from the iOS App Store) on another iOS device.

Find My Friends

Use the Find My Friends app (available from the iOS App Store) to locate people. iOS users who share their location with you appear on a map. Privacy controls let you turn off location-sharing or share temporarily with a specific group of people. Parental restrictions let you manage how your children use Find My Friends.

Internet Accounts

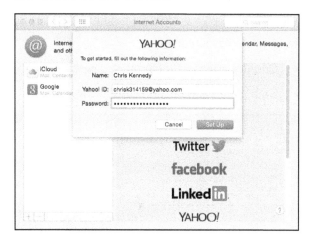

Use the Internet Accounts panel to enter and edit your internet accounts with iCloud, Microsoft Exchange, Google, Twitter, Facebook, LinkedIn, Yahoo, and other service providers so that you can quickly access them in Mail, Calendar, Reminders, Messages, Notes, and other account-based apps. You can sync account information to iCloud.

To add an account: Click a service provider on the right (if your provider isn't listed, click Add Other Account), enter your account information, click Set Up, and then select the apps with which to associate the account. The account list on the left shows accounts created within this panel, as well as accounts created within other account-based apps and services (such as Mail or iCloud).

To edit an account: Select the account in the list and then toggle the app checkboxes on the right or click Details or Manage.

To delete an account: Select the account in the list and then click (-).

Keyboard

Configures the keyboard (page 16).

Language & Region

Use the Language & Region panel to set:

- The display language
- Country-specific ("localization") settings
- Date, time, number, and currency formats

Preferred languages
> Set the language used on menus, dialog boxes, and buttons. Drag the desired language to the top of the list. To add or remove languages, click (+) or (−). If a program can't show the first language in the list, it shows the second, and so on. To effect the change in a particular program, quit and then reopen the program. To effect the change systemwide, log out and then log back in.

Region
> Choose a geographic region for date, time, number, and other formats.

First day of week
> Designate the first day of the week for displaying calendars and doing date arithmetic.

Calendar
> Choose the civil calendar for your country or region.

Time format
> Show the time as a 24-hour or 12-hour clock.

List sort order
> Determines the order of icons when they are sorted by name in Finder.

Keyboard Preferences
> Add international keyboards (page 18).

Advanced
> Fine-tune the formats for dates, times, numbers, currencies, and measurement units displayed in programs and Finder.

Mission Control

Configures Mission Control (page 45).

Mouse

Configures the mouse (page 19).

Network

Configures online connections (Chapter 8).

Notifications

Configures Notification Center (page 47).

Parental Controls

Configures Parental Controls (page 166).

Printers & Scanners

Configures printing, scanning, and faxing (Chapter 6).

Security & Privacy

Configures security and privacy settings (Chapter 9).

Sharing

Configures sharing settings (Chapter 7).

Sound

Use the Sound panel to configure your Mac's sound system, including volume, alert sounds, playback, and recording. Shortcut: Option-click the Sound menu ◀)) to view or set input/output audio devices.

To adjust the master volume: Do any of the following:

- Drag the "Output volume" slider at the bottom of the Sound panel (or select the Mute checkbox).

- Drag the volume slider ◀)) in the menu bar (if necessary, select "Show volume in menu bar" in the Sound panel).

- Press and F10 ◀, F11 ◀), or F12 ◀)) to mute, decrease, or increase the volume, respectively (you may have to hold down the Fn key too). To adjust by fine increments, hold down Shift+Option as you press these keys.

- On an Apple Remote, press the Volume Up and Volume Down buttons.

Sound Effects Pane

Use this pane to set the alert sound and volume.

Select an alert sound
Sets the sound that OS X makes to get your attention or when you click or type somewhere that you shouldn't.

Play sound effects through
Sets the output speakers or headset for sound effects.

Alert volume slider
Adjusts the alert volume relative to the master volume (never exceeding the master volume). You can also adjust this setting by Option-dragging the volume slider ◀)) in the menu bar. Dragging this slider all the way to the left mutes the alert sound but plays music, games, and movies at the volume set by the master "Output volume" slider.

Play user interface sound effects
Determines whether sound effects play during some Finder operations such as dragging an item into the Trash, off the dock, or into a folder.

Play feedback when volume is changed
Determines whether the volume is muted when you adjust the volume. To temporarily reverse this setting, hold down Shift as you adjust the volume.

Output Pane

Use this pane to adjust the left–right balance of the selected speakers or headset.

Input Pane

Use this pane to adjust the input volume (sensitivity) of the selected microphone or line input. For mics, select "Use ambient noise reduction" to mute background noise during dictation.

Spotlight

Configures Spotlight search (page 93).

Startup Disk

Sets which drive (page 99) to use when starting (booting) the computer (page 8).

Time Machine

Configures Time Machine (page 172).

Trackpad

Configures the trackpad for multitouch gestures (page 21).

Users & Groups

Configures user accounts (page 9) and login options (page 12).

Files, Folders & Drives

OS X uses files and folders to organize your information so that you aren't overwhelmed by long file lists and can distinguish one set of content from another. A **file** is the basic unit of computer storage; it can be a program, a program's configuration data, a log that the computer itself maintains, or a document that you create or receive. You organize files in containers called **folders** (or **directories**), which can hold additional folders (called **subfolders** or **subdirectories**) to form a treelike hierarchy. Folders in turn are stored on **drives** (or **volumes**) such as hard drives, USB flash drives, CDs, DVDs, and network servers. OS X creates a few system folders to store its own files and settings but otherwise doesn't care how you structure your tree of folders and files. This chapter explains how to use Finder to navigate and manage your stored information.

System Folders

The drive on which OS X is installed, called the **system drive** or **startup drive**, usually Macintosh is in the desktop's upper-right corner and is labeled *Macintosh*. If this drive icon isn't on your desktop, switch to Finder and then choose Go > Computer (Shift+Command+C) to see a list of available drives. Double-click the system drive to browse the following **system folders** in the OS X folder structure.

Applications contains all the programs—iTunes, Word, Photoshop, and so on—that Applications you, another user, the OS X installer, or an administrator installed, along with all the programs' support files. In general, you shouldn't touch the files in here except to open them or delete (uninstall) them.

Library contains operating-system support files and components (drivers, fonts, preferLibrary ences, sounds, help files, keyboard layouts, and so on).

System contains critical Unix operating-system files that control OS X's basic operations. System Most of its contents are invisible. Look but don't touch.

Users contains the home folder for each user account. These folders contain the users' Users personal settings and files. If you're not an administrator, you can't open or see other users' home folders. The Shared folder (page 149) stores files that are available to every user.

User Guides And Information contains links to User Guides, Welcome guides, and other User Guides And documentation from Apple. Information

Other System Folders

Depending on your setup, you may see other folders with self-explanatory names like Network, Developer, Previous System, or Incompatible Software. If you upgraded from OS 9 or earlier, other folders may appear: your personal files and folders preserved during the upgrade, pre-OS X applications, and old system files.

Home Folder

Your **home folder**, labeled with your user account's short name, stores your files and foldchris ers in one place. A unique home folder is associated with the user account of whoever is logged in. Other users (besides administrators) can't see what's in your home folder; neither can you see what's in theirs.

To open your home folder: Do any of the following:

- In Finder, choose Go > Home (Shift+Command+H).

- In a Finder window, click the Home icon in the sidebar.

- Click an empty area on the desktop and then choose Go > Enclosing Folder (Command+↑).

To make new Finder windows open your home folder: In Finder, choose Finder > Preferences > General pane. Select your home folder from the "New Finder windows show" pop-up menu.

Tip: You can create a Home folder shortcut in the dock by dragging the Home folder's proxy icon (page 81) from the title bar to the dock.

Home Subfolders

The home folder contains specialized subfolders, each of which is intended for the type of file that its name suggests:

Applications
> Contains programs that you install. This folder (~/Applications, where ~ denotes your home folder) has more-restrictive sharing permissions (page 146) than the Applications system folder (/Applications). By default, other users can run the programs in this folder but can't delete them.

Desktop
> For desktop files and shortcuts. Anything that you put in here appears on your desktop (and anything that you drag to your desktop lands in the Desktop folder). You can't delete or rename this folder.

Documents
> For word-processing files, spreadsheets, databases, presentations, text files, and other user-created documents.

Downloads
> For files downloaded from the internet.

Library
> For personal preferences, fonts, email, and so on. This folder is hidden by default; to open it in Finder, hold down the Option key and then choose Go > Library. To unhide Library, open your home folder, choose View > Show View Options (Command+J), and then select Show Library Folder.

Movies
> For videos and clips from your digital camera or camcorder, or video files downloaded or ripped (copied) from a DVD.

Music
> For MP3s and digital music, downloaded or ripped from a CD.

Pictures
> For digital pictures from a camera or scanner.

Public
> For files and folders that other users can access without a password, over a network or while sitting at the machine.

Sites
> For websites, if you're using OS X as a web server.

These folders are just helpful anchors to help you organize your files without having to start from scratch, but this storage scheme doesn't work when things get complicated. It's better to ignore file types and nest folders deeply. If you create a shallow or "flat" folder structure, then you're forced to use long, descriptive file names rather than succinct ones. A flat structure also makes you fill each folder with so many subfolders that it's hard to discern the structure quickly. If you're, say, running an advertising campaign, it's more sensible to organize all the photos, graphics, copy, layouts, videos, and spreadsheets in a dedicated project folder rather than disperse them to the factory-installed subfolders.

You don't *have* to store your stuff in your home folder (OS X doesn't care where you put your files), but doing that is a good idea because:

- It's easy to open from Finder.

- It's indexed by OS X automatically so you can find files instantly by using a search box.

- It's where programs expect you to save and open files.

- It segregates your work and programs, preventing accidental document deletion when you remove or upgrade programs.

- It makes it easier to back up your work by archiving only your home folder (and its subfolders) rather than folders scattered about your hard drive.

- It keeps your personal files private.

Finder

Finder is the key tool for working with files and folders on your computer or network. The term "folder window" actually refers to a Finder window. It's common to have several Finder windows or tabs open at the same time, each one looking a little different depending on the settings and filters in effect for that folder. Apple presets folders to show their contents a certain way; you'll see icons grow or shrink or regroup, depending on which folder you click. You can change views globally or by folder. Finder itself always is open, even if no folder windows are. Finder windows work like other windows, but also have specialized parts. Finder supports full-screen view.

To activate Finder: Do any of the following:

- Click the Finder icon in the dock.
- Click an empty area on the desktop.
- Command+Tab to Finder.
- Click any folder window.

To open a new Finder window: In Finder, choose File > New Finder Window (Command+N). The new window opens the folder set by Finder > Preferences > General pane > "New Finder windows show".

To explore the folder hierarchy: Double-click a folder to open it and explore its contents. Keep double-clicking folders to drill down to the folder you want. To return to a previous folder, click ‹ or right-click the folder name in the title bar.

To print a list of files: Open the desired Finder window, choose Edit > Select All (Command+A), choose Edit > Copy (Command+C), switch to a text editor or word processor (such as TextEdit), and then choose Edit > Paste (Command+V). A list of all the files in the Finder window appears, ready to format and print.

Finder Tabs

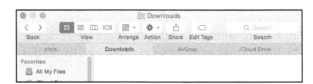

Finder **tabs** let you declutter your desktop by consolidating multiple Finder windows into a single, tabbed window (similar to web browsers, where each webpage appears as a separate tab in the same window). Each tab behaves like its own Finder window, so you can change the view of each one independently.

Open tabs are listed in the **tab bar** near the top of a Finder window (below the toolbar). By default, the tab bar is visible only when multiple tabs are open. To always show the tab bar, choose View > Show Tab Bar (Shift+Command+T).

A Finder window can hold an unlimited number of tabs. You can open folders in new tabs, switch among them, move them, close them, drag files between them, and more.

To open a new tab: Do any of the following:

- In Finder, choose File > New Tab (Command+T).

  The new tab opens the folder set by Finder > Preferences > General pane > "New Finder windows show".

- Hold down the Command key and then double-click a folder icon.

- Hold down the Command key and then click a folder in the sidebar.

- Right-click a folder icon in Finder and then choose Open in New Tab in the shortcut menu.

Tip: To choose whether Open in New Tab or Open in New Window appears in the shortcut menu, choose Finder > Preferences > General pane > "Open folders in tabs instead of new windows". To swap between these two options when the shortcut menu is already open, press and hold the Option key.

- Click + on the right edge of the tab bar.

- Right-click a tab in the tab bar and then choose New Tab in the shortcut menu.

- Drag the proxy icon from the title bar of a Finder window to the + on the tab bar of another Finder window.

To view and manage tabs: Do any of the following:

- To view a different tab, click it in the tab bar.

- To cycle forward through tabs, press Ctrl+Tab repeatedly. To cycle backward, press Shift+Ctrl+Tab repeatedly. Alternatively, choose Window > Show Next/Previous Tab.

- To view hidden tabs (if the tab bar is filled with tabs), click » on the rightmost tab.

- To reorder tabs, drag them left or right in the tab bar.

- To move a tab to its own Finder window, right-click the tab in the tab bar and then choose Move Tab to New Window in the shortcut menu. Alternatively, activate the tab and then choose Window > Move Tab to New Window.

- To consolidate all open Finder windows in a single tabbed window, choose Window > Merge All Windows.

To close a tab: Do any of the following:

- Hover the pointer over the tab in the tab bar and then click × when it appears.

- Activate the tab and then choose File > Close Tab (Command+W).

- Right-click the tab in the tab bar and then choose Close Tab in the shortcut menu.

- To close all tabs but one, right-click the tab that you want to keep in the tab bar and then choose Close Other Tabs in the shortcut menu.

To move or copy files and folders by using tabs:

1 Open tabs for the source and destination folders.

2 Drag files or folders from the source folder and drop them onto the tab of the destination folder in the tab bar.

   To copy an item instead of moving it, hold down Option when you drop it. To alias (page 88) an item instead of moving or copying it, hold down Option+Command when you drop it.

Tip: If you hover over the destination tab before you drop, the destination tab behaves like a spring-loaded folder (page 88) and becomes active, letting you drop items into a nested folder.

Sidebar

The **sidebar**—on the left side of a Finder window—shows icons for frequently visited locations. Click an icon to show the contents of that location in the main part of the Finder window. An icon in the sidebar is only a pointer; removing it doesn't delete the original, nor does dragging an item to the sidebar move the original. Each sidebar icon has its own shortcut menu, available via a right-click. The sidebar is divided into categories:

Favorites

Lists files, folders, smart folders, programs, drives, and other locations that you use frequently. It's common to customize this section.

Shared

Lists the shared computers on your local network.

Devices

Lists storage devices: internal and external drives, CDs, DVDs, iPods, USB flash drives, and so on. Removable devices are marked with ⏏, which you can click to eject that device.

Tags

Lists recently used tags (page 89).

To add items to the sidebar: Drag the icon of a file, folder, or program to the Favorites section, or select an icon (or group of icons) on the desktop or in any folder window and then choose File > Add to Sidebar (Ctrl+Command+T).

To remove an item: Drag its icon out of the sidebar, or right-click it and then choose Remove from Sidebar. (You can't remove icons from the Shared section.)

To rearrange items: Drag icons or categories up and down to reorder them. (You can't rearrange icons in the Shared category.)

To show or hide the sidebar: Choose View > Show/Hide Sidebar (Option+Command+S).

To change the width of the sidebar: Drag its right edge to the left or right.

To customize the sidebar list: Choose Finder > Preferences > Sidebar pane.

To resize sidebar icons: Choose > System Preferences > General > "Sidebar icon size".

Toolbar

The toolbar—running along the top of a Finder window—works like a normal toolbar and provides a customizable set of Finder-specific buttons:

- Back ‹ and Forward › move among previously visited locations (you can click-and-hold these buttons for a location history, letting you jump two or three folders at a time).

- View ⊞ ≡ ⊞ ▥ changes the size or arrangement of the icons in the folder window.

- Arrange ▥˅ sorts icons by the selected criterion.

- Action ✱˅ is a context-sensitive pop-up menu. Its commands change depending on which icons, if any, are selected.

- Share ⬆ lets you share files via Mail, Messages, or AirDrop.

- Edit Tags ◯ button lets you assign tags (descriptive labels) to a file or folder.

- Quick Look ◉ button previews a file or folder without opening it.

- Path ≡˅ shows the current location in the folder hierarchy.

To show or hide the toolbar: Choose View > Show/Hide Toolbar (Option+Command+T).

To customize the toolbar: Open or activate any Finder window and then choose View > Customize Toolbar, or right-click the toolbar of any Finder window and then choose a command. When the Customize Toolbar panel is open, you can drag icons on or off the toolbar, or drag them left or right to reorder them. Use the Show pop-up menu to show toolbar icons, icon labels, or both.

Proxy Icon

The **proxy icon**—the tiny icon 🏠 chris next to the window's name on the title bar—stands in for the folder or drive itself. Use this icon to manipulate the folder or drive without having to first close its window. To move a folder, hold down the mouse button on the proxy icon until it darkens, and then drag it to a different folder or drive, into the dock, to the sidebar's Favorites section, or into the Trash. To copy the folder, hold down Option while you drag.

Dragging the proxy icon of a *document* window will alias (page 88) the document rather than move or copy it. (Not all document windows have proxy icons.)

Path Bar

The **path bar**—the long strip under the folder contents—appears when you choose View > Show Path Bar (Option+Command+P) and shows your current location in the folder hierarchy as a "breadcrumb trail" of links separated by arrows. These links are operational: double-click a link to jump

to that location, drag items into a tiny folder icon, or right-click a link for a shortcut menu. See also "Paths" on page 2.

Status Bar

3 of 9 selected, 39.6 GB available

The **status bar**—running along the bottom of a Finder window—appears when you choose View > Show Status Bar (Command+/) and shows the number of icons selected and the remaining free space on the drive.

Navigating in Finder

Use the Go menu to move among folders on your computer or network.

The following commands are available on the Go menu:

- Back (Command+[) and Forward (Command+]) move among previously visited locations.

- Enclosing Folder (Command+↑) moves up the hierarchy tree to the parent of the current folder.

- All My Files (Shift+Command+F) is a smart folder that shows all your files.

- Documents (Shift+Command+O), Desktop (Shift+Command+D), and so on jump to common locations.

- Recent Folders tracks where you've been lately. To cover your tracks, choose Recent Folders > Clear Menu.

- Go to Folder (Shift+Command+G) lets you jump to a folder by typing its Unix path: ~/Downloads, for example (~ denotes your home folder and / separates folder names).

- Connect to Server (Command+K) connects to Macs that have File Sharing turned on (page 146), Windows machines with shared folders, wireless drives, network servers, and FTP servers.

Tip: To reveal a hidden shortcut to the Library folder in your home folder (~/Library), hold down the Option key when you click the Go menu.

To jump quickly to any folder up the hierarchy tree from the current folder, right-click the name in the folder window's title bar, and then choose a destination from the pop-up menu. (This feature works like the path bar.)

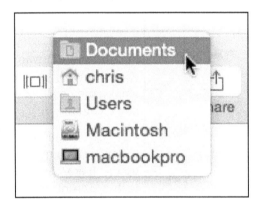

When you open a folder, Finder replaces the window's current contents with those of the new folder. To open a new window instead of replacing the current one (which can quickly crowd your desktop), choose Finder > Preferences > General pane > select "Always open folders in a new window".

Folder Views

You can change the size and arrangement of the items in a folder by choosing to view them as icons, in a list, in columns, or as large thumbnail images (Cover Flow). Finder lets you fine-tune each view via the View Options dialog box and remembers each folder's view settings independently. In general, the view that you choose for a folder depends on the type and number of files that it contains.

To switch views: In a Finder window or tab, do any of the following:

- In the View menu, choose As Icons (Command+1), As List (Command+2), As Columns (Command+3), or Cover Flow (Command+4).

- Click a view in the toolbar.

- Right-click an empty area in a folder and then choose from the View submenu.

To set view options: In a Finder window or tab, do any of the following:

- Choose View > Show View Options.

- Press Command+J (this keyboard shortcut also closes the View Options dialog box).

- Click ⚙ > Show View Options.

- Right-click an empty area in a folder and then choose Show View Options.

Tip: The available options change depending on which view is active and apply to only the active folder.

To apply the current view options as defaults for all windows: In the View Options dialog box, click Use as Defaults. To undo this action, hold down the Option key and then click Restore to Defaults.

To override the default view for the active window: Select a view and then, in the View Options dialog box, select the "Always open" checkbox.

Icon View

⊞ This view shows items as icons and works best for sparsely populated folders or folders containing mostly pictures.

To align icons to a grid: To align an individual icon, Command-drag it. To align some or all icons, choose View > Clean Up Selection (with some icons selected) or View > Clean Up (nothing selected). These commands also appear in the shortcut menu when you right-click an empty area in a folder window. To swap commands or show alternative commands temporarily, hold down Option when you right-click or open a menu. To lock all icons to the grid, in the View Options dialog box (Command+J), choose Snap to Grid from the "Sort By" pop-up menu. To override the Snap to Grid setting for an individual icon, Command-drag it.

To sort icons: To sort temporarily, choose View > Arrange By submenu (Ctrl+Command+[0–7]). To sort permanently, hold down the Option key and choose View > Sort By submenu (Option+Ctrl+Command+[0–7]). Alternatively, use the "Arrange By" or "Sort By" pop-up menu in the View Options dialog box (Command+J). These commands also appear in the shortcut menu when you right-click an empty area in a folder window. To swap commands or show alternative commands temporarily, hold down the Option key when you right-click or choose a menu command.

List View

☰ This view shows a columnar list of files, folders, and their attributes indicated by column headings (Name, Date Modified, Size, Kind, and so on). This view works best for general file management and crowded folders.

To set up columns: To choose which columns appear, right-click any column heading to open its shortcut menu, or use the "Show Columns" check-boxes in the View Options dialog box (Command+J). To reorder columns, drag the column headings left or right (the Name column must be first). To resize a column, drag the right edge of its column heading left or right. To resize a column to fit its widest entry, double-click its right edge.

To sort the list: Click the heading of the column to sort by. To reverse the sort order, click it again. A small arrowhead near the column name points up ⌃ for an ascending sort or down ⌄ for a descending sort. Alternatively, use the "Arrange By" or "Sort By" commands in the View menu. To swap commands or show alternative commands temporarily, hold down the Option key when you choose a menu command.

To show or hide the contents of a folder: Click ▶ or ▼ next to the folder icon (or select the folder and then press → or ←). To show all subfolders, hold down the Option key and then click ▶ (or select the folder and then press Option+→).

Column View

⊞ This view shows the contents of the current folder and its subfolders in a series of side-by-side vertical panes. The first pane shows the current folder or drive. Clicking a folder in the first pane shows that folder's contents in the second pane, and so on—click a folder in any pane to show its contents in the pane to its right. If panes slide left out of view, use the horizontal scroll bar to show them again. This view works best when you want to see nested folders and their parent folders in the same window.

To resize columns: To view more or fewer columns, resize the window. To change a column's width, drag the handle ⫴ at the bottom of the column's right edge. To change all column widths simultaneously, Option-drag ⫴. To resize a column to fit its widest entry (called *right-sizing*), double-click ⫴. To resize all columns to fit their widest entries, hold down Option and then double-click ⫴. Alternatively, right-click ⫴ to right-size a column or columns.

To navigate columns: To jump from column to column, press → or ←. To go to a specific folder, use the sidebar or Go menu. To choose an item within a column, click it, press ↑ or ↓, or type the first few letters of the item's name. To open a selected item, double-click it (Command+O) or press Command+↓.

To sort columns: Use the "Arrange By" or "Sort By" commands in the View Options dialog box (Command+J), View menu, or shortcut (right-click) menu. To swap commands or show alternative commands temporarily, hold down the Option key when you right-click or choose a menu command.

Cover Flow View

▢ This view splits the windows into two horizontal panes. The top pane shows items as a scrolling row of large preview images that you can "flip" through by using arrow keys, Tab and Shift+Tab, the mouse wheel, or the horizontal scrollbar just below the images. The bottom pane shows an ordinary list view. Selecting an item in the list view flips to its preview image in the top pane. Special controls appear when you point to certain types of files: a Play button plays a video file in place, for example, and circled arrows page through a PDF document without actually opening the file. This view works best for sparsely populated folders containing pictures or movies.

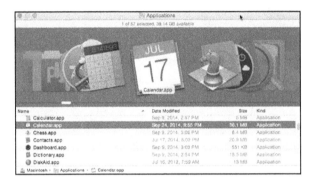

To resize Cover Flow panes: Drag the horizontal divider that separates the panes up or down.

Quick Look

Quick Look lets you quickly preview the contents of a file or folder without opening it, switching views, or starting a program. The preview appears in a large pop-up window whose contents depend on the type of file that you're viewing. Quick Look supports share sheets and full-screen view.

Tip: To preview the selected file directly in a Finder window panel without using Quick Look, in Finder, choose View > Show Preview (Shift+Command+P).

The types of files that Quick Look natively supports include:

- Photos and graphics (GIF, JPEG, Photoshop, PNG, RAW, and TIFF)
- PDF files
- Text files
- TextEdit files
- Webpages (HTML) and Safari archives
- Audio and video formats (AAC, AIFF, H.264, MP3, MPEG-4, and so on)
- Apple iWork documents (Pages, Numbers, and Keynote)
- Microsoft Office documents (Word, Excel, and PowerPoint)
- Fonts
- vCards

Quick Look is also available in programs other than Finder. For example, you can preview:

- Webpage links in Mail
- Street addresses in Mail, Safari, and Contacts
- Spotlight results (a preview of the selected result appears in the Spotlight window)
- Any item in Mission Control or in a stack

To get third-party plugins that support other file types (such as ZIP or Adobe formats), go to *quicklookplugins.com*. Quick Look works in Finder, Time Machine, Exposé, the Trash, Messages, Spotlight, and elsewhere.

To preview items by using Quick Look: Select the item(s) and then do any of the following:

- Choose File > Quick Look (Command+Y).
- Press Spacebar.
- Click 👁 .
- Click ⚙ ˅ > Quick Look.
- Right-click a selected item and then choose Quick Look.
- Tap three fingers.

Tip: To preview full-screen instead of in a small window, hold down Option when you choose a Quick Look command (Option+Spacebar or Option+Command+Y, for example).

The Quick Look window opens to show the first item. To preview multiple items, press the arrow keys or click the arrow buttons in the preview window. The other controls in the preview window let you go full-screen, scroll through images or pages, open or share files, and so on. To preview items that weren't in the original selection, Command-click their icons in a Finder window. To exit the Quick Look window, click ×, press Esc, or repeat any of the commands listed above.

Managing Files & Folders

To manage your information, create a folder hierarchy in your home folder and organize files within it. You can rename, move, copy, alias, label, and delete files and folders.

Creating Folders

untitled folder

You can create a folder on the desktop, anywhere in your home folder, in a shared location, on a network server, or anywhere you have permission.

To create a folder: On the desktop or in a folder window, choose File > New Folder (Shift+Command+N), or right-click an empty area and then choose New Folder. Type a name for the folder and then press Return. (If the New Folder command is dimmed, then you lack permission to create a folder at the current location.)

Naming Files and Folders

TXT
Memo to self.txt

You can rename a file or folder to make its name longer, shorter, or more explicit. The name can contain up to 255 characters, including letters, numbers, spaces, punctuation, and symbols (_, #, &, μ, π, •, and so on). A name can't start with a dot (.) or contain a colon (:) or, in some cases, a slash (/). To use a file with a pre-OS X application, limit its name length to 31 characters. Don't rename applications or system folders.

Finder sorts files that begin with numbers numerically (1, 2, 3, 10, 200) rather than alphabetically (1, 10, 2, 200, 3), so leading zeros aren't required. Punctuation and symbols are significant for sorting; case is not. The usual way to force a file to the top of a sorted list is to start its name with a space, an underscore (_), or a tilde (~).

To rename a file or folder: Select it and then press Return (or click the icon's name, wait a moment, and then click it again). When the existing name highlights, type a new name and then press Return (or Enter or Tab) or click outside the name box. Before editing, you can press ← or → to jump to the start or end of the name. While editing, you can use the keyboard shortcuts for Cut (Command+X), Copy (Command+C), Paste (Command+V), Undo (Command+Z), and Select All (Command+A). To cancel and revert to the original name, press Esc. When you rename a file, be careful not change its filename extension accidently.

Tip: You can rename a file from the title bar by using Auto Save (page 107).

To rename a set of files or folders (batch rename): Right-click (or Ctrl-click) a set of selected files or folders and then choose Rename Items. You can add custom text and numbers to each filename.

Moving and Copying Files and Folders

epub

You can move or copy files and folders to reorganize your folder structure, make backup copies in a safe location, or move files to the Shared folder to share them with other users. To copy or move items, you must select (highlight) them on the desktop or in a folder window. A progress bar appears during long operations. To cancel mid-operation, press Command+dot (.) or click ×.

Same-named items can't occupy the same folder. When a naming conflict occurs, OS X asks you what to do: keep both files (under different names), stop the operation, or replace the existing file; an "Apply to All" option applies your chosen action to any further conflicts for the current operation.

You can drag items to the desktop, into an open window, or onto a folder or drive icon. The rules that determine whether an item is copied, moved, or aliased (page 88) are:

- If you drag an item to another place on the same drive, it's moved.

- If you drag an item from one drive to another, it's copied.

- If you drag a drive to another drive (a CD to a hard drive, for example), it's aliased.

- To copy an item instead of moving or aliasing it, hold down Option when you drop it.

- To move an item instead of copying or aliasing it, hold down Command when you drop it.

- To alias an item instead of moving or copying it, hold down Option+Command when you drop it.

To move or copy items by dragging: Make sure that the destination folder or icon is visible. Select the item(s) that you want to move or copy. Drag the items to the destination. As you drag, a translucent image of the selected icons moves with the pointer. The pointer itself sprouts a circled number that indicates how many items you're moving.

To move or copy items by pasting: Select the item(s) that you want to move or copy. Choose Edit > Copy (Command+C), or right-click a selected item and then choose Copy. Open the destination folder. Choose Edit > Paste (Command+V), or right-click an empty area and then choose Paste. The Copy and Paste commands are also available in the ⚙ ˅ menu in the toolbar and are labeled with the selection ("Copy 2 Items" or "Paste Item", for example). To move items instead of copying them, hold down the Option key when you paste.

To move or copy items by using Finder tabs: In a Finder window, open tabs for the source and destination folders, and then drag items from the source folder and drop them onto the tab for the destination folder in the tab bar. To copy items instead of moving them, hold down the Option key when you drop. For details, see "Finder Tabs" on page 78.

To move or copy a folder by dragging its proxy icon: Make sure that the destination folder or icon is visible. Drag the proxy icon from the title bar to the destination.

To duplicate items: Select the item(s) that you want to duplicate and then do any of the following:

- Choose File > Duplicate (Command+D).

- Right-click a selected item and then choose Duplicate.

- Click ⚙ ˅ > Duplicate.

- Option-drag a selected item.

To merge items: If you drag a file or folder into a folder that already contains a file or folder with the same name, Finder gives you three options:

- Cancel the operation (Stop).

- Replace the existing items with the ones that you're dragging (Replace or Replace All).

- Keep everything (Keep Both Files or Keep Both).

If you're dragging or pasting *files*, then Keep Both renames the incoming files by appending a number (2, 3,…) to their file names (the names of the existing files in the destination aren't changed). If you're pasting *folders*, then Keep Both merges the contents of the folders (renaming the files inside, if necessary). When merging folders, the Keep Both options appear when you're *pasting* a folder into a new window—not dragging it. The Keep Both options also appear when you Option-drag a folder into a new window to copy it there, or when you drag it to a different drive.

Spring-Loaded Folders

The spring-loaded folders feature pops open closed folders automatically so that you can drop items into a nested folder without first opening it.

To set up spring-loaded folders: In Finder, choose Finder > Preferences > General pane > select "Spring-loaded folders and windows". Drag the Delay slider to adjust the delay until a folder opens automatically. (Even when spring-loaded folders is turned off, you still can press Spacebar to open a folder that you're dragging to.)

To use spring-loaded folders: Drag an item (or group of items) onto a folder or drive icon (or onto a location in the sidebar). Keep the mouse button pressed and hover the pointer over the icon until it opens automatically (or press Spacebar to open it immediately). Either release the mouse button to drop the selection in the current folder or hover the pointer over an inner folder to open it automatically, and so on. If a target folder isn't visible, drag near the window's edge to autoscroll to it.

Aliases

 An **alias** is a convenient link to a file, folder, drive, or program. When you double-click an alias, its linked item opens. You can Memo to create an alias to any item and store it self.txt anywhere; it's a tiny file. A small curved arrow distinguishes an alias from the original item to which it's linked.

Moving or renaming an alias or the original won't break the link. Deleting an alias has no effect on the original. (An alias is the same as a Windows *shortcut*.)

To alias items: Select the item(s) that you want to alias and then do any of the following:

- Choose File > Make Alias (Command+L).
- Right-click a selected item and then choose Make Alias.
- Click ☼ ⌄ > Make Alias.
- Option-Command-drag a selected item.

To show the original items linked to aliases: Select an alias (or group of aliases) and then do any of the following:

- Choose File > Show Original (Command+R).
- Right-click a selected alias and then choose Show Original.
- Click ☼ ⌄ > Show Original.

To alias a webpage: In your web browser, go to the page that you want to alias. Drag the small icon on the left end of the address bar to the desktop or a folder window. (The resulting file isn't a true alias, but it acts like one.)

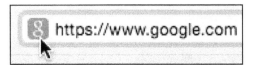

Tags

Tags are meaningful words and phrases that you can assign to files and folders to make them easy to sort and find—tag a batch of photos with *san francisco* and *2015*, for example. OS X comes with some sample tags (Red, Green, Home, Work, Important, and so on) that you can use, edit, or delete, and you can create your own tags to describe and organize your files.

Tip: The built-in colored tags (Red, Orange, and so on) are holdovers from earlier versions of OS X, where they were called colored labels. On pre-Mavericks Macs (OS X 10.9 or earlier), files with colored tags behave like files with colored labels. If a file has more than one colored tag assigned to it, only the most recently applied colored tag is visible.

Finding tagged files. In the sidebar of every Finder window (and in some Open dialog boxes), is a Tags list showing recently used tags. Click a tag to show all the files on your Mac that have that tag. Or click All Tags to open a complete list of tags. If you start typing the name of a tag in a Finder window's search box, an option to search for files that have that tag appears. Note that you can't select multiple tags in the sidebar; instead, use Spotlight search to find files with any or all of a set of tags.

Tip: You can drag a tag from the Finder sidebar to the dock for quick access to all the files with that tag.

Setting up tags in Finder. You can identify tagged files by color as well as by keyword. To set up tags in Finder, choose Finder > Preferences > Tags pane.

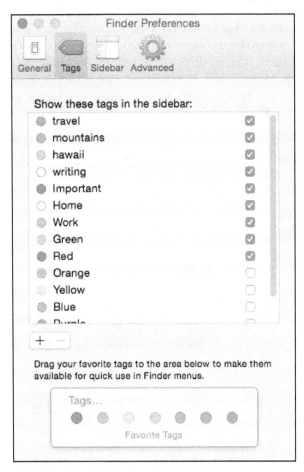

To rename, delete, or assign a color to a tag, right-click the tag in the list. To reorder tags in the sidebar, drag tags up or down the list. To choose which tags appear in the sidebar, select or clear the checkboxes in the list. To choose which tags appear in Finder's File, shortcut (right-click), and ✽ ⌄ menus, drag tags from the list to the Favorite Tags box.

When a tag that's never been added to any file is added to a file for the first time, that tag appears automatically in the Finder sidebar and a crossbar (instead of a checkmark) appears in its checkbox in Preferences.

Tip: You can also edit or reorder tags by right-clicking or dragging them directly in the sidebar. To show or hide the Tags list in the sidebar, choose Finder > Preferences > Sidebar pane > Tags.

Tag indicators in file lists. In file lists in Finder windows, a small colored circle appears next to the name of each file tagged with a color. If a file has multiple colored tags, an overlapping stack of colored circles appears, up to a maximum of three, showing the three most recently applied thereafter. (No circle appears for tags assigned no color.)

Tagging files in apps. You can add tags to a file when you first save it in an app. The standard Save dialog box (page 107) has a Tags box where you can tag the file. You can choose an existing tag in the pop-up suggestions list, or type to create a new tag.

To accept a suggestion, click it or press Return. If you're typing a new tag, select Create New Tag or type a comma—tags are essentially lists of comma-separated items, meaning your tags can be more than one word long, if you like. OS X remembers the tags that you've already created and offers them as autocomplete suggestions. After naming and tagging your file, click Save. The tags live with the file, whether you copy, move, or rename it.

You can also hover the pointer over the document name in a window's title bar and then click the small arrowhead ▼ that appears. The pop-up menu lets you edit that document's tags. For details, see "Auto Save and Versions" on page 107.

Tagging files in Finder. You can also tag selected files and folders via Finder:

- Click the Edit Tags button ▭ in the toolbar. The process of adding or creating tags here is the same as that for the Save dialog box.

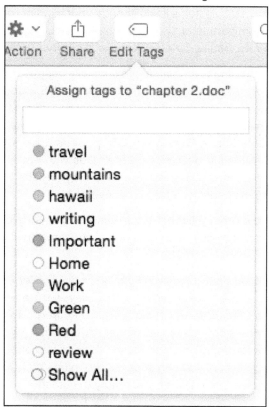

- Drag files or folders onto a tag in the sidebar to add that tag to those items.

- Choose the Tags command in the File, shortcut (right-click), or ✿ ˅ menu.

- Add tags in an item's Info window (select the file or folder and then choose File > Get Info or press Command+I).

Tip: You can also tag documents stored in iCloud libraries.

Deleting Files and Folders

 When you delete a file or folder, it's not actually erased but moved to the Trash (in the dock). The Trash is a safeguard from which you can recover (undelete) items if you change your mind or delete them permanently. The Trash's icon tells you whether it contains deleted items or is empty.

Emptying the Trash doesn't actually destroy data; it just makes those data harder to find. OS X doesn't erase files but *marks* them as deleted, making them invisible to you and to programs but leaving their data intact. Only when OS X needs drive space later will it overwrite deleted files with newly created ones. OS X lets you **secure-empty** the Trash to make deleted files unrecoverable.

To protect a file or folder from accidental deletion, lock it by selecting the Locked checkbox in its Info window (page 28).

To set up the Trash: In Finder, choose Finder > Preferences > Advanced pane. To always secure-empty the Trash, select "Empty Trash securely". To suppress confirmation messages, clear "Show warning before emptying the Trash". (Even if this option is turned on, you can suppress warnings by holding down Option when you empty the Trash.)

To move files and folders to the Trash: Select the item(s) to trash and then do any of the following:

- Choose File > Move to Trash (Command+Delete).
- Right-click a selected item and then choose Move to Trash.
- Click ☼ ˅ > Move to Trash.
- Drag a selected item to the Trash icon in the dock.

To recover items from the Trash: Click the Trash icon to open it and then drag the desired items out of the Trash window. To recover an item that you *just* deleted, choose Edit > Undo (Command+Z). To restore selected items to their original locations, choose Put Back (Command+Delete) from the File menu, shortcut (right-click) menu, or ☼ ˅ menu.

To empty the Trash: Choose Finder > Empty Trash (Shift+Command+Delete), or right-click (or click-and-hold) the Trash icon in the dock and then choose Empty Trash.

To empty the Trash securely: Choose Finder > Secure Empty Trash. This operation can take much longer than emptying the trash normally.

To erase a drive securely: Choose Applications > Utilities > Disk Utility > select the drive > Erase pane > Security Options.

Compressing Files and Folders

 Compressing files and folders reduces the space they occupy on your drives (fixed or removable). OS X uses the standard **ZIP** compression scheme, which is useful for emailing large attachments, archiving files that you no longer use regularly, transferring files over the internet or via FTP, and gaining the maximum amount of drive space.

To compress files and folders: Select the item(s) that you want to compress and then do any of the following:

- Choose File > Compress.
- Right-click a selected item and then choose Compress.
- Click ☼ ˅ > Compress.

A single item is compressed into a file of the same name, but with the extension .zip. Multiple items are compressed into a file named Archive.zip (you can rename it).

To uncompress a ZIP archive: Double-click it. If the ZIP archive contains multiple items, a folder with the same name as the archive appears, containing uncompressed copies of the original items.

Spotlight

`Q Spotlight Search`

Spotlight, OS X's search feature, returns results instantly and is available systemwide. You can trigger the main Spotlight window from the menu bar or use Spotlight search boxes in search windows, the System Preferences window, any Finder window, and Help menus. Spotlight is also available in some applications, including Photos, iTunes, and Mail.

You can find all files that meet certain criteria, including:

- File names containing specific text
- Files containing a specific phrase
- Files of a given file type (type *.doc* or *.docx* for Word files, for example)
- Files with specific tags (page 89)
- Documents written by a given author
- Photos taken after a certain date
- Photos of certain people (using the Faces feature in the Photos application)
- Photos taken at a certain place (using the Places feature in the Photos application)
- Graphics wider than a fixed number of pixels
- People in your Messages buddy lists
- Files downloaded from a specific source (type *google.com*, for example, to find programs that you downloaded from that site)
- Messages from a specific sender (a name or email address)

When you type in a search box `Q Search`, Spotlight returns a results list or filters the view based on what you're typing. You can type things like file and folder names, tags, program names, text contained within a file, file types, and file attributes (metadata).

Spotlight can find:

- Files and folders
- Installed applications
- Media files (video, audio, and images)
- PDF documents
- iWork documents (Pages, Numbers, and Keynote)
- Microsoft Office documents (Word, Excel, PowerPoint, Outlook, and Entourage)
- Safari bookmarks and history
- System Preferences
- Email
- Messages transcripts
- Contacts
- Calendar events
- Reminders
- Dictionary definitions
- Fonts
- Recently used documents (type the name of the application that you were working in)

You can set preferences to expand or limit the scope of the search.

In some cases, Spotlight is context sensitive, basing its results on your current location and activity. Searching from the System Preferences window, for example, finds only relevant System Preferences tasks; and searching from Photos finds matching pictures only in your photo library.

Tip: You can also find files by using the **mdfind** command in Terminal.

Other Types of Search Results

This section concentrates on searching for files, applications, and settings, but Spotlight can also find:

- Locations in Maps

- Digital media in the iTunes and iBooks stores

- Software in the Mac App Store

- Wikipedia articles

- Bing.com search results

- Unit conversions (type *100 yards* to get 91.44 meters, for example)

- Mathematical calculations (type *6*7* to get 42, for example)

- Local movie showtimes (type *movies*)

- Local restaurants (type *pizza*, for example)

Tip: You can toggle and reorder Spotlight's search categories in > System Preferences > Spotlight > Search Results pane.

Search Tips

- Search text is case-insensitive: Spotlight considers *Egg*, *egg*, and *EGG* to be the same search term.

- In a search box, you can use the keyboard shortcuts for Cut (Command+X), Copy (Command+C), Paste (Command+V), Undo (Command+Z), and Select All (Command+A).

- Spotlight usually lists results instantly, but you don't have to wait until a search ends to open an item in the results list.

- For better results, type from the start of a word. If you're searching for *bicycle*, for example, type *bic* rather than *cyc*.

- Spotlight lists results from only your user account and the public system folders; not anyone else's home folder.

- If a search spans multiple drives, drive names appear in the results list.

- Typing the first few letters of a program's name in Spotlight is often the fastest way to open that program.

- Spotlight can evaluate mathematical expressions like *2.3+3* and *pow(exp(sqrt(pi)), log(3))*. For a list of functions, type the command `man math` in Terminal.

Advanced Searches

If a search returns too many results, you can refine it by specifying quoted phrases, metadata (data about data) attributes, and boolean operators:

Quotes

 Surround a search phrase with quotes to find files or attributes that contain that exact phrase. *"aspen tree"* finds files in which *aspen* and *tree* are right next to each other, in that order. Without the quotes, the results would include items that contain any of those words, in any order, not necessarily next to each other.

Attributes

 Most items contain metadata attributes about their own content (the creation date of a document or the resolution of a photo, for example). Separate the attribute name and the search value with a colon (:). For example, *author:stewart* finds only files with *stewart* in the Author field; *kind:pdf* finds PDF files; and *kind:folder* finds only folders. See "Getting Help" (page 31) for using Spotlight to search for specific kinds of items.

 Use the <, <=, >, >=, and - operators to specify numerical and date ranges. For example, *modified:1/1/2014-1/1/2015* finds files modified during a one-year date range. *width:>=800* finds all images that are 800 or more pixels wide.

 For yes/no (or true/false) attributes, use 1 (one) for yes and 0 (zero) for no. For example, *flash:1* finds all photos that were taken with the camera's flash on and *flash:0* finds photos taken with the flash off.

To restrict a search chronologically, use a date keyword: *this year*, *this month*, *this week*, *yesterday*, *today*, *tomorrow*, *next week*, *next month*, or *next year*. The latter four items, which specify future dates, are useful for finding upcoming Calendar events. For example, *date:yesterday* finds files that you last opened yesterday; *modified:today* finds files that you changed today; and *created:this year* finds files that you created since January 1.

You can string words together. For example, *created:today kind:pdf* finds all PDFs that you created today, and *created:today kind:pdf coastal* further restricts the search to PDFs created today that contain the word *coastal*.

You can view a file's metadata attributes in its Info window. If an attribute has a space in its name—*pixel width*, *musical genre*, or *phone number*, for example—then omit the space in the Spotlight search (*pixelwidth:*, *musicalgenre:*, or *phonenumber:*).

Boolean operators

 Type AND, OR, and NOT in uppercase to combine search words by using boolean logic. *word1* AND *word2* finds both *word1* and *word2*, even if those words aren't next to each other. *word1* OR *word2* finds either *word1* or *word2* (or both). NOT word excludes word from the search; *aspen NOT tree*, for example, finds files or attributes that contain *aspen* but not *tree*. A hyphen (-) is shorthand for AND NOT: *aspen -tree* is the same as *aspen AND NOT tree*. Parentheses are shorthand for AND: (*word1 word2*) is the same as *word1* AND *word2*. Booleans work with attribute searches: *kind:pdf OR kind:jpeg* shows both PDF files and JPEG photos in a single results list.

Using Spotlight

To set up Spotlight: Choose > System Preferences > Spotlight. In the Search Results pane, specify the categories and order in which results appear, and the keystrokes that activate Spotlight. In the Privacy pane, specify any drives or folders that you don't want Spotlight to track for privacy reasons (Spotlight rebuilds its entire search index whenever you modify this list).

Tip: For privacy, turn off Spotlight Suggestions in Spotlight (> System Preferences > Spotlight > Search Results) and in Safari (Safari > Preferences > Search). Turning off this setting prevents your search terms and location from being sent to Apple and third parties.

To search from the Spotlight window: Click in the menu bar or press Command+Spacebar. Type text in the Spotlight Search box. As you type, items that match your text appear in the results list, grouped by category (Top Hit, Applications, Definition, System Preferences, Documents, Folders, PDF Documents, Images, and so on). A preview of the selected result appears to the right of the results list.

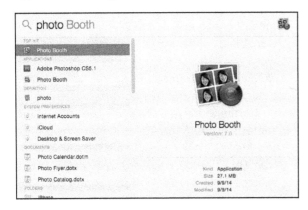

In the Spotlight window, do any of the following:

- To see a preview of an item in the results list, click it, or use the arrow keys to select it.

- To open an item in the results list, double-click it, or use the arrow keys to select it and then press Return.

- To open the item that Spotlight has autoselected (Top Hit), just press Return.

- To show an item in a Finder window instead of opening it, hold down Command and then double-click it, or use the arrow keys to select it and then press Command+Return.

- To see a complete list of results instead of only the best matches, double-click "Show all in Finder" at the bottom of the results list.

- To jump from category to category in the results list, press Command+↓ or Command+↑.

- Drag and drop an item from the Spotlight window (onto the desktop, into a window or a folder, into the Trash, to an email message, onto the AirDrop icon in the sidebar, to another drive, and so on).

- To get Info about an item, select it and then press Command+I.

- To clear the search text, backspace over it or press Esc.

- To cancel the search, press Command+Spacebar, press Esc twice, or click off the Spotlight window.

To search from a search window: Do any of the following:

- To search from the current folder, in Finder, choose File > Find (Command+F) or File > New Smart Folder (Option+Command+N).

- To search all your files starting from a new window, press Option+Command+Spacebar.

- To start from any Finder window, click in the search box in the upper-right corner (the window will change into a search window when you start to type).

The search results will be the same for all the preceding starting points.

In the search window, do any of the following:

- To do a basic search, type text in the search box. As you type, items that match your text appear in the window. To clear the search text, click × or backspace over it.

- To change the scope of the search, click a location in the location bar: This Mac (includes external drives), *"current_folder"*, or Shared (includes networked computers). To change the default scope, choose Finder > Preferences > Advanced pane > "When performing a search".

- To specify search criteria, click + on the right side of the location bar. Use the menus and controls on the criteria bar to refine the search results. Click + or − to add or remove rows as needed. Each row is connected with the preceding one by using AND logic (that is, the results must match all rows).

- To find hidden files, set a criteria bar to Other > File invisible > Invisible items.

- To save the search results as a smart folder, click Save in the location bar.

Smart Folders

If you work regularly with a certain group of files and do the same search repeatedly to find them, you can save your search as a **smart folder**. When you open a smart folder, Spotlight repeats the search and then lists the most current files that match the original search criteria. Finder includes the All My Files smart folder in the sidebar's Favorites section, where you can add your own smart folders. Smart folders are actually files with the extension .savedSearch, stored by default in ~/Library/Saved Searches (~ denotes your home folder). They can be copied, moved, renamed, and deleted like any other files.

To create a smart folder: Use a Spotlight search window to find your files. Click Save on the right side of the location bar. Specify the folder's name and location, and choose whether it appears in the sidebar. (You can drag smart folders on or off the sidebar at any time.)

To open a smart folder (run the search): Click the smart folder in the sidebar, or double-click it on the desktop or in a folder window.

To edit a smart folder: Open the smart folder (run the search), choose ⚙ ˅ > Show Search Criteria, make the desired changes, and then resave the folder.

Burning CDs & DVDs

If your Mac has an internal or external Combo drive or SuperDrive, you can **burn** (copy) files to a writable disc. Combo drives can burn to writable CDs (but not DVDs). SuperDrives can burn to most writable CDs and DVDs. You can burn a disc quickly by dragging files to it and then using the Burn command, or you can create a burn folder. The burn-folder method saves space (because it doesn't make temporary copies of the files to burn), lets you burn the same disc multiple times (each time with the latest versions of your files), and doesn't require you to have a blank disc on hand. You can't burn discs on a remote (networked) drive. OS X might not recognize an inserted disc if you're running VMware or Parallels virtual-machine software. iTunes can also burn discs. To set the default action for an inserted disc, use CDs & DVDs preferences (page 54).

To determine which kinds of discs you can burn: Choose Applications > Utilities > System Information > Hardware > Disc Burning.

To burn a disc by dragging files to it: Insert a writable CD or DVD into the disc burner. If a dialog box appears, choose Open Finder and then click OK.

Double-click the disc's icon on the desktop.

Drag to the disc's window the files and folders that you want to burn (alternatively, you can drop items on the disc icon without opening it). The items appear as aliases, which you can add, delete, or rename (the original files aren't changed). The status bar shows the remaining disc space. To burn the disc, do any of the following, and then follow the onscreen instructions:

- Choose File > Burn.
- Drag the disc icon to the Trash.
- Click the Burn icon next to the disc's name in the sidebar.
- Click the Burn button in the disc window.

To create a burn folder: In Finder, choose File > New Burn Folder. Type a name for the folder, and then press Return.

To add items to a burn folder: Drag the files and folders that you want to burn to the burn folder. The items appear as aliases, which you can add, delete, and rename (the original files aren't changed). The status bar shows the total size of the items.

To burn a disc: Select the burn folder and then do any of the following:

- Choose File > Burn.
- Click the Burn button in the burn-folder window.
- If the burn folder is in the sidebar, click the burn icon beside it. Insert a writable CD or DVD into the disc burner, and then follow the onscreen instructions.

To eject a disc: Quit any programs that are using files on the disc and then do any of the following:

- Select the disc's icon and then choose File > Eject (Command+E).
- Drag the disc's icon to the Trash.
- Click the Eject button ⏏ next to the disc's name in the sidebar.
- Hold down the Eject key ⏏ until the disc ejects.
- Right-click the disc's icon and then choose Eject.
- Click the Eject icon (if there is one) in the menu bar.
- Hold down the left mouse button or F12 key when you start or restart your computer.
- If your drive has an eject hole, put the computer to sleep and then firmly push a straightened paper clip into the hole.

If a busy disc won't eject, OS X will open a dialog box telling you which program is using the disc. Switch to that program, quit it, and then eject the disc.

To duplicate a disc: Choose Applications > Utilities > Disk Utility > select the disc > Restore pane.

Drives

Hard Drive   USB Flash Drive

Macs recognize internal and external hard drives (spinning disk or solid state), USB flash drives, CDs, DVDs, network servers, and mobile devices such as smartphones, media players, ereaders, and iDevices (in their role as removable storage). When you insert a disc or connect a drive or device, its icon appears on the right side of the desktop, in the sidebar, and in the Computer window (Shift+Command+C). To see what's on a drive, double-click its icon.

When you start your Mac, it looks for a system or startup drive (that is, one that has a System folder). If it can't find one, it waits until you insert a disc or connect a drive with a bootable System folder. Installing OS X onto a hard drive (internal or external) or DVD turns it into a startup drive. If multiple startup drives are connected, you can choose which one to boot from. You can also use Disk Utility (page 116) to manage drives.

To show or hide drives on the desktop: In Finder, choose Finder > Preferences > General pane > "Show these items on the desktop".

To eject a removable drive: Quit all programs that are using files on the drive and then do any of the following:

- Select the drive icon and then choose File > Eject (Command+E).

- Drag the drive's icon to the Trash.

- Click the Eject button ⏏ next to the drive's name in the sidebar.

- Right-click the drive's icon and then choose Eject.

Tip: For more ways to eject CDs and DVDs, see "Burning CDs & DVDs" on page 98.

To choose a startup drive: Choose > System Preferences > Startup Disk. See also "Startup" on page 8.

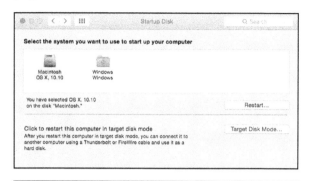

Tip: To select the current startup drive, in Finder, hold down the Shift key and then choose Go > Select Startup Disk on Desktop.

To repair a drive: Choose Applications > Utilities > Disk Utility > select the drive > First Aid pane.

To erase a drive: Choose Applications > Utilities > Disk Utility > select the drive > Erase pane. To secure-erase the drive (to make its contents unrecoverable), click Security Options. You can't erase the current startup drive or write-only CDs and DVDs.

To copy or restore a drive image: Choose Applications > Utilities > Disk Utility > select the drive > Restore pane.

To encrypt a drive: In Finder or on the desktop, right-click the drive icon and then choose Encrypt. See also "FileVault" on page 163.

Programs & Documents

O S X is a launching pad for programs, or **applications** (or **apps**, for short). Apple and sound design enforce substantial consistency, so you can apply knowledge of a few common operations to many programs. Most programs share user-interface elements—scrollbars, copy-and-paste operations, menus, buttons, dialog boxes, and so on—as well as setup and management options. OS X provides consistent ways to manage programs and **documents**, which are self-contained pieces of work (files) that you create with programs.

Installing & Removing Programs

How you install a program depends on where its installation files are located. Most shrink-wrapped programs are installed from a CD or DVD. You can also install programs that you've downloaded from the internet, a local network, or the Mac App Store (● > App Store). Programs from the App Store are downloaded, installed, and updated automatically; programs from other sources require some manual labor. OS X's **Gatekeeper** security feature helps prevent you from inadvertently installing viruses, spyware, and other **malware** (malicious software). Gatekeeper works by restricting which downloaded apps you can install.

 A downloaded program lands by default in your Downloads folder (which is in your home folder). If the TextWrangler.dmg file arrives as a **disk image** (.dmg file), then you can start the installation.

If the program arrives as a compressed file, then you must decompress it before you install. The usual compression formats are:

ZIP (.zip files)
A standard format that OS X can decompress natively (double-click the file to decompress it).

StuffIt (.sit files)
A proprietary format that the widely available, free program StuffIt Expander (*stuffit.com/mac-expander.html*) can decompress.

Unix formats (.tar, .gz, .tar.gz, and .tgz files)
Standard formats that OS X can decompress natively (double-click the file to decompress it).

The decompressed file will contain a .dmg file and possibly other files, such as release notes, readme files, special instructions, or companion utilities.

To enable app installations (Gatekeeper): Choose ● > System Preferences > Security & Privacy > General pane (click 🔒 if the settings are dimmed).

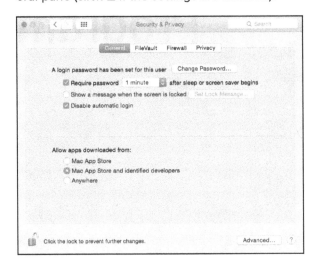

Below "Allow applications downloaded from", choose one of the following options:

Mac App Store
Download and run apps from only the Mac App Store. The App Store is the safest place to get apps because it's curated, meaning that Apple vets the developers and reviews their apps before accepting them to the store. If there's a problem with an app, Apple removes it from the store. Before you download and install an app, you can read reviews from other users.

Mac App Store and identified developers

Download and run App Store apps and non-App Store apps that have a Developer ID. Developers that register with Apple get a unique Developer ID, which they can use to digitally sign the apps that they create. This digital signature is cryptographically secure and lets Gatekeeper verify that the app hasn't been tampered with since it left the hands of the developer. Signed apps aren't necessarily sold through the App Store and aren't pre-screened by Apple, but if Apple discovers any problems with apps created by a registered developer, they can block that developer's apps and revoke their credentials. OS X updates its list of blacklisted developers once each day.

Anywhere

Download and run apps from anywhere. Note that Apple charges a yearly fee for a Developer ID and takes a large cut (30%) of all apps sold through the App Store, so plenty of unregistered but legitimate developers avoid the "Apple tax" by selling their apps through their own websites and other non-Apple stores.

Gatekeeper works only the first time that you try to launch an app, and only when that app has been downloaded via a web browser, an email client, or a similar program (Gatekeeper doesn't check apps copied from USB or network drives, and won't stop Flash and Java programs). After an app has been launched once, it's beyond the reach of Gatekeeper.

Tip: To manually override your Gatekeeper setting, right-click an unsigned app in Finder and then choose Open.

Installer

To install a program: If you have an installation CD or DVD, insert it, double-click its desktop icon if it doesn't auto-open, and then follow the onscreen instructions. If you have a .dmg file, double-click it. The disk image will appear as a new drive icon on the desktop.

Double-click the drive icon to open the installer window. Drag the program's icon to the Applications folder or to your home folder, or double-click the installer (if it appears) and then follow the onscreen instructions.

If you're an administrator, you can install a program in:

- The Applications system folder (page 111), where everyone can use it.

- Your home folder (page 76), where only you can see and use it.

- The Applications subfolder in your home folder, where everyone can see and use it but only you can uninstall it.

Nonadministrators can install in only their home folder (or its subfolders).

After installation, you can eject the disk-image (drive) icon and delete the original compressed file and the .dmg file (unless you need to reinstall someday).

To uninstall a program: Drag it (or its folder) from the Applications folder (or your home folder) to the Trash. (Unlike Windows programs, OS X programs usually don't have separate uninstall utilities.) Uninstalled programs sometimes leave minor parts of themselves behind, typically in /Library/Application Support and /Library/Preferences in the system folder and in your home folder. If you downloaded a program from the App Store, you can use Launchpad (page 105) to uninstall it.

To see a program's support files: Right-click its icon in a Finder window, and then choose Show Package Contents.

Opening, Switching & Quitting Programs

An open program appears in the dock (with a dot next to its icon if you've selected > System Preferences > Dock > "Show indicators for open applications"). Only one program at a time is **active** (frontmost, receiving your keystrokes). The bolded application menu, next to the menu, identifies the active program. Quitting a program lets OS X reclaim its memory for other use. If an individual program **freezes** ("hangs"), you can **force-quit** (and then re-open) it without destabilizing or restarting OS X. The "spinning beachball" cursor is a sign of a frozen program. Force-quitting loses any unsaved changes.

To open a program: Do any of the following:

- Click its icon in the dock or sidebar.

- Click the Applications stack in the dock and then click the program's icon.

- Press Command+Spacebar to open the Spotlight search window, type the first few letters of the program's name until it highlights, and then press Return.

- Choose > Recent Items > Applications submenu.

- Double-click its icon in a Finder window (hold down Option to autoclose the window).

- Select its icon and then choose File > Open (Command+O or Command+ ↓).

- Open any document associated with the program.

- Use Launchpad (page 105).

- Use the open command in Terminal.

To restore your previous document windows when re-opening programs: Choose > System Preferences > General > clear "Close windows when quitting an app". See also "Auto Save and Versions" on page 107.

To open a program automatically at login: Choose > System Preferences > Users & Groups > Login Items pane.

To switch to an open program: Do any of the following:

- If any of the program's windows is visible in the background, click it.

- Click its dock icon.

- Use Exposé or Spaces.

- Command+Tab to it.

To use Command+Tab: Hold down Command and press Tab repeatedly until the desired program highlights in the pop-up list, and then release both keys (to cycle backward, press Shift+Command+Tab). If you release Tab but keep Command pressed, you can click an icon in the list. If you press and release Command+Tab quickly, you swap between only two programs instead of cycling through them all.

To switch to the next window of the active program: Press Command+~ (or Shift+Command+~).

To quit a program: Do any of the following:

- Choose Quit from the program's application menu (Command+Q).

- Right-click (or click-and-hold) its dock icon, and then choose Quit.

- Command+Tab to highlight its icon, and then press Q without releasing the Command key.

To force-quit a program: Do any of the following:

- Choose > Force Quit (Option+Command+Esc).

- Right-click (or click-and-hold) its dock icon, hold down Option, and then choose Force Quit.

- In Terminal, use the kill command (type man kill for usage).

Launchpad

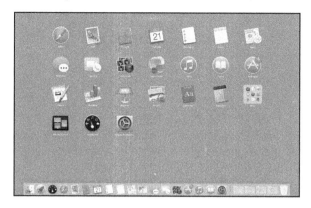

Launchpad displays a full-screen grid of application icons that lets you open, switch, or (in some cases) delete apps. All apps installed on your computer—specifically, in the / Applications and ~/Applications folders—appear automatically, including those downloaded from the App Store. New Launchpad pages sprout automatically to accommodate an icon overflow as you add more apps. (Launchpad mimics the Home screen of iOS devices like the iPad or iPhone.)

To show Launchpad: Do any of the following:

- Click the Launchpad (rocket ship) icon in the dock or in the Applications folder.

- Pinch three fingers and your thumb (> System Preferences > Trackpad > More Gestures pane).

- Press the Launchpad key F4 (on newer Macs).

- Press the Launchpad keyboard shortcut (> System Preferences > Keyboard > Shortcuts pane > Launchpad & Dock > Show Launchpad).

- Move the pointer into one of the screen's four corners (> System Preferences > Mission Control > Hot Corners > Launchpad).

To dismiss Launchpad without opening an app, press the keyboard shortcut again, reverse the multitouch gesture, press Esc, or click an empty area.

To open or activate an app from Launchpad: Do any of the following:

- Click or tap the app's icon.

- Use the arrow keys to highlight the target app and then press Return.

- In the search box at the top of the screen, type the first few letters of the app's name until it highlights, and then press Return. (You don't need to click in the search box; just start typing as soon as Launchpad opens.)

To switch among Launchpad pages: Do any of the following:

- Drag the pointer left or right on an empty area.

- Flick two fingers left or right.

- Hold down Command and then press the left or right arrow key.

To rearrange Launchpad icons: Drag icons within a page or off the edge of one page and onto the next. (You can also drag icons from Launchpad to the dock).

To group apps into folders in Launchpad: To create a folder, drag one app's icon over another, and then drag other apps to add to the folder. To change a folder's name, click the folder to open it, click the current name, and then type the new name. To move an app out of a folder, click the folder to open it, and then drag the app out of the folder.

To uninstall an app from Launchpad: Click-and-hold any app icon (or press-and-hold the Option key) until all the icons wiggle. Click the target app's ⊗ button to uninstall the app. If an icon doesn't have a ⊗ button, you can't uninstall it by using Launchpad. You can always uninstall apps downloaded from the App Store and reinstall them for free at any time.

Resume

When you open an app, it starts where you left off the last time you ran it, with the same windows open in the same positions. Resume also works when you log out of OS X or shut down your Mac: log back in or restart and all the apps that you were using automatically relaunch with the same open windows.

If you prefer a clean desktop, you can turn off this feature: choose > System Preferences > General > select "Close windows when quitting an app". This setting stops OS X from opening windows when you open an app, but doesn't affect how Resume works when you log in or restart. To turn off Resume, when you log out or restart, clear "Reopen windows when logging back in".

Running Older Programs

If you're upgrading from an older version of OS X, consider the following changes that have been made to OS X over the years:

- OS X 10.8 (Mountain Lion) and later don't include **X11**, an environment used to host X Window System programs (graphical Unix apps that don't supply a native OS X interface). If you launch an X11-dependent program, OS X prompts you to install X11 separately.

- In OS X 10.7 (Lion), Apple stopped supporting all **PowerPC** applications, including Photoshop CS2, Quicken 2007, Microsoft Office 2004, AppleWorks, and many classic games. The translation software that runs PowerPC apps, called **Rosetta**, isn't available as an optional add-on; to run PowerPC apps, partition your hard drive and dual boot to OS X 10.6 (Snow Leopard) or earlier. Lion also doesn't include the **Java Development Kit** (JDK), which must be installed separately.

- In OS X 10.5 (Leopard), Apple stopped supporting "Classic" mode, which ran pre-Intel, pre-2001, OS 9 programs.

- **Cocoa** and **Carbon** refer to the programming libraries ("APIs") that the program's developers used to create it. Cocoa programs are true OS X programs. Carbon programs look (and mostly behave) like true OS X programs but really are repackaged versions of older OS 9 programs—"Carbonized" programs can't use all OS X's special features. With each new version of OS X, Apple deprecates (phases out) more parts of Carbon.

Saving Documents

Most applications let you save your work as documents, which you can return to later, print, send to other people, back up, and so on. Nearly all programs use OS X's standard Save dialog box. The first time that you save a document, OS X asks you to name it and pick a location to store it in. (Two files in the same folder can't have the same name.)

Tip: To perform common file operations, you can right-click, drag, Command-drag (move), or Option-drag (copy) files in the Save dialog box.

To save a document: To save the document in its current state, choose File > Save (Command+S). To save a copy of a file under a different name or in a different folder, choose File > Save As (Option+Shift+Command+S) or File > Duplicate (Shift+Command+S).

Tip: If the Save As command doesn't appear in the File menu, hold down the Option key when the menu is open.

To use Finder-like navigation to choose a destination for the file, click ⌄ to expand the dialog box (you can drag a folder icon from the desktop or a Finder window to the expanded dialog box to jump to that location). If the application supports iCloud storage, you can choose it in the iCloud section of the sidebar. In the Save As box, type the name of the file. While editing, you can use the keyboard shortcuts for Cut (Command+X), Copy (Command+C), Paste (Command+V), Undo (Command+Z), and Select All (Command+A). Name the file according to OS X's file-naming rules (page 86). Many programs offer the option to save a file in a format other than the program's default (native) format.

Tip: The standard Save dialog box also lets you add tags to documents (page 89).

Auto Save and Versions

Documents in applications that support OS X's **Auto Save** feature are saved automatically in the background, without pauses or progress bars (meaning you don't have to press Command+S every few minutes). Auto Save saves during pauses in your work and, if you work continuously, it will save after 5 minutes.

Tip: If you prefer to be prompted to save changes, choose > System Preferences > General > select "Ask to keep changes when closing documents".

The **Versions** feature lets you save and browse past versions of documents by using a Time Machine-like interface (page 172) that shows document snapshots cascading back to earlier versions. Versions automatically creates a new version of a document each time that you open it and every hour while you're working on it. You can also create versions manually (choose File > Save or press Command+S). Versions doesn't actually create a copy of a document for each new version (otherwise, your drive would quickly fill to capacity); instead, Versions saves only the *changes* ("deltas", in geekspeak) to the document over time and applies them as needed to show different versions of the original. When you share a document with someone, you share only the most recent version.

Applications that support Auto Save and Versions include some built-in OS X apps (TextEdit, Preview, and Automator, for example) and Apple iWork (Pages, Numbers, and Keynote). Third-party developers are free to update their own apps to support Auto Save and Versions. To use Auto Save and Versions, you can:

- Use File menu commands (Save, Duplicate, Move To, Revert To, and so on).

- Hover the pointer over the document name in the window's title bar until a small arrowhead Down-pointing arrowhead appears, and then click to open the menu.

Tip: To use the Save As command in an application that supports Auto Save, hold down the Option key when you click the File menu, or press Option+Shift+Command+S.

Do any of the following:

- Tag the document.

- Rename the document.

- Move the document to iCloud storage.

- Move the document to a different folder or drive.

- Create a duplicate of the document next to the original (type a new name for the copy).

- Lock the document to prevent inadvertent changes (if you try to change a locked document, you're prompted to unlock it or copy it). Two weeks after the last edit, OS X automatically locks the document for you.

- Revert (roll back) the document to the state it was in when you last opened or saved it (if you're unhappy with your recent changes).

- Bring up the Versions interface (choose Revert To > Browse All Versions).

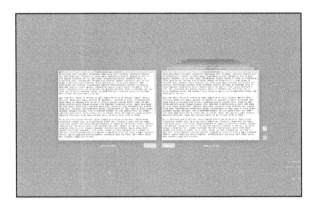

The Versions interface lets you:

- See your document in its current state (on the left) and past incarnations (use the timeline on the right edge of the screen to scroll through old versions).

- Copy and paste between versions.

- Delete old versions.

- Make side-by-side version comparisons.

- Revert to an earlier version.

Opening Documents

To open a document: Do any of the following:

- In the program that created the document, choose File > Open (Command+O). The standard Open dialog box works like the Save dialog box (page 107). If the application supports iCloud, you can open documents from iCloud storage.

- Click its icon in the dock or sidebar.

- Click its stack in the dock, and then click the document's icon.

- Press Command+Spacebar to open the Spotlight search window, type the first few letters of the document's name until it highlights, and then press Return.

- Choose ● > Recent Items > Documents submenu.

- Double-click its icon in a Finder window (hold down Option to autoclose the folder window when the document opens).

- Select its icon and then choose File > Open (Command+O or Command+↓).

- Drag its icon onto the icon of any program that can open it (in the dock, the sidebar, or in a Finder window).

- Use the open command in Terminal.

To open a document automatically at login: Choose ● > System Preferences > Users & Groups > Login Items pane.

Tip: To perform common file operations, you can right-click, drag, Command-drag (move), or Option-drag (copy) files in the Open dialog box.

Associating Documents with Programs

OS X tracks file types to determine which program to launch when you open a document. If you haven't set a default program with "Always Open With", OS X consults its own database. Finally, it checks the document's filename **extension**—the few characters appearing after the filename's last dot (.txt for text files, for example). The Info window (page 28) shows a file's type and default program. Note that setting your preferences with "Always Open With" overrides filename extensions.

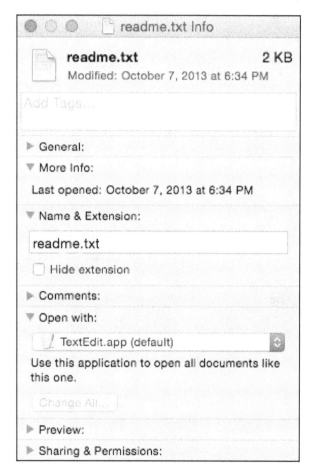

OS X hides extensions by default to appear friendlier. But you should show extensions because they impart the types of like-named files quickly (readme. doc vs. readme.txt vs. readme.html, for example) without making you discern icons or read the Kind column in Finder. If a newly installed program hijacks an extension's association without asking your permission, you can reassociate the extension with your preferred program.

To show or hide filename extensions in Finder: In Finder, choose Finder > Preferences > Advanced pane > "Show all filename extensions".

To show or suppress warnings when you change filename extensions: In Finder, choose Finder > Preferences > Advanced pane > "Show warning before changing an extension".

To open specific document(s) in a nondefault program: In Finder, select the document(s) that you want to open and then do any of the following:

- Choose File > Open With.

- Right-click a selected icon and then choose Open With.

- Click ⚙ ⌄ > Open With.

- Drag a selected icon onto the program's icon in Finder or the dock.

Tip: If a program isn't listed in the "Open With" menu, choose Other to locate it, or choose App Store to find a compatible app. Alternatively, you can open the desired program and then choose File > Open (Command+O).

To change the default program for specific document(s): In Finder, select the document(s) whose default program you want to change and then do any of the following:

- Hold down Option and then choose File > Always Open With.

- Hold down Option, right-click a selected icon, and then choose Always Open With.

- Hold down Option and then click ⚙ ⌄ > Always Open With.

- If only one document is selected, choose File > Get Info (Command+I) > "Open with" pop-up menu. If multiple documents are selected, hold down Option and then choose File > Show Inspector (Option+Command+I) > "Open with" pop-up menu (don't click Change All).

Tip: If a program isn't listed in the "Always Open With" menu, choose Other to locate it.

To change the default program for all documents of a specific file type: In Finder, select any document of the target file type, choose File > Get Info (Command+I), select the desired program from the "Open with" pop-up menu, and then click Change All.

Tip: If a program isn't listed in the "Open with" pop-up menu, choose Other to locate it.

To open a file that has an unknown extension (or no extension): Double-click the mystery file and then click Choose Application.

Applications & Utilities

The Applications folder teems with free programs (.app files) that are part of the standard OS X installation. Inside the Applications folder is the Utilities folder, which holds smaller-scale tools for more-technical tasks. To get help for a specific program, open it and use its Help menu.

To open the Applications folder: In Finder, choose Go > Applications (Shift+Command+A) or click Applications in the sidebar. Alternatively, click the Applications stack in the dock and then choose Open in Finder.

To open the Utilities folder: In Finder, choose Go > Utilities (Shift+Command+U). You can add a Utilities icon to the sidebar or create a Utilities stack in the dock.

Activity Monitor

Use the Activity Monitor utility to identify the programs and processes running on your computer, monitor their activity, and show statistics and graphs about CPU load, memory allocation, power consumption, drive activity, drive usage, and network traffic. If you select a process, you can inspect its details (View > Inspect Process or Command+I) or kill it (View > Quit Process or Option+Command+Q). The Activity Monitor dock icon shows a real-time activity graph (View > Dock Icon).

AirPort Utility

Use AirPort Utility to set up and manage AirPort base stations (Apple's wireless routers). Click Continue to step through a series of setup screens, or click Manual Setup to skip the hand-holding interview and configure the router manually. A free AirPort Utility app is also available for iOS devices.

App Store

Use the App Store application to find, buy, download, install, and update OS X system software and applications directly from Apple's online store. The Mac App Store works like the iOS App Store for iPhone, iPad, and iPod touch. To open App Store, choose > App Store. Thousands of free or paid apps from Apple and third-party developers are available, with new or updated apps arriving every day. App Store supports notifications, parental controls, full-screen view, and share sheets.

The store is curated, meaning that Apple must approve every app. Apple can also yank an app from the store if it crashes too much, violates store policy, is complained about excessively, or whatever. Yanked apps disappear from the store but not from your Mac; after you download an app and back it up, it's yours.

You can read program descriptions and customer reviews before you buy. App Store programs have cost advantages (no box, no disc, and no shipping) and tend to be cheaper than traditionally distributed software (many programs in the store are free). Apple controls the transaction as middleman between you and the developer and identifies you by your Apple ID. If you uninstall an app that you bought from the App Store, you can reinstall it for free at any time on any of your Macs.

You can find apps by using the store's browse and search tools. Apps are available in many languages, though store content varies by country. In App Store, click one of the following buttons in the toolbar:

Featured
> The Featured pane (Command+1) shows new and notable apps spotlighted by Apple's staff (via editorial fiat or paid placement). Scroll down to see apps organized in various special categories.

Top Charts

The Top Charts pane (Command+2) lists the currently most popular paid, free, and top-grossing apps in the store. To show more apps, click See All. To show only a certain type of top apps, click an item in the Top Charts Categories list. These lists are updated many times each day.

Categories

The Categories pane (Command+3) lists apps by type (Games, Productivity, Weather, and so on). Click a category name or icon to see new, popular, or featured apps in that category.

Purchases

The Purchases pane (Command+4) lists the apps (paid or free) that you've downloaded previously. To restore an app that you deleted, find it in the list and then click Install. You don't have to pay again for previously purchased apps, though substantial revisions may cost money.

Updates

The Updates pane (Command+5) lists apps that have been updated by their developers since you downloaded or last updated them. All OS X and other Apple software updates (page 170) are also available here.

Tip: Flick two fingers left or right on the trackpad to navigate through your history in App Store.

Audio MIDI Setup

Use the Audio MIDI Setup utility to add and configure MIDI (Musical Instrument Digital Interface) devices connected to your computer. You can select audio-channel input and output devices, configure output speakers, set clock rates, and control levels. In GarageBand, Audio MIDI Setup helps connect your guitar, keyboard, and other instruments.

Automator

Use the Automator application to create drag-and-drop workflows that automate repetitive tasks such as renaming groups of files and converting image formats. Automator works with Apple programs (Finder, Calendar, Contacts, iTunes, Safari, Mail, iWork, and so on) and third-party programs such as those in Microsoft Office and Adobe Creative Suite. Automator doesn't require programming knowledge, as does AppleScript. To use Automator, drag Actions for programs to the Workflow area, and then save the actions as a workflow or application to run whenever you want. You can also save workflows as services, plugins, and other types of documents. To download and share Automator Actions, choose Automator > Display Automator Website. Automator supports Auto Save.

Bluetooth File Exchange

Use the Bluetooth File Exchange utility to share files with Bluetooth-enabled devices. You can receive a photo from a mobile phone, for example, or send multiple selected documents to an iPad or tablet. To send a file, drag its icon from a Finder window to the Bluetooth File Exchange icon in the dock. You can create remote folders and double-click to navigate folders.

Bluetooth Firmware Update

Use the Bluetooth Firmware Update utility to update low-level Bluetooth software.

Boot Camp Assistant

Use the Boot Camp Assistant utility to install Windows 7 or later on an Intel-based Mac. (For upgraders, existing Boot Camp installations support Windows XP Service Pack 2 or later.) Boot Camp Assistant partitions your Mac's hard drive and steps you through installing Windows on the new partition.

After you install Windows on a Boot Camp partition, you can choose to boot either OS X or Windows at startup. To choose, hold down the Option key during the startup process, and then select the desired system when the partition list appears. To set the default partition for future startups, choose > System Preferences > Startup Disk.

As an alternative to (or in addition to) Boot Camp, you can use VMware Fusion (*vmware.com*), Parallels Desktop (*parallels.com*), or VirtualBox (*virtualbox.org*) to run Windows (or other operating systems) in a virtual machine simultaneously with OS X.

Calculator

Use the Calculator application to perform the basic operations of arithmetic.

Calculator includes these features:

- Switch among Basic (Command+1), Scientific (Command+2), and Programmer (Command+3) modes.

- To operate Calculator, click the onscreen buttons or press the corresponding number and symbol keys on the keyboard.

- To clear the display, click the C button or press C on the keyboard.

- To make Calculator speak keystrokes aloud, use the Speech menu.

- To convert between standard units of measurement, use the Convert menu.

- To copy the calculated result for pasting into another program, choose Edit > Copy (Command+C).

- To toggle algebraic and RPN entry (like Hewlett–Packard calculators), choose View > RPN Mode (Command+R).

- To view the calculation history, choose Windows > Show Paper Tape (Command+T). To export the calculation history to a text file, choose File > Save Tape As (Shift+Command+S).

***

Tip: A quick alternative to Calculator: type or paste a mathematical expression in the Spotlight search window (Command+Spacebar); the answer appears in the results list.

***

Calendar

Use the Calendar application to manage your calendars and events (appointments). Calendar identifies you by your Apple ID (Calendar > Preferences > Accounts pane) and is integrated with Contacts. Calendar supports Auto Save and full-screen view.

Calendar includes these features:

- View individual calendars or multiple color-coded calendars at the same time (choose View > Show Calendar List or click Calendars in the toolbar).

- Add new events (File > New Event).

- Edit existing events (Edit > Edit Event).

- View and search recent and upcoming events.

- Enter repeating events (such as birthdays or weekly meetings).

- Specify what hours constitute a workday and what weekday starts the week (Calendar > Preferences > General pane).

- Receive onscreen, audio, email, or message alerts of upcoming events (Edit > Edit Event > Alert).

- Send notifications for events and invitations (Calendar > Preferences > Alerts pane).

- Create multiple calendars for home, work, and so on (File > New Calendar).

- Set the default calendar for new events (Calendar > Preferences > General pane > Default Calendar).

- Switch among daily (Command+1), weekly (Command+2), monthly (Command+3), and yearly (Command+4) views.

- Import, export, and print calendars (File menu).

- To use iCloud to sync calendars wirelessly across your Macs and iOS devices, choose > System Preferences > iCloud > Calendars.

- To sync Calendar with Gmail, Yahoo, or other services that support calendars, choose > System Preferences > Internet Accounts, select the account, and then turn on Calendars/Reminders.

- To turn on notifications for calendar events, choose > System Preferences > Notifications > Calendar.

- See maps for event locations.

Calendar also lets you view the online calendars of people who have published them on the internet. You can subscribe to **iCalendar** (.ics) or **CalDAV** calendars, including iCloud, Yahoo, Google, and Calendar for iOS calendars. You can read events from subscribed calendars, but you can't add or edit events. To subscribe to a calendar, choose File > New Calendar Subscription (Option+Command+S).

You can also subscribe to web calendars by clicking a link to the calendar in Safari. Open Safari, go to a site such as *icalshare.com*, find a calendar that you like (holidays, sports schedules, movie releases, and so on), and then click Subscribe to Calendar. The new calendar is added to your subscription list, and its events appear in Calendar. To show or hide those events, click the Calendars button in the toolbar and then toggle the target calendar.

To edit or delete a calendar subscription, right-click the calendar in the Calendars list.

If you get an iCalendar (.ics) file attached to an email message, you can open the attachment to import its events into Calendar.

Chess

Use the Chess application to play chess and chess variants on a 3D board, optionally logging games. To make moves by speaking or to make Chess speak moves aloud (handy if you drift off during slow games), choose Chess > Preferences > Speech. Chess supports Game Center and full-screen view.

ColorSync Utility

Use ColorSync Utility to manage color profiles and filters used in Apple's PDF workflow, and to apply filters to PDF documents. Click one of the buttons in the toolbar:

- Profile First Aid repairs ColorSync profiles so they conform to the ICC specification.

- Profiles browses and compares installed profiles.

- Devices lists registered ColorSync devices and displays and their default profiles.

- Filters builds and modifies systemwide PDF filters.

- Calculator converts among RGB, CMYK, and other color-value schemes.

Console

Use the Console utility to view text logs of interaction messages passed between OS X and programs (useful for software developers).

Contacts

Use the Contacts application to store names, addresses, telephone numbers, email addresses, birthdays, and other contact information. Contacts supports Auto Save and share sheets.

Contacts includes these features:

- In its default view, Contacts resembles an address book. On the left page, browse contacts by clicking, scrolling, or searching. On the right page, scroll contact info, or click a field or button to perform an action such as sharing a contact or opening a contact's home page.

- To create a new contact, choose File > New Card (Command+N) or click (+). Your contacts are available in Mail, Messages, FaceTime, Calendar, file sharing, AirDrop, and other apps and services that tap into Contacts.

- To edit an existing contact, select the contact and then choose Edit > Edit Card (Command+L) or click the Edit button.

- To specify which fields appear in all cards, choose Contacts > Preferences > Template pane. To add a field to a specific card, select the card and then choose Card > Add Field.

- To change how contacts are sorted and displayed, choose Contacts > Preferences > General pane.

- To sync your contacts with iCloud, Yahoo, or other contact lists, choose Contacts > Preferences > Accounts pane. Alternatively, choose > System Preferences > Internet Accounts, select the account, and then turn on Contacts.

- To use iCloud to sync your contacts across your Macs, Windows PCs, and iOS devices, choose Contacts > Preferences > General pane > Default Account > iCloud. To store your contacts on only your Mac, choose On My Mac as the default account.

- Each Contacts entry is a customizable "card". You can use the File menu to import and export cards in common formats, organize them into fixed or self-updating ("smart") groups, or print contact lists and address labels.

- To display groups, choose View > Show Groups (Command+1).

- Contacts exchanges contact information with other programs (including Windows programs) mainly through **vCards** (.vcf files). If you get a vCard file attached to an email, drag the file into your Contacts window to create a contact. To create a vCard file, drag an entry (or Command-drag multiple entries) out of your Contacts list to the desktop or into an outgoing message. To change the vCard format, choose Contacts > Preferences > vCard pane.

- To control which apps and services can access your contacts, choose > System Preferences > Security & Privacy > Privacy pane > Contacts (click if the settings are dimmed).

- Facebook friends appear in Contacts with profile photos and up-to-date information.

- See maps for contact addresses.

Dashboard

Opens the dashboard (page 42).

Dictionary

Use the Dictionary application to look up word definitions, pronunciations, synonyms, Apple terms, and Wikipedia articles. It includes American, British, Japanese, Simplified Chinese, Spanish, German, and other dictionaries and thesauri (Dictionary > Preferences). Dictionary supports parental controls for profanity.

You can look up a word in any of the following ways:

- In Dictionary, type or paste the word in the search box and then click it in the results list.

- In TextEdit, Mail, Messages, Safari, and other OS X programs, point to a word and then press Ctrl+Command+D.

- In any program that taps into Dictionary, right-click a word and then choose Look Up or double-tap a word or phrase with three fingers.

- In a web browser, type *dict://word* in the address bar, replacing *word* with the actual word to define.

- Use the Dictionary widget in Dashboard.

Tip: Flick two fingers left or right on the trackpad to navigate through your history in Dictionary.

DigitalColor Meter

Use the DigitalColor Meter utility to show the color value of any onscreen pixel (useful for print and web designers). Open DigitalColor Meter and point anywhere on your screen. A magnified view appears in the meter window, along with the RGB (red-green-blue) color value of the selected pixel(s). To change the format of the color value, click the pop-up menu. To get the *average* color value of multiple pixels, increase the aperture size. To move the pointer precisely, tap the arrow keys.

Disk Utility

Use Disk Utility to perform drive-related tasks.

- Get size, format, hardware, and other information about any drives attached to your Mac.

- Fix drives that misbehave or won't appear on your desktop.

- Erase, secure-erase, format, and partition drives (partitioning a drive subdivides it into multiple **volumes**, each of which appears on the desktop as a separate drive icon).

- Manage partitions (you can create or enlarge partitions without erasing the entire drive).

- Mount, unmount, and eject drives and disk images.

- Verify and repair a drive's integrity and permissions.

- Erase rewritable CDs and DVDs.

- Create, convert, compress, and encrypt disk images (.dmg, .iso, and other formats).

- Burn disk images (.dmg files) to CDs and DVDs.

- Create and manage RAID sets (a cluster of separate drives that acts as a single volume).

- Toggle journaling.

Disk Utility's Repair Disk feature can solve a huge number of small, quirky, and disparate problems. Also, use the Repair Disk Permissions feature if OS X ever tells you that you lack sufficient access privileges for a file, folder, or program.

Tip: The command-line interface for Disk Utility is the `diskutil` command in Terminal.

DVD Player

Use the DVD Player application to play DVD movies on your computer. It supports multiple audio, video, and subtitle tracks, Dolby audio, closed captions, and other standard DVD features. To circumvent DVD restrictions (such as unskippable warnings and ads), use VLC media player (*videolan.org*) instead. To open a player automatically when you insert a movie DVD, use CDs & DVDs preferences.

FaceTime

Use the FaceTime application to make video calls to other FaceTime users over a high-speed internet connection. The other caller must have an iPhone, iPad, or iPod touch with a forward-facing camera, or a camera-equipped Mac running FaceTime. To use a specific camera or microphone, use the Video menu.

FaceTime identifies you by your Apple ID (FaceTime > Preferences > Settings pane) and is integrated with Contacts. To make a FaceTime call, double-click a contact in the FaceTime window, or right-click the FaceTime dock icon and then choose a contact under Recent Calls.

After you connect, you can:

- Resize the window (drag any window edge, click the green Zoom button in the top-left corner, or choose Window > Zoom).

- Go full-screen (choose Video > Enter Full Screen, press Ctrl+Command+F, or spread two fingers on the trackpad).

- Drag the small inset picture of you to a different corner of the video window.

- Mute the mike (choose Video > Mute or click the microphone button at the bottom of the video window).

- Pause the call (minimize FaceTime, choose FaceTime > Hide FaceTime, press Command+H, or right-click the FaceTime dock icon and then choose Hide).

- Rotate your picture (choose Video > Use Portrait/Landscape, press Command+R, rotate two fingers on the trackpad, or click the curved arrow in the inset picture of you).

For incoming FaceTime calls:

- FaceTime doesn't have to be running for you to receive a call.

- When someone calls you, FaceTime posts a message on your screen and plays a ringtone (FaceTime > Preferences > Settings pane > Ringtone).

- If your screen is locked, you can answer the call from the login screen without having to enter your password.

- If iTunes is playing, it pauses automatically.

- You can accept the call and start talking, or decline it to tell the caller that you're unavailable.

- FaceTime can send notifications for missed calls.

- If you don't want to be interrupted, you can turn off FaceTime by choosing FaceTime > Turn Face-Time Off (Command+K), or by signing out of FaceTime or disabling your account (FaceTime > Preferences > Settings pane).

- To stop specific contacts from calling you, choose FaceTime > Preferences > Blocked pane.

- When you receive a FaceTime call while you're having another FaceTime call with someone else, you can put your current conversation on hold and answer the incoming call (call waiting).

Font Book

Opens Font Book (page 140).

Game Center

Use the Game Center application to play games on Apple's online multiplayer social gaming network, which Apple says has more than 100 million members around the world. You can get Game Center-compatible games from the Mac App Store to play against friends or strangers on iPhones, iPads, iPods, or Macs.

Tip: Chess supports Game Center.

Game Center offers features common to most gaming networks:

- You can add people to your friends list or receive friend requests from others.

- Friends can invite each other to play or find equally matched opponents.

- You can earn bonus points for games that reward points for completing certain tasks, and you can see what your friends have achieved.

- Game leaderboards rank the best players.

- In-game voice chat lets you talk with your opponents or team members during multiplayer games.

Game Center supports parental controls, full-screen view, and notifications for friend requests and game invitations.

To use Game Center, you need an internet connection and an Apple ID. If you like, you can create a separate Apple ID for gaming and still use your main Apple ID for iCloud, App Store, iTunes, and so on.

The first time that you sign in to Game Center, you must create a **nickname**, which is your unique user name in Game Center. If you pick a nickname that someone is already using, Game Center suggests alternatives, which you're free to ignore. If you see your nickname at the top of the Me pane, you're already signed in. You can change your nickname at any time in account settings, but only one nickname at a time can be associated with an Apple ID. Other players can search for you by using your nickname. Account settings also let you configure privacy-related options, such as whether to accept game invitations or display your real name to nonfriends.

After you sign in, click the buttons in the toolbar to edit your account, play or buy games, or manage your friends:

Me

View or buy top games, add or take a photo, or declare your status, which you define.

Tip: You don't need to sign out each time you quit Game Center.

Friends

Invite people or contacts to be friends, respond to friend requests or search for requests, get friend recommendations, invite friends to play, see games that friends play, buy a game that a friend has, check a friend's scores, search your friends list, list a friend's friends, remove (unfriend) a friend, or report problems or cheaters.

Tip: No friends? Unresponsive friends? Use Auto-Match to have Game Center find another player for you.

Games

Play a game, get game recommendations, search for Game Center games, tell a friend about a game, view leaderboards (rankings) and achievements, or get a game from the App Store. Not all Game Center-compatible games feature multiplayer play.

Challenges

Send or receive challenges to beat friends' scores or earn achievements.

Turns

Keep track of turn-based games.

Tip: Apple maintains and updates your Game Center **profile** automatically. Your profile contains your nickname, friends list, achievement points, photo, status, Game Center-compatible games owned, and more.

In many multiplayer games—racing and cooperative games being obvious examples—all players play at the same time. Other games—particularly board and card games such as backgammon, Scrabble, and poker—are **turn-based**, in that each player waits until the other acts before proceeding. Game Center keeps track of each player's turn and can manage multiple games if you're playing more than one. If it's taking a long time between moves, Game Center can send you notifications when it's your turn.

GarageBand

Use the GarageBand application to create music or podcasts. Its features include audio recording, virtual instruments, MIDI editing, and music lessons. GarageBand supports full-screen view.

Grab

Use the Grab utility to take screenshots (image files that record what's on your display). Use the Capture menu to take a picture of a selected part of the screen (Shift+Command+A), a selected window (Shift+Command+W), or the entire screen (Command+Z). The Timed Screen command (Shift+Command+Z) waits 10 seconds before snapping the picture, giving you time to set up the shot or open a menu. To show or hide the pointer in screenshots, choose Grab > Preferences.

Grab's image format is TIFF; to convert to another format, use the File > Export command in Preview (page 125). Note that Preview has its own File > Take Screen Shot command.

Instead of Grab, you can use OS X's own built-in keyboard shortcuts to take screenshots:

- To capture the whole screen, press Shift+Command+3. The screenshot appears on the desktop as a PNG-format file named *Screen Shot YYYY-MM-DD at HH.MM.SS*. You can open, edit, and convert these files in Preview.

- To capture part of the screen, press Shift+Command+4, and then drag a rectangular area (hold down Shift to constrain the drag vertically or horizontally, or hold down Option to drag from the center outward), or press Spacebar and then click a screen object. To cancel the screenshot, press Esc.

- To copy a screenshot to the clipboard (ready for pasting), rather than saving it as a file, also hold down Ctrl when you take the shot.

- To change the screenshot keyboard shortcuts, choose > System Preferences > Keyboard > Shortcuts pane > Screen Shots.

You can also take screenshots by using the screencapture command in Terminal.

To create screen recordings—videos of what takes place on your computer screen—open QuickTime Player (page 126) and then choose File > New Screen Recording (Ctrl+Command+N).

Grapher

Use the Grapher utility to create 2D and 3D graphs of equations.

Grapher includes these features:

- To see sample graphs that you can use as starting points, use the Examples menu.

- To fine-tune a graph, use the Format, Object, View, and Window menus, or choose Window > Show Inspectors.

- To move a 2D graph in the window, choose View > Move Tool (Command+2) and then drag. To move a 3D graph, Command-drag it.

- To rotate a 3D graph, drag in any direction, or Option-drag to flip the graph on one axis.

- To export a graph as an image file, choose File > Export.

- To copy an equation for pasting into another program, select the equation in the edit field above the graph, right-click it, and then choose Copy As or Copy LaTeX Expression.

- To create animations and do higher-math calculations, use the Equation menu.

iBooks

The iBooks application is Apple's ebook reader for the Mac, iPad, iPhone, and iPod touch. Like the Amazon Kindle and other ereaders, iBooks lets you download books and read them onscreen.

- Shop for books in Apple's iBooks Store (click iBooks Store, choose Store > Store Home, or press Shift+Command+H). You can browse by title, author, or genre. And click to see details, read reviews, or download a free sample.

- Use iCloud to download iBooks Store purchases to all your Macs and iOS devices automatically (iBooks > Preferences > Store pane > "Download new purchases automatically").

- Download EPUB-format books from the internet and add them to your iBooks library (File > Add to Library).

- Add PDF files to your iBooks library to read in Preview (File > Add to Library).

- Sort the books in your library manually or automatically (View > Sort By).

- Organize your books into collections on topics of your choosing (File menu).

- Open multiple books at the same time to view side by side, each in its own window.

- Read books in one-page or two-page view (View > Single Page/Two Pages or Command+1/2).

- Turn pages by clicking, flicking, or using the Go menu keyboard shortcuts.

- Zoom images by double-clicking or pinching.

- Move the pointer to the top of the window to show the reading and navigation controls.

- Annotate books with bookmarks, highlights, and notes (use the Edit menu or drag to select text). Annotations and reading progress (furthest page read) are synced across all your devices.

- Share quotes from books via Mail, Messages, Twitter, or Facebook (File > Share).

- Change a book's typography and layout.

- Use the Night (View menu) theme to make reading in the dark easier on your eyes.

- Change to full-screen view to focus on the words without distraction.

- Find all occurrences of a word or phrase in a book.

- Double-click a word to see its definition in the built-in dictionary.

- Copy text from a book and paste it in other apps.

- Set parental controls (iBooks > Preferences > Parental pane).

Image Capture

Use the Image Capture application to transfer images to and from a digital camera, or grab images from a scanner. Image Capture lacks the organizational tools of Photos but is smaller and faster and lets you create slideshows and rescale images for printing or email. You can also share cameras and scanners attached to your Mac with other users on a network, or control a camera remotely to monitor a room.

To set up photo transfer, connect your camera to your Mac, turn on the camera, select the camera in the Devices list (on the left), and then use the "Connecting this camera opens" pop-up menu.

You can also use Preview (page 125) to import camera images or operate a scanner.

iMovie

Use the iMovie application to edit home movies.

iMovie lets you:

- Import footage from movie files, tape camcorders, digital video cameras, iPhones, iPads, iPod touches, or DVD camcorders.
- Record live video from a built-in FaceTime/iSight camera, a third-party webcam, or an external camera (via a FireWire or USB connection).
- Storyboard and edit a movie.
- Add transitions, themes, travel maps, and animatics.
- Add video effects.
- Crop, rotate, color-fix, and stabilize video.
- Add titles, subtitles, and credits.
- Add narration, music, and sound.
- Add photos and still images.
- Create trailers.

- Play the final movie in QuickTime Player; share it on the web (YouTube, Facebook, and so on); download it to your iPhone, iPad, or iPod touch.
- Go full-screen.

iTunes

Use the iTunes application to buy, play, and organize your digital library of music, video, audiobooks, and other media. iTunes supports full-screen view.

iTunes lets you:

- Play CDs, rip (copy) songs from CDs, burn custom music CDs, and organize and play audio files.
- Create playlists and smart (self-updating) playlists (File > New > Playlist or File > New > Smart Playlist).
- Download media (free or paid) from Apple's iTunes Store, including music, movies, TV shows, podcasts, audiobooks, iOS apps and games, and ringtones.
- Download free university lectures from iTunes U.
- Get automated Genius recommendations and playlists based on the media in your library (Store > Turn On Genius).
- Share (stream) your media library on your local network (iTunes > Preferences > Sharing pane).
- Copy music and videos from one Mac to another one (File > Home Sharing).
- Sync or back up an iPhone, iPad, or iPod.
- Use iCloud to sync music, iOS app, and book purchases across iOS devices (iTunes > Preferences > Store pane > Automatic Downloads).
- Read, write, and convert between MP3, AIFF, WAV, MPEG-4, AAC, and Apple Lossless audio formats.
- Read CD track names from an online database when a music CD is inserted (iTunes > Preferences > General pane).

- Listen to internet radio stations around the world.

- Listen to iTunes Radio, Apple's ad-supported internet radio service.

- Set parental controls (iTunes > Preferences > Parental pane).

Java Preferences

The Java Preferences utility holds settings of interest mainly to Java programmers.

Keychain Access

Opens Keychain Access (page 164).

Launchpad

Opens Launchpad (page 105).

Mail

Use the Mail application to send, receive, and manage email. Mail supports parental controls and full-screen view. See also "Internet Accounts" on page 71.

Mail includes these features:

- Read, reply to, forward, redirect, print, file, flag, find, archive, or delete messages.

- Open or search attachments.

- Add or edit multiple email accounts (Mail > Add Account or Mail > Preferences > Accounts pane).

- iCloud support (Mail > Preferences > Accounts pane).

- Notification Center support for incoming email from all senders, only contacts, or only VIP senders (Mail > Preferences > General pane > "New message notifications"). To flag a person as a VIP, click the little star icon that appears when you hover the pointer over a sender's name in a message.

- Contacts integration.

- See maps for addresses in messages.

- Import mailboxes from Apple Mail, Netscape/Mozilla, Thunderbird, Eudora, and other email programs that use the mbox format (File > Import Mailboxes).

- Export mailboxes for backups (Mailbox > Export Mailbox).

- Rebuild mailboxes to repair and compact message files (Mailbox > Rebuild).

- Threaded conversations (Mail > Preferences > Viewing pane > "View conversations").

- Data detectors recognize postal addresses, phone numbers, dates, times, flight numbers, and so on.

- Message-filtering rules (Mail > Preferences > Rules pane).

- Rich (formatted)-text or plain-text message composition (Mail > Preferences > Composing pane).

- Junk-mail (spam) filtering (Mail > Preferences > Junk Mail pane).

- Self-updating smart mailboxes or folders (Mailbox > New Smart Mailbox or Mailbox > New Smart Mailbox Folder).

- Spotlight-indexed messages.

- Attachment searches.

- Use Mail Drop to send large attachments (up to 5GB).

- Use Markup to annotate images and fill out forms without leaving Mail.

- Fill out PDF forms without leaving Mail.

- Message-priority flags.

- Photo-resizing tools.

- Slideshow views of received photos.

- Signatures (Mail > Preferences > Signatures pane).

- Stationery templates.

- Inline images.

- Custom fonts and colors (Mail > Preferences > Fonts & Colors pane).

- Microsoft Exchange support.

Maps

The Maps application is Apple's mapping and navigation program for the Mac, iPad, iPhone, and iPod touch. Maps supports full-screen view.

- Open multiple maps in separate windows.

- Find a location, business, or other point of interest and get the complete address, telephone number, website link, photos, reviews, and more.

- Mark a spot on a map by dropping a pin.

- Find your current location by using Location Services (page 168).

- Get travel directions (walking or driving). You can plan a trip on your Mac and then send the map directly to your iPhone, where Maps can give you turn-by-turn voice navigation as you go.

- Show real-time traffic conditions and incident reports.

- Show 3D views and photo-realistic Flyover views (for major cities and landmarks).

- Zoom, pan, tilt, or rotate the map by using the mouse, multitouch gestures, menu commands, or keyboard shortcuts.

- Bookmark your favorite places.

- Switch to satellite view.

- Share locations via Mail, Messages, Facebook, Twitter, or AirDrop.

- Add locations as new contacts.

- Print a map or export it as a PDF file.

- Reorient to North.

- See maps for addresses within Mail, Contacts, Calendar, and Reminders.

Messages

Use the Messages application for instant text messaging, audio/video chatting, and file exchange. Messages supports notifications and full-screen view.

In addition to supporting the ubiquitous SMS and MMS messaging services used on mobile phones and the web, Messages supports Apple's **iMessage** service. iMessage is a free alternative to SMS/MMS that lets you send unlimited free text messages, photos, videos, and more to people who are also running Messages on their iPads, iPhones, iPod touches, or Macs, and with whom you've exchanged email addresses. iMessage identifies you by your Apple ID email address and requires an internet connection. iMessages are displayed on all your Macs and iOS devices logged in to the same account. You can start a conversation on, say, your iPad and then continue it on your Mac. Set up Messages on each device, using the same email address.

Messages includes these features:

- Support for iMessage, AIM (AOL Instant Messenger), Jabber, Google Talk, and Yahoo Messages accounts (Messages > Preferences > Accounts pane).

- Contacts integration.

- One-to-one or group typed conversations.

- Add or remove people in group conversations at any time.

- Leave a group conversation at any time.

- Give group conversations titles to make them easier to find and manage.

- Mute notifications for conversations when you don't want be bothered, and read the messages later.

- Delivery and read receipts (iMessage only).

- End-to-end encryption secures iMessage conversations.

- Search messages by text or recipient.

- Video and audio chat via FaceTime/iSight camera (or other webcam or microphone).

- Soundbites: record your voice in Messages and send the audio clip to others, who can play the recording inside their conversation.

- Automatically find other Messages users on your local network.

- Background, image, and video effects.

- Multiple chats in a single window or in separate windows.

- Message forwarding (right-click selected messages and then choose Forward).

- Unified buddy list.

- Unified status.

- Buddy search.

- Screen-sharing for getting live help from other Mac users.

- Timestamped chat histories.

- Formatted text and smileys.

- File exchange (Buddies > Send File). iMessage allows attachments of up to 100MB.

- Send email (Buddies > Send Email).

Tip: To sync Messages with Gmail (Google Talk), Yahoo (Yahoo Messages), or other services that support messages, choose > System Preferences > Internet Accounts, select the account, and then turn on Messages.

Migration Assistant

Use the Migration Assistant utility to transfer your user accounts, files, programs, and settings from one Mac to another, or from a Windows PC to a Mac. Migration Assistant is useful when you buy a new Mac or when you need to recover data from Time Machine, a secondary hard drive, or a partition. On-screen instructions guide you through the process.

Mission Control

Opens Mission Control (page 45).

Network Utility

Network Utility is a graphical frontend for standard Unix networking commands: netstat, ping, lookup, traceroute, whois, and finger. (These commands are also available in Terminal.) Network Utility also shows information about network connections and scans open ports for a given domain name or IP address.

Notes

Use the Notes application to type notes on a virtual pad of scratch paper. It's also a handy place to paste text and photos copied from Safari, Mail, or other apps. Notes supports Auto Save, share sheets, and full-screen view.

Notes includes these features:

- To create a new note, choose File > New Note (Command+N) or click New Note button.

  A list of notes appears on the left, and the current note is highlighted. Notes are listed chronologically, with the most recently modified note at the top. Each item in the list shows the first few words of the note.

- To view or edit a note, click it in the notes list.

- Paste or drag text, images, or web addresses (URLs) into notes.

- To format a note, select the target text and then use the Format menu. You can format a note with fonts, rich text, bulleted items, and numbered lists.

- To find a note, type or paste text in the search box.

- To open a note in a separate window, double-click it in the notes list. These notes stay visible even when Notes is minimized.

- To delete a note, right-click it in the notes list and then choose Delete, or click the Trash icon at the bottom of the note.

- You can organize notes in a hierarchy of folders. To view a list of folders, choose View > Show Folders List. To create a new folder, choose File > New Folder (Shift+Command+N). To view a folder's notes, click the folder in the folders list. To move a note to a different folder, drag the note from the notes list to the target folder. To nest folders, drag a folder onto another. To delete or rename a folder, right-click it in the folders list (deleting a folder also deletes its notes and subfolders).

- To use iCloud to sync notes wirelessly across your Macs and iOS devices, choose > System Preferences > iCloud > Notes.

- To sync Notes with Gmail, Yahoo, or other services that support notes, choose > System Preferences > Internet Accounts, select the account, and then turn on Notes.

Notification Center

See "Notification Center" on page 47.

Photo Booth

Use the Photo Booth application to take photos or video with an FaceTime/iSight camera, webcam, or camcorder. (Photo Booth won't open if your Mac doesn't have a camera.) Before you shoot, you can apply special effects, distortions, color changes, and background images or video. After you shoot, you can trim video clips. Photo Booth supports share sheets and full-screen view.

Photos

Use the Photos application to import, organize, edit, print, and share digital photos. Photos supports share sheets and full-screen view. To get started, read the Apple support article "Get started with Photos for OS X" at *support.apple.com/HT204655*.

Photos includes these features:

- Import images in JPEG, TIFF, RAW, and other image formats.

- Import images from digital cameras, iOS devices (iPhone, iPad, and iPod touch), mobile phones, tablets, hard drives, flash drives, CDs, DVDs, SD cards, emails, text messages, webpages, and My Photo Stream.

Tip: Use My Photo Stream (> System Preferences > iCloud > Photos > Options) to sync your photos across Macs, Windows PCs, and iOS devices.

- Import and manage videos.

- Use **iCloud Photo Library** (> System Preferences > iCloud > Photos > Options) to store every photo and video that you take, making them accessible from your Mac, iPhone, iPad, or iPod touch, and on *icloud.com*. For details, read the Apple support article "iCloud Photo Library FAQ" at *support.apple.com/HT204264*.

- Use **iCloud Photo Sharing** (> System Preferences > iCloud > Photos > Options) to create shared albums, control who sees what, and see updates to your shared albums across your devices. For details, read the Apple support article "iCloud Photo Sharing FAQ" at *support.apple.com/HT202786*.

- Use editing tools to fix red-eye, adjust contrast and brightness, crop and resize images, change saturation and color balance, apply filters, and so on. Install third-party extensions (page 66) to add more editing tools.

- Use Moments, Collections, and Years views to organize your photos and videos automatically by when (timestamp) and where (geolocation) they were taken. Or use the Faces facial-recognition feature to organize photos by people.

- Add geotags to images manually or use geotags embedded in photos taken with a GPS-enabled camera.

- Title, tag, and sort images.

- Create slideshows, albums, and smart (self-updating) albums.

- Make your own prints or order prints online.

- Create photo books, calendars, and cards.

- Use Spotlight (page 93) to find photos based on their Faces and Places information in Photos, as well as their file names and attributes.

- Email photos from within Photos, automatically optimizing your message so that it's not too big to send.

- Publish photos to the web (Facebook, Twitter, Flickr, and so on).

- Set a photo as your desktop picture (wallpaper).

- Use an Apple TV to view photos and videos on your HDTV.

Preview

Use the Preview application to view image files, PDF files, and other documents. Preview has basic image-correction, cropping, and rotation tools. You can view, edit, search, encrypt, annotate, and page-shuffle PDF documents, and much more. Preview supports Auto Save, share sheets, and full-screen view.

Tip: To preview the selected file directly in a Finder window panel without using Preview, in Finder, choose View > Show Preview (Shift+Command+P).

Preview includes these features:

- To customize the Preview toolbar, choose View > Customize Toolbar. To rearrange toolbar icons, Command-drag them sideways. To remove toolbar icons, Command-drag them downward.

- Like Photos and Image Capture, Preview can import pictures directly from a digital camera, iPhone, or iPod touch. Connect your camera, open Preview, and then choose File > Import from Camera.

- Like Image Capture, Preview can operate a scanner, autostraighten the scanned images, and save or export them to various formats (PDF, JPEG, and so on). Connect your scanner, Open Preview, and then choose File > Import from Scanner.

- To save documents and images in iCloud, choose File > Move To > iCloud.

- Use the Preview sidebar to work with multiple PDF files, multiple photos, multiple fax pages, and so on. You can switch among views by using the View menu or pressing Option+Command+1–6.

  Choose View > Thumbnails to view a scrolling vertical list of miniature pages or photos. Click one of the thumbnails to see it at full size in the main section of the window. To make the thumbnails larger or smaller, drag the right edge of the sidebar.

  Choose View > Table of Contents to view a list of photo names, file names, or PDF chapter and section headings.

  Choose View > Contact Sheet to view a full screen of thumbnail miniatures. To make the images bigger or smaller, click the Zoom buttons in the toolbar.

- To mix and match pages from different PDF documents into a single new one, drag thumbnails from one Preview window's sidebar into another.

- If you select multiple image files in a Finder window and then open them all at the same time (by pressing Command+O, for example), Preview shows the first one and lists the thumbnails of the group in the sidebar. To step through the images, press the arrow keys. To open a full-screen slideshow, choose View > Slideshow (Shift+Command+F). To reorder the photos, drag them in the sidebar (in any sidebar view).

- To crop an image, drag across the part of the image that you want to keep, adjust the crop area by dragging its handles, and then choose Tools > Crop (Command+K). If necessary, you can use Auto Save to return to the original image.

- To rotate or flip images or PDF documents, select one or more thumbnails in the sidebar and then use the Rotate or Flip commands in the Tools menu.

- Preview has a few Photoshop-like tools. To fix up photos, use the Show Inspector, Adjust Color, and Adjust Size commands in the Tools menu.

- To convert file formats, choose File > Export.

- To bookmark your place in a PDF document, choose Tools > Add Bookmark (Command+D).

- To annotate a PDF document or image, you can type notes in a box or a bubble, add clickable links (to web addresses or other parts of the document), or add circles, arrows, rectangles, strikethrough, underlining, or highlighting. To do so, choose Tools > Annotate or use the Edit toolbar (choose View > Show Edit Toolbar or press Shift+Command+A). To see a list of your annotations, choose Tools > Show Inspector (Command+I) or View > Highlights and Notes (Option+Command+4). You can search annotations either by author or by content.

- To inspect part of a graphic or PDF closely, choose Tools > Show Magnifier (or press the ` key).

- You can fill out PDF forms within Preview. Type or paste in text-entry areas such as underlining and textboxes or click to select checkboxes.

- To add your "written" signature to a PDF document, choose View > Show Markup Toolbar (Shift+Command+A), click the Sign button (signature icon), and then choose Trackpad (to sign the trackpad with a stylus or finger) or Camera (to take a photo of your written signature). For Camera, hold up your signature (black ink on white paper) to the FaceTime/iSight camera and then take a snapshot. You can store multiple signatures to sign or initial documents.

Preview can open many types of files, including:

- AI (Adobe Illustrator)

- BMP (Windows Bitmap)

- DNG (Digital Negative)

- EPS (Encapsulated PostScript)

- FAX (faxes)

- FPX (FlashPix)

- GIF (Graphics Interchange Format)

- ICNS (Apple Icon Image)

- ICO (Windows icon)

- JPEG (Joint Photographic Experts Group)

- PS (PostScript)

- PSD (Adobe Photoshop)

- PICT (QuickDraw)

- PDF (Portable Document Format)

- PNG (Portable Network Graphics)

- RAW (Raw)

- SGI (Silicon Graphics Image)

- TGA (Targa Graphic)

- TIFF (Tagged Image File Format)

- Apple iWork (Pages, Numbers, and Keynote)

- Microsoft Office (Word, Excel, and PowerPoint)

QuickTime Player

Use the QuickTime Player application to:

- Play or edit QuickTime movie files (File, Edit, and View menus). QuickTime Player supports full-screen view.

- Convert (export) media to a web-friendly format (File menu).

- Stream audio and video in your web browser.

- Make audio, video, and screen recordings (File menu).

- Export, stream, or share video via YouTube, iTunes, Facebook, Vimeo, Flickr, iMovie, Mail, Messages, or AirDrop (File > Share).

RAID Utility

Use RAID Utility to create a RAID array (multiple-drive system), provided you have a RAID card and can access a system running OS X Server.

Reminders

The Reminders application lets you create and manage to-do lists. You can add reminders to custom lists, assign them to future due dates, receive notifications when they come due, and mark them as completed to hide them from view. You can create multiple to-do lists to keep your work, personal, and other tasks separate. Reminders comes with two lists: Reminders for active reminders and Completed for finished tasks. Reminders supports Auto Save.

Reminders includes these features:

- To view reminder lists, choose View > Show Sidebar (Option+Command+S). To create a new list, choose File > New List (Command+L). To view a list's reminders, click the list in the sidebar. To move a reminder to a different list, drag the reminder to the target list or right-click it and then choose Move to List. To reorder lists, drag them up or down. To delete or rename a list, right-click it in the sidebar (deleting a list also deletes its reminders).

- To create a new reminder, click the target list and then choose File > New Reminder (Command+N) or click (+).

- To edit a reminder, right-click it and then choose Show Info, or click the reminder's *i* button, which appears when you point to a reminder. You can add a due date, set a priority, add a location-based (geofenced) alert, and more.

- To delete a reminder, right-click it and then choose Delete.

- To mark a reminder as completed, select its checkbox or right-click it and then choose Mark as Completed. Completed reminders are moved to the Completed list.

- To reorder reminders, drag them up or down.

- To open a reminder list in a separate window, double-click it in the sidebar. These lists stay visible even when Reminders is minimized.

- To import or export reminders as iCalendar (.ics) files, use Import or Export commands in the File menu. iCalendar is a standard format that many email and calendar programs can read.

- To show a calendar in the sidebar, choose View > Show Calendar (Option+Command+K). Days with active reminders are marked with dots. To jump to today's date, choose View > Go to Today (Command+T).

- To use iCloud to sync reminders wirelessly across your Macs and iOS devices, choose > System Preferences > iCloud > Reminders.

- To sync Reminders with Gmail, Yahoo, or other services that support reminders, choose > System Preferences > Internet Accounts, select the account, and then turn on Calendars/Reminders.

- To turn on notifications for reminders, choose > System Preferences > Notifications > Reminders.

- See maps for reminder locations.

- Flick two fingers left or right on the trackpad to move quickly among reminder lists.

Safari

Use the Safari application to browse the web. Safari has features common to most browsers, as well as a few Apple touches. Safari supports parental controls, share sheets, and full-screen view.

Safari includes these features:

- Tabbed browsing.

- Top Sites (History > Show Top Sites) shows a thumbnail array of frequently visited sites. You can add sites from your bookmarks and rearrange the thumbnails by dragging them.

- The sidebar (View > Show Sidebar) lists your bookmarks, Reading List, or Shared Links alongside the page you're currently on. You can also add pages to your Reading List with one click.

- Shared Links shows you links from people you follow on Twitter and LinkedIn.

- Tab View (View > Show All Tabs) shows your open tabs (pinch to see them all or flick to switch among them).

- Launch with previously open webpages.

- Bookmark management.

- Multitouch gestures (pinch or spread to zoom; two-finger double-tap to magnify a block; and two-finger flick for Back or Forward).

- Download manager.

- AutoFill automatically fills in your name, address, contact info, user names, and passwords.

- View PDF pages in the browser window.

- Resume webpages you had open last.

- Pop-up blocking.

- History and bookmark search.

- Text search.

- Unified search/address bar.

- Integration with Photos, Mail, and Contacts.

- Web Clips for Dashboard.

- Reader view for distraction-free reading.

- Reading List saves webpages for later reading offline.

- HTML5 and CSS3 technologies.

- MathML support.

- Private Browsing mode.

- Sandboxing (personal data protection).

- Third-party extensions.

- iCloud support for bookmarks, Reading List, and open tabs. To view synced tabs in Safari, click the iCloud button ☁ in the toolbar.

Script Editor

Use the Script Editor utility to write programs (.scpt files) in AppleScript, a natural-language-like scripting language with OS X-specific commands that automate tasks such as renaming groups of files and converting image formats. To set the default editor or toggle the Script menu in the menu bar, choose Script Editor > Preferences > General pane. To see sample scripts to get you started, choose Help > Open Example Scripts Folder. To open the online reference to the AppleScript language, which includes syntax and sample code, choose Help > Show AppleScript Language Guide. To set up AppleScript folder actions, right-click a folder icon in Finder and then choose Folder Actions Setup.

Script Editor also supports JavaScript for Automation for creating applets and accessing Cocoa frameworks.

Tip: To automate tasks without programming, use Automator (page 112).

Stickies

Use the Stickies application to post virtual notes on your screen, similar to the paper reminders that you stick to the edge of your actual monitor.

System Information

Use the System Information utility to get detailed technical information about your Mac's hardware, software, and network. You can save this report to a file or use it to diagnose problems. Shortcut: hold down the Option key and choose > System Information.

System Preferences

Opens System Preferences (Chapter 3).

Terminal

Use the Terminal utility to interact with OS X through a command-line interface. Running invisibly beneath OS X's graphical interface is a complete Unix operating system. Terminal supports full-screen view.

Terminal includes these features:

- Type Unix commands at the Terminal prompt (to list the contents of the current directory, for example, type ls).

- Copy or paste text commands in a Terminal window.

- Drag a file, folder, or proxy icon into Terminal to enter its path on the command line. Or drag an icon onto Terminal's icon in the dock or in a Finder window.

- Use multiple tabs in the same Terminal window (Shell > New Tab and View > Show Tab Bar).

- Customize Terminal (Terminal > Preferences).

- Import or export Terminal settings (Shell menu).

OS X includes hundreds of standard Unix commands (derived from BSD Unix), common tools, and scripting languages such as Perl and Python. To learn how to use a command, read the command's manual page by typing man *command_name*. (man ls, for example). To learn how to use man, type man man. Manual pages are written by programmers for programmers, so they may take some deciphering. To learn some basic Unix commands, in Terminal, choose Help.

TextEdit

Use the TextEdit application as a text editor or word processor. TextEdit has some high-end word-processing and typography features, supports Auto Save, and can share selected text. You can use TextEdit to read and write the following types of files:

- Plain text (.txt)

- Rich Text Format (.rtf)

- Rich Text Format with Attachments (.rtfd)

- HTML (.htm or .html)

- Web Archive (.webarchive)

- Microsoft Word (.doc, .docx, or .xml)

- Open Document Text (.odt) files

To save documents in iCloud, choose File > Move To > iCloud.

Tip: Pinch the trackpad to zoom a document.

Time Machine

Opens Time Machine (page 172).

VoiceOver Utility

Use VoiceOver Utility, an Accessibility feature (page 53), to make your Mac describe aloud what appears onscreen and speak the text in documents and windows.

X11

See "Running Older Programs" on page 106.

Services

Services lets you apply the features of other programs to content selected in the current program (the service-providing program doesn't have to be open). In TextEdit, for example, you can define the selected word by using the service provided by Dictionary. TextEdit, in turn, provides its own services to other programs: you can highlight webpage text in Safari and then send it to a new TextEdit document. Services commands are contextual (text-related commands won't appear when a photo is selected, for example) and some programs neither provide nor accept services. OS X comes with built-in services and third-party programs—Skype, for example—can add their own services. You can also create custom services by using Automator (page 112).

To choose a service: In any Services-compatible program, select the content that you want to apply a service to (text, pictures, or Finder icons, for example) and then do any of the following:

- Choose from the Services submenu, which is in the program's application menu.

- In Finder, choose a service from the ⚙ ⌄ menu in the toolbar.

- Right-click the selection and then choose a service. (Services commands usually appear at the bottom of menus, sometimes grouped into a Services submenu.)

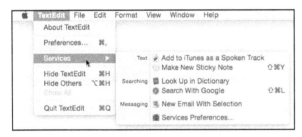

To configure Services: Choose > System Preferences > Keyboard > Shortcuts pane > Services. Alternatively, choose Services > Services Preferences from the application menu.

To assign or change keyboard shortcuts, click a service's name and press Return (or double-click to the right of a service's name), and then type the new keystroke. Use the checkboxes to toggle services (many are turned off by default). Commonly used services include:

Pictures

The Capture services use Grab to take a picture of all or part of the screen. The Import Image service imports a digital photo from an attached scanner, digital camera, or webcam. These services are available only in programs that accept pasted graphics. The Set Desktop Picture service makes the selected picture your desktop wallpaper.

Messaging

These services open Mail with a newly created message containing the selected file or text or addressed to the selected email address in a text document.

Development

These services invoke Automator and AppleScript.

Files and Folders

The Open Selected File in TextEdit service opens the TextEdit document specified by the selected path (~/Documents/readme.txt, for example). The New Terminal services open a Terminal window or tab with the selected folder as the working directory. The Encode services encode (convert) selected video or audio files. The Folder Actions Setup service configures AppleScript folder actions for the folder specified by the selected path. The Open, Reveal, and Show Info services invoke Finder for the file specified by the selected path. The Send File to Bluetooth Device service (Shift+Command+B) transfers the selected file wirelessly via Bluetooth to a laptop or other Bluetooth device; you can select a file icon in Finder or a file path in a text document. For all these services, an error message appears if the selected text is an invalid path.

Searching

The Look Up in Dictionary service defines the selected word. The Search with Google service (Shift+Command+L) opens the default browser and then searches for the selected text by using Google. The Spotlight service (Shift+Command+F) searches systemwide for the selected text by using Spotlight.

Text

The Add Contact service adds the selected text as a new contact. The Call and Send services call or send messages to the highlighted recipient. The Add to iTunes as a Spoken Track service saves the selected text or the path of the selected icon as an audio file by using Text to Speech. The Convert services convert the selected file or text from Simplified Chinese to Traditional Chinese, or vice versa. The Create services create a Font Book collection or library of fonts used for the selected text. The Make New Sticky Note service (Shift+Command+Y) opens Stickies with a newly created sticky note containing the selected text. The New TextEdit Window Containing Selection service opens TextEdit with a newly created document containing the selected text. The Show Address in Google Maps service opens the default browser with the selected text address or location highlighted in Google Maps. The Summarize service creates a concise version of a selected passage (as if someone had highlighted the important bits); to vary the length of the summary, use the slider that appears in the pop-up Summary window.

Internet

The Add to Reading List service adds the selected URL to the Safari reading list. The Open URL service opens the selected web address (google.com, for example) in the default browser.

Printing, Faxing & Fonts

In OS X, the operating system—not individual programs—handles printing. When you print something in any program, you activate OS X's intermediary printing system, which accepts print jobs from programs and feeds them to the printer. This process, called **background printing**, lets you keep working in your program while your documents print.

Installing and configuring a printer is easy. After connecting and setting up your hardware, you can print individual documents with the default settings or override them for special printouts. If you have an analog modem, you can fax documents as easily as print them. You can use Font Book to install and manage font files.

Setting Up a Printer

A printer connects to your computer through a USB or FireWire port, an Ethernet jack, or a wireless signal (wi-fi, Bluetooth, or Bonjour). Computers on a network can share a network printer.

When you connect a printer to your computer, OS X often recognizes it and searches its extensive collection of built-in drivers. **A printer driver** is software that lets programs send commands to a particular printer. If your printer isn't in OS X's library, you can use the driver on the disc that came with the printer or download the driver from the manufacturer's website. If you upgraded from an earlier version of OS X, you inherited the existing printer driver and settings, and your printer will usually work fine.

If you have several printers, you can designate one to be the default printer—the one selected automatically when the Print dialog box opens. You can save drive space by deleting unneeded printer drivers from /Library/Printers. Printers that you add manually are stored in ~/Library/Printers (~ denotes your home folder).

To set up a printer: Connect the printer to your computer and then turn on the printer. Open a document to print (any document will do) and then choose File > Print (Command+P). In the Print dialog box, choose the printer's name from the Printer pop-up menu. (If the printer isn't listed in the menu, then OS X couldn't detect and autoconfigure it—you have to add it manually.)

Tip: "Nearby Printers" refers to printers that aren't connected directly to your Mac, but are still accessible. For example, a shared printer connected to another Mac, a network printer that speaks Bonjour, or a printer connected to an AirPort base station or an Apple Time Capsule.

To add a printer manually: Open a document to print (any document will do) and then choose File > Print (Command+P). In the Print dialog box, choose Add Printer from the Printer pop-up menu. If your printer is listed in the "Default" pane, click it and then click Add. If your printer isn't listed, click the icon in the toolbar for your type of printer:

- Click "IP" if you have an internet printer, a network printer, an LPR (Line Printer Remote) printer, a wireless (wi-fi or Bluetooth) printer, or an old AppleTalk printer.

- Click "Windows" if you have a Windows-only network printer.

In the list, click the printer that you want to use (only connected and turned-on printers appear). Optional: to use a specific printer driver, choose "Select Printer Software" from the Use pop-up menu. When you're done, click Add.

To designate a default printer: Choose > System Preferences > Printers & Scanners > "Default printer" pop-up menu.

To create a desktop printer icon: Choose > System Preferences > Printers & Scanners. Drag a printer icon from the Printers list to the desktop, to a Finder window, or to the dock. You can drag documents to this icon to print them.

To delete a printer: Choose > System Preferences > Printers & Scanners. Select a printer in the Printers list and then click (–).

Printing Documents

Most programs have a Print command, which prints a document, and a Page Setup command, which sets basic printer options. The Print and Page Setup dialog boxes vary by program and printer model, but they have some common settings.

To set up a printout: Choose File > Page Setup (Shift+Command+P). Choose a paper size, change the orientation (landscape or portrait), or reduce or enlarge the pages' content (the standard Print dialog box actually has better scaling controls than the Page Setup dialog box). You must configure Page Setup independently in each program.

To set the default paper size: Choose > System Preferences > Printers & Scanners > "Default paper size" pop-up menu.

To print a document: Open the document and then choose File > Print (Command+P). To print using the default settings, click Print.

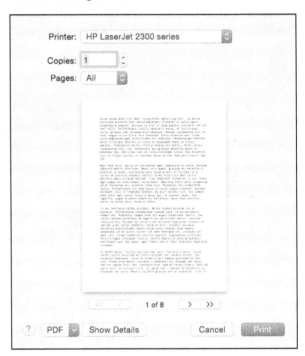

Otherwise, click Show Details to expand the dialog box.

Choose preset settings or set new ones, and then click Print. Options vary by program and printer; some common ones are:

Printer
> Choose a printer (if you have more than one).

Presets
> Use this pop-up menu to save your print settings. Change the other settings in this dialog box (paper orientation, layout, colors, two-sided

printing, and so on), choose Save Current Settings as Preset from the Presets pop-up menu, and then name the preset ("Two-sided landscape", for example). The presets that you save appear in the Presets pop-up menu.

Copies

Set the number of copies to print.

Pages

Print all the pages or only a subset. Leave the From box empty to print from the start of the document; leave the To box empty to print to the end. Specify physical page numbers (1, 2, 3,…), not logical ones (roman numerals, for example).

Paper Size

Choose a standard paper size or choose Manage Custom Sizes to define odd sizes.

Orientation

Choose portrait (tall) or landscape (wide).

PDF

Set PDF options. PDF (Portable Document Format) is a standard file format for digital documents; it renders even complex documents faithfully on every modern operating system without font, layout, viewing, or printing problems. The PDF pop-up menu lets you save any document as a PDF file (instead of printing it). Other options let you preview or send PDFs, or add them to your iBooks library. Spotlight search indexes the content of PDF files. See also "Preview" on page 125.

Supplies

Open the printer manufacturer's website to a page shilling ink and printer supplies.

Additional Printing Options

Use the options pop-up menu (on the divider line) to change settings unique to the printer and program that you're using. Some common choices are:

Layout

Print multiple shrunken page images on a single sheet of paper.

Color Matching

Set the color-matching system of a color printer: ColorSync (page 114), your printer manufacturer's, or none.

Paper Handling

Set the pages to print and their printout order. The Odd and Even options can be used for double-sided printing. The Reverse option flips the printed stack. For multiple copies, clear the "Collate pages" checkbox to print pages 1, 2, 3, 1, 2, 3, or select it to print pages 1, 1, 2, 2, 3, 3.

Paper Feed

Choose which pages come from which tray of a multitray printer. These options are typically used to print the first page on letterhead and the remaining ones on blank paper.

Cover Page

Set an optional cover sheet to accompany the printout.

Scheduler

Delay printing until a specific time of day. These options are usually used to print long documents at low-traffic times.

Other settings

Other printer-specific and program-specific settings include color options, print quality (resolution), media type, paper path, paper type, and booklet printing.

Summary

Show a text summary of your current print settings.

Tip: If you're technically inclined, open a web browser and go to the address http://127.0.0.1:631. You land on the web interface for **CUPS** (Common Unix Printing System), OS X's underlying printing technology. From this administration page, you can access older printers that don't have OS X drivers, print test pages, manage networked printers and print jobs, stop printers, and more. If the CUPS web interface is disabled, run the indicated Terminal command to enable it.

Controlling Printouts

When you print a document, it's intercepted by an intermediary program, called a **print spooler**, on its way to the printer. The print spooler holds your documents (on drive or in memory) until your printer can accept them. The delay is usually short but can be substantial for large graphic files. The spooler puts each document in a **print queue**, where it waits its turn to be printed. You can pause or resume printing, change the printer for pending printouts, or cancel specific print jobs. Spooling occurs in the background, so you can keep working in your program—or even quit the program—and documents still print. You can use the print queue to print a document without opening its program.

To manage the print queue: If printing is in progress, click the printer's icon in the dock; otherwise, choose > System Preferences > Printers & Scanners. Select the printer, click Open Print Queue, click a printout (or Command-click multiple printouts) in the queue, and then use the toolbar buttons and Jobs menu to delete, hold (pause), or resume printouts. You can't reorder printouts by dragging but you can drag them to print queues in other printer windows.

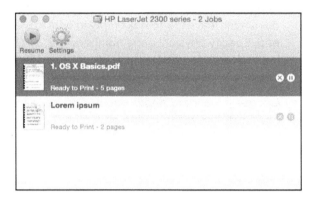

To print a document by using the print queue: Drag the document's icon from the desktop or a Finder window to the print queue or to the printer icon in the dock or on the desktop.

 To remove a printer icon from the dock: Right-click (or click-and-hold) the icon and then choose Quit. To autoremove the icon when all printouts finish, choose Auto Quit (if present).

Sharing a Printer

You can share a printer connected to your computer with other Macs on the same (wired or wireless) network. Your computer (with the attached printer) must be turned on for others to print. Everybody's print jobs go through your copy of OS X, draining your system resources. Windows users who have installed Bonjour (which comes with the Windows version of iTunes) can use a Mac's shared printer.

To share a printer: On the Mac connected to the printer, choose > System Preferences > Sharing. Turn on Printer Sharing and then select the checkbox for each printer that you want to share. To restrict a printer to certain users, select the printer and then click (+) or (–). You can also turn on printer sharing in > System Preferences > Printers & Scanners.

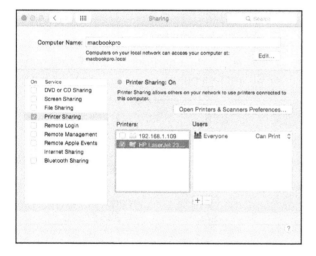

To use a shared printer over a network: Open a document to print and then choose File > Print (Command+P). In the Print dialog box, choose Add Printer from the Printer pop-up menu. Select the shared printer in the list and then click Add. The shared printer appears in the Printer pop-up menu from now on.

Faxing

Computer-based faxing conserves paper, saves money on ink and paper, and generates cleaner, more-legible faxes than ones sent via fax machine. Unfortunately, OS X doesn't support native faxing or even Apple's own (discontinued) USB modem. If you need to send or receive faxes, you have these options:

- Sign up for a service like eFax (*efax.com*) or Faxaway (*faxaway.com*), which let you send and receive faxes online.

- Buy a non-Apple analog (fax) modem, some of which work fine—try Zoom (*zoomtel.com*) or USRobotics (*usr.com*), for example. The modem comes with its own software and instructions.

Fonts

A **font** is a collection of letters, numbers, symbols, and other characters that describes a certain typeface, along with size, spacing, and other qualities. OS X includes many **OpenType** (.otf) and **TrueType** (.ttf) fonts, which look smooth and clear in all sizes, onscreen and in print. OS X also supports **PostScript Type 1** fonts but not the old OS 9 bitmapped fonts. Installed fonts appear on all Font menus and in font lists. You can install and manage fonts by using Font Book. Other tools—the Fonts, Typography, and Characters panels—let you apply fonts within documents, typeset text, and insert special characters.

Font Locations

Where a font is installed determines who can use it:

- User fonts, located in ~/Library/Fonts (~ denotes the home folder), are available only to the user who installs them.

- Computer fonts, located in /Library/Fonts, are available to all users and must be installed by an administrator.

- System fonts, located in /System/Library/Fonts, are used by OS X itself in the user interface—don't touch them.

- Application-specific fonts, located in /Library/Application Support/*product_name*, appear when you install certain programs (Adobe and Microsoft products, for example).

Tip: If you're on a network, your administrator can make additional fonts available on a network server.

Font Book

Use Font Book to install, uninstall, find, group, preview, and disable fonts. Font Book organizes fonts into libraries and collections. **Libraries**, which appear at the top of the Collection (leftmost) column, group fonts by folder location or language (All Fonts is a library, for example). **Collections**, listed below libraries, assign fonts to user-defined groups (Fixed Width is a collection, for example). Font Book comes with built-in libraries and collections, and you can create your own. A typeface has variations (regular, italic, bold, condensed, and so on), each contained in a separate font file. You can disable fonts (without uninstalling them) to keep your font menu uncrowded. Font Book supports full-screen view.

To open Font Book: Do any of the following:

- Choose Applications > Font Book.

- Double-click a font file.

- Click ⚙ ˅ > Manage Fonts in the Fonts panel or Characters panel.

To set up Font Book: In Font Book, choose Font Book > Preferences and then set the following options:

Default Install Location
Set the default library for installed fonts. Choose Computer if you want fonts that you install to be available to everybody (/Library/Fonts). Choose User if you want them to be available to only you (~/Library/Fonts).

Resolve duplicates by moving files to the Trash
Prevent Font Book from installing duplicate fonts.

Automatic font activation

Autoenable (with optional warning) any disabled fonts when you open a document that uses them.

To install a font: Insert the disc that contains the new font, or copy or download the font to your drive, and then do any of the following:

- Drag the font file to a Fonts folder.

- Double-click the font file and then click Install Font in the font preview window.

- In Font Book, choose File > Add Fonts (Command+O) or click (+) in the toolbar.

- Drag font files to a library or collection in Font Book.

To remove a font: Do any of the following:

- In Font Book, select the font in the Font column and then choose File > Remove "*name*" or press Delete.

- In Finder, drag the font file out of its Fonts folder (typically /Library/Fonts or ~/Library/Fonts).

Tip: You can't remove critical system fonts. If your system fonts become corrupted, choose File > Restore Standard Fonts.

To preview or print fonts: Select a library or collection in the Collection column. In the Font column, select a font to see a preview in the rightmost column. Use the mouse or the four arrow keys to move up and down the font list or expand and collapse the font variations (regular, italic, bold, and so on). Click the toolbar buttons to see different font views or technical information. To change the preview size, use the Size box or the slider on the right of the preview column. Use the View menu to determine which characters are displayed—Sample, Repertoire (all characters), or Custom. To print a font reference sheet, choose File > Print (Command+P).

To create a library: Choose File > New Library (Option+Command+N), and then type a name for the library.

To add fonts to a library: In the Collection column, select the target library. Choose File > Add Fonts (Command+O) or click (+) in the toolbar. Select the folder that contains the fonts that you want to add, and then click Open. Adding a font to a library doesn't move or copy font files.

To create a collection: Choose File > New Collection (Command+N) or click + below the Collection column, and then type a name for the collection.

Tip: You can also create a **smart collection** (File > New Smart Collection) that self-updates to display fonts based on search criteria.

To add fonts to a collection: In the Collection column, select All Fonts or a library or collection that has the fonts you want to add. Drag the desired fonts from the Font column to the target collection. Adding a font to a collection doesn't move or copy font files.

To remove fonts from a library or collection: In the Collection column, select the library or collection that you want to change. In the Font column, select the target font(s), and then choose File > Remove "*name*" or press Delete. Removing fonts from a built-in library moves the font files to the Trash (they're gone from your system). Removing fonts from a user-created library leaves the font files untouched but invisible to programs (they can be reinstated later). Removing fonts from a collection removes them from that collection but not from Font Book (they're still available to programs).

To delete a library or collection: In the Collection column, select the target library or collection, and then choose File > Delete "*name*" or press Delete. Deleting a library or collection doesn't delete font files. Deleting a library makes its fonts unavailable to programs (you can't delete built-in libraries). Deleting a collection doesn't affect font availability. (It may be more convenient to disable, rather than delete, a font, library, or collection.)

To disable a font: In the Collection column, select All Fonts or a library or collection that has the font that you want to disable. In the Font column, select the target font, and then choose Edit > Disable "*font_name*" (Shift+Command+D). To enable the font, repeat these steps. Disabling a font in a collection hides it in the Fonts column when that collection is selected. Disabling a font in a library makes it unavailable to programs.

To disable a library or collection: In the Collection column, select the target library or collection, and then choose Edit > Disable "*collection_name*" (Shift+Command+E). To enable the library or collection, repeat these steps. Disabling a library disables all its fonts. Disabling a collection turns off its fonts in the Fonts column. Fonts in a disabled collection are disabled if they appear only in that collection.

To resolve duplicate-font conflicts: In the Collection column, select All Fonts. In the Font column, select any font (or font variant) marked with a yellow triangle ▲, and then choose Edit > Look for Enabled Duplicates (or Resolve Duplicates).

To validate a font: In the Collection column, select All Fonts or a library or collection that has the font you want to validate. In the Font column, select the target font, and then choose File > Validate Font.

To open the Fonts, Typography, and Characters panels: Look for a program's Font and Special Characters commands. In TextEdit, for example, choose Format > Font > Show Fonts (Command+T). To show the Typography panel, click ✿˅ > Typography in the Fonts panel. To show the Characters panel, choose Edit > Special Characters (Ctrl+Command+Spacebar). These panels also are available in iMovie, Photos, Mail, Pages, Keynote, Numbers, and many other programs.

Networks & Sharing

You create a **network** when you connect two or more computers to exchange data or share equipment. Setup is easy, thanks to OS X's built-in tools (but the hassle of buying and installing network hardware remains). You can add computers running Windows to your network too. Networks let you share files (you can designate drives and folders as shared network resources); share printers, scanners, backup drives, and other devices; and share an internet connection.

This book covers small local (peer-to-peer) networks, common in homes and small businesses with ten or fewer computers, not large work or school networks maintained by full-time administrators.

Types of Networks

Before you can set up OS X's network software, you must install and configure network hardware. Your choice of network depends on your budget, the proximity of the computers to be networked, and your inclination to lay cable.

Ethernet (IEEE 802.3)

The most popular network standard, **Ethernet**, is cheap, fast, and reliable, and it imposes few limits on where the networked machines are placed. To create an Ethernet network, you'll need three components along with your computers:

Network adapter

Each computer must have a network adapter that provides a physical connection to the network. An adapter has an RJ-45 jack that you connect an Ethernet cable to. If you have an older computer that has no built-in Ethernet jack, buy a network interface card (NIC) or a USB plugin network adapter.

Ethernet cables

The cables used in Ethernet networks are a little thicker than telephone cables, and the **RJ-45 connectors** at each end are wider than ordinary phone (RJ-11) connectors. You can buy Ethernet cables—called 10BaseT, 100BaseT, CAT5, CAT5e, CAT6, or twisted-pair cables—of common lengths with attached connectors. For custom lengths, you (or someone at the store) can cut the cable off a spool and attach connectors. Or you can join two lengths by using an RJ-45 female/female coupler. A connection's length shouldn't exceed 100 meters (328 feet). If you're drilling through walls to lay cable, consider hiring an installer (or using a wireless network).

Hub/router

On an Ethernet network, you connect each cable from a computer's network adapter to a central connection point called a **hub**—a small box with a row of five to eight or more jacks (called **ports**) that accept RJ-45 connectors. Small green lights on the hub glow or flicker to signal an active connection. Computers communicate through the hub, so there's no direct connection between any two machines. One port (an **uplink** port) connects to a router, broadband modem, or another hub to expand the network. The other ports are numbered, but it doesn't matter which port you plug which cable into. You can also connect shared devices, such as printers, to the hub. If you have an internet connection, use a **router** instead of an ordinary hub to share the connection.

Wireless (IEEE 802.11)

Wireless networks are versatile and don't require cables. The wireless standard is called **wi-fi** or 802.11 (say *eight-oh-two-eleven*).

Each computer on a wireless network needs a wireless network adapter. Every laptop has a built-in wireless adapter. For a desktop computer, you may need to install a wireless adapter card. Wireless networks transmit and receive radio waves over a range of about 150 feet (through walls). To share a broadband internet connection, you need a **base station**. You can use any base station (Linksys, Belkin, and so on) but Apple's AirPort base stations are easiest to set up by using AirPort Utility (page 111).

To stop neighbors or passersby from stealing your internet bandwidth and eavesdropping, turn on the password or encryption option—usually labeled WPA or WPA2. (Don't use WEP, an older and easily broken protocol.) Also, change the default router password. Other security methods—hiding or changing the SSID, disabling DHCP, and restricting MAC addresses—are less effective.

Wireless equipment comes in these flavors: 802.11a, 802.11b, 802.11g, 802.11n, and 802.11ac. These protocols vary by compatibility, band, range, and speed. To make a long story short, buy only *g*, *n*, or *ac* equipment (*ac* being the latest standard). Note that faster wireless equipment doesn't make your internet connection faster; the modem is the bottleneck.

FireWire (IEEE 1394)

You can form a simple "IP over FireWire" network if your computers all have FireWire (IEEE 1394) jacks, which usually are used to capture digital video from camcorders. (You can buy a 1394 adapter to get these jacks.) Just hook together the computers with 6-pin-to-6-pin IEEE 1394 cables. There's no need to buy a hub or router. FireWire networks usually have only two computers, but you can chain more than two if each has two free FireWire ports. The computers have to be close; 1394 cables can't be more than 15 feet (4.5 meters) long. And you can't use this arrangement to share a printer or DSL/cable modem.

To set up a FireWire network: Connect two Macs with a FireWire cable. Choose > System Preferences > Network. Select FireWire in the network connection services list (click 🔒 if the settings are dimmed). If FireWire isn't listed, click (+), choose FireWire from the Interface pop-up menu, and then click Create. You typically don't have to enter the DNS and search domain addresses. When you're done, click Apply.

File Sharing

Public-folder sharing (simple) and any-folder sharing (more flexible but a bit more complex) let people on the same computer or network share files, folders, and drives among themselves. AirDrop lets you share quickly and wirelessly with other nearby AirDrop users.

The Public Folder

The easiest way to share files is to put them in your Public folder. Everyone with a user account on your Mac or on the same network can access your Public folder, no password needed. You can't choose who can access it—either everyone can or no one can. You must move or copy files to the Public folder—aliases won't work. Every user account has its own Public folder in its home folder.

To share your Public folder: Choose > System Preferences > Sharing and then select the File Sharing checkbox. All files and folders that you put in your Public folder become available to all users locally and over the network.

The Drop Box folder, located within your Public folder, lets others securely give *you* files. People can drop files and folders into your Drop Box, but they can't actually open it. This folder, too, is available both locally and over the network. (Don't confuse the Drop Box folder with the online Dropbox service.)

Any-Folder Sharing

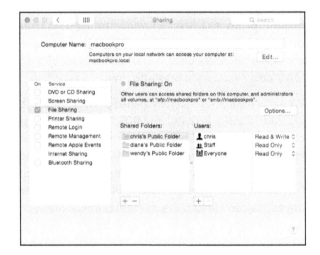
Using the Public folder can be inefficient. If you're sharing hundreds of photos, for example, it's wasteful to store copies in both your (unshared) Pictures folder and your Public folder. If you create or update files frequently, it's cumbersome to keep copying them to your Public folder.

Use any-folder sharing to share files and folders directly from the location where they're stored (typically, in your Documents, Pictures, or Music folder). You can set sharing permissions for individual users rather than for everyone on your network, giving some people more or less access (or no access).

To share any folder by using the Info window: Choose > System Preferences > Sharing and then select the File Sharing checkbox.

In Finder, select the folder or drive that you want to share and then choose File > Get Info (Command+I). In the Info window, expand the General panel and then select "Shared Folder". (Type your administrator password, if prompted.) Expand the Sharing & Permissions panel (click 🔒 if the settings are dimmed).

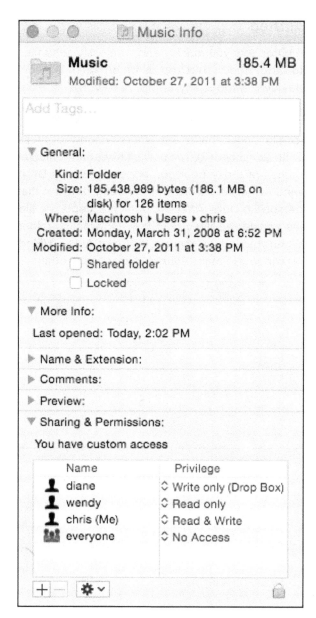

Select an existing user or group. Or add a new user: click (+), click New Person, type a name and password for the account, click Create Account, select the user in the list, and then click Select. To add an address-book contact, click Contacts, select the contact, click Select, assign a password to the new sharing account, and then click Create Account.

To choose a permission for yourself or another user, select from the pop-up menus in the Privilege column:

Read & Write
Lets a user add or delete a file, or open a file and change its contents.

Read Only
Lets a user open a file to see or copy its contents, but not change, move, or delete the original file.

Write only (Drop Box)
Lets a user copy files to the shared folder, but not see or change the folder's contents. Only the drop box's owner can open it to take out files.

No Access (available only to "everyone")
Blocks all access. Users can see the folder or drive icon but can't open, change, or copy it.

To apply the same permissions to every item contained in the selected folder or drive, click ⚙▾ > "Apply to enclosed items".

To change the item's owner, select the new owner in the Name column, and then click ⚙▾ > "Make '*name*' the owner".

To remove a user or group, select the user or group in the Name column, and then click (–). The entry Everyone refers to everyone who's not specifically listed in the Name column.

To share any folder by using the Sharing preferences panel: Choose > System Preferences > Sharing and then select the File Sharing checkbox. The permissions table works the same way as it does in the Info window, except that the extra column, Shared Folders, shows all shared folders and drives in a master list (you can drag items from the desktop or a Finder window to this list). Use the (+) or (–) buttons to add and delete folders and users in the list (you can also turn off sharing for Public folders here).

To share with Windows users: Choose > System Preferences > Sharing, and then select the File Sharing checkbox. Click Options and then select "Share files and folders using SMB". (Windows uses the SMB—Server Message Block—protocol). Select the On checkbox for each account that will share files with a Windows computer.

To connect to a shared folder: In a Finder window, choose Go > Network (Shift+Command+K) to show the computers that you can access. To connect as a registered user, select the computer's icon, and then click Connect As in the connection bar near the top of the window. (Alternatively, you can connect as a no-login guest to access only Public folders.) Double-click a computer icon or click its name in the sidebar (if necessary, choose Finder > Preferences > Sidebar, and then select items under Shared). Use shared drives, folders, and files as you would any other Finder items (subject to their read–write permissions). To disconnect from a computer, click ⏏ next to its name in the Finder sidebar. To connect to an internet or unlisted server (by, say, WebDAV, DNS, NFS, FTP, or IP address), choose Go > Connect to Server (Command+K). You can also navigate to shares from within the Save and Open dialog boxes. To wake a sleeping computer for network access, see "Energy Saver" on page 64.

To get information about or troubleshoot a network: Choose Applications > Utilities > Network Utility.

AirDrop

AirDrop lets you quickly and wirelessly send files to other nearby AirDrop users on Macs and iOS devices, without any setup, passwords, special settings, or base stations. To see other people nearby who are using AirDrop, click the AirDrop icon in the sidebar of any Finder window (or press Shift+Command+R). The user pictures and computer names of those near you appear in the AirDrop window. To share a file with someone, drag it to that person's picture. After the person accepts the file, it's transferred directly to their Downloads folder. When you're done sharing, close the AirDrop (Finder) window to make your Mac invisible to others.

AirDrop encrypts files for transfer and creates a private firewall between you and the other person. AirDrop can also use an Apple ID to verify the identity of the person trying to send you a file. If senders are in your Contacts list and are signed in with their Apple IDs, their names will appear below their photos in AirDrop. To cancel an incoming transfer, open the Downloads folder or stack and then click the × that appears on the icon. AirDrop uses wi-fi to transfer files (to turn on wi-fi, choose > System Preferences > Network > Wi-Fi > Turn Wi-Fi On).

When you use AirDrop to send a file between two devices that have the same Apple ID, the file is downloaded automatically on the receiving device, making it easy to transfer files between two of your own devices.

See also "Ad-hoc Networks" on page 158.

Tip: You can receive files even when AirDrop isn't selected in Finder. You can choose to make yourself available to only your Contacts or to everyone. When a file is sent to you, it appears as a notification. Click to download the file.

The Shared Folder

You can share files with other users on your computer (without a network) by using the Shared folder.

To share across accounts: Open the Shared folder, in the Users folder on your system drive. The Shared folder is a single folder available to every account on the Mac (it doesn't belong to any particular user). Each user, administrator or not, can add, open, or delete files without restriction.

Tip: If your family members all share the same Mac but have different accounts, and you all want to listen to the same music collection (MP3 files) by using the iTunes application, then move all the audio files into a new folder (named Music or whatever) and then move that music folder into the Shared folder, where it's available to everybody. Each account holder can log in, open iTunes, choose iTunes > Preferences > Advanced, and then click Change to choose the shared music folder.

Screen Sharing

You can connect to another computer on your network and show that computer's screen on your own monitor, controlling the other computer as if you were sitting in front of it—opening its programs and documents; moving, copying, renaming, or deleting files and folders; rearranging windows; and even restarting or shutting down. You can also share your own screen with others on your network.

Screen sharing is useful for accessing you own computer from afar, collaborating on projects, and giving technical support. OS X uses the standard VNC (Virtual Network Computing) remote-control protocol. If you use iCloud, you can click Back to My Mac in the sidebar to connect (over a local or remote network) to the computer where you've registered in the iCloud preferences panel.

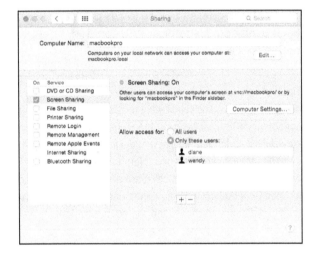

To set up screen sharing: Choose > System Preferences > Sharing, select the Screen Sharing checkbox, and then do any of the following:

- Select "All users" to let anyone with a user account on your computer share your screen.

- Select "Only these users" to restrict screen sharing to specific users.

- Click (+) and then select a user from Users & Groups, Network Users, or Network Groups.

Click Computer Settings to set the following options:

Anyone may request permission to control screen
Lets anyone on your network request to share your screen.

VNC viewers may control screen with password
Sets the password needed by third-party VNC viewers to control your screen. (Don't bother setting a password if you share by using only OS X's built-in screen sharer.)

To share another computer's screen: In a Finder window, click the computer whose screen you want to share in the sidebar's Shared section, and then click Share Screen. Sign in if you're on the other person's "Only these users" list; otherwise, ask permission (which can be granted only if someone is seated at the other computer). To connect by using an IP address or DNS name, in Finder, choose Go > Connect to Server (Command+K), and then type vnc://*ip_address* or vnc://*name.domain*. (To see a computer's name or address, choose > System Preferences > Sharing > Screen Sharing.)

Tip: When you're screen sharing, you can drag and drop to swap files.

CD & DVD Sharing

You can let other network users use the disc in your CD/DVD drive.

To share a CD or DVD: Choose > System Preferences > Sharing, select the DVD or CD Sharing checkbox, and then set the sharing options.

Bluetooth Sharing

You can transmit files wirelessly to and from Bluetooth devices (page 54).

To share over Bluetooth: Choose > System Preferences > Sharing, select the Bluetooth Sharing checkbox, and then set the sharing options. In the Bluetooth menu *, choose the Send or Browse command to invoke Bluetooth File Exchange (page 112).

Share Sheets

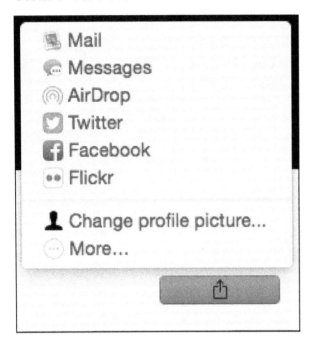

A **share sheet** is a menu that appears when you click the Share button ⬆️ or Share menu in an application that supports sharing. Share sheets let you share quickly and easily, with no need to switch apps or drag files. You can share via Mail, Messages, or Air-Drop, or post straight to Twitter, Facebook, Vimeo, or Flickr (to sign in to your accounts, choose > System Preferences > Internet Accounts). Third-party developers can also add their apps and services to share sheets. To select and reorder items in share sheets choose > System Preferences > Extensions > Share Menu.

Depending on the app you're using, you can share text, documents, links, photos, contacts, locations, or videos. Apps that support sharing include Safari, Notes, Preview, Finder, Maps, iBooks, Photo Booth, Contacts, Photos, QuickTime Player, and Quick Look. To share selected text from TextEdit, right-click the selection and then choose Share.

Twitter Integration

Twitter (*twitter.com*) is a popular third-party micro-blogging service. It's available systemwide in OS X.

- To sign in to your Twitter account, choose > System Preferences > Internet Accounts > Twitter.

- You can send **tweets**—140-character messages—with attachments from several apps, including Safari, Preview, Photo Booth, Photos, TextEdit, Quick Look, and more. To tweet a link or photo, click the Share button ⬆️ and then choose Twitter. To tweet selected text, right-click the selection and then choose Share > Twitter. While you're composing a tweet, the number at the bottom of the Tweet window shows the number of characters remaining that you can enter (up to 140). Attachments use some of a tweet's characters.

- To get notifications for direct messages and mentions, choose > System Preferences > Notifications > Twitter.

- Tweets can pick up your approximate location by using Location Services (page 168).

- To add a Twitter field to a contact, open Contacts, select the contact, and then choose Card > Add Field > Twitter.

Facebook Integration

Facebook (*facebook.com*) is the dominant social-networking service. It's available systemwide in OS X.

- To sign in to your Facebook account, choose > System Preferences > Internet Accounts > Facebook.

- You can use share sheets to post photos, links, and comments straight to Facebook from Safari, Preview, Photo Booth, Photos, TextEdit, Quick Look, and more.

- To get Facebook notifications in Notification Center, choose > System Preferences > Notifications > Facebook. Click Options to specify which types of Facebook notifications to show (friend requests, comments, wall posts, and so on).

- Facebook posts can pick up your approximate location by using Location Services (page 168). Click the location indicator in the Facebook share sheet to add a location to your post.

- Facebook friends appear in Contacts with profile photos and up-to-date information.

- Facebook is integrated with Game Center.

AirPlay Mirroring

You can use **AirPlay**, Apple's wireless file-streaming technology, to mirror (duplicate) whatever is on your Mac's screen—videos, apps, games, photos, presentations, websites, anything—to a high-definition TV (HDTV), up to 1080p HD. AirPlay also lets you use an HDTV as a full-fledged display, complete with dock and menu bar—so while you're, say, running a slideshow on your TV, you can send email or chat on your Mac. You need an Apple TV (second generation or later, *apple.com/appletv*) that's on the same wireless network as your Mac—OS X detects the Apple TV automatically. Click the AirPlay icon on the menu bar and then select Apple TV to start mirroring. If the AirPlay icon isn't visible, choose > System Preferences > Displays > Display pane > "Show mirroring options in the menu bar when available".

AirPlay mirroring scales your Mac's desktop image to fit your HDTV screen. For a sharper image, set the resolution of your desktop to best match that of your Apple TV. For privacy, signals between your Mac and your Apple TV are encrypted. AirPlay mirroring requires a 2011 or newer Mac.

Tip: AirPlay mirroring sends audio (as well as video) from your Mac to your Apple TV. You can use the audio feature independent of AirPlay mirroring by selecting your Apple TV in Sound preferences.

Continuity & Handoff

Continuity is Apple's umbrella term for deep integration between Macs and iOS devices (iPhones, iPads, and iPod touches). Continuity encompasses several features and technologies, and requires OS X 10.10 (Yosemite) or later on the Mac side and, for most features, iOS 8 or later on the iDevice side.

Handoff (a major part of Continuity) lets you transition easily between devices while continuing to work on the same task. Suppose that you're composing an email on your iPhone on the way to work. When you arrive at the office, you can complete the email on your Mac and send it. Handoff makes the transition from iPhone to Mac frictionless by eliminating the usual steps of saving a draft of the outgoing message on a server, launching Mail on the Mac, syncing with the server, and finding the saved draft. Instead, when you log in to your Mac, Handoff places a Mail icon to the left of the dock (or on top, if your dock is on the side of the screen). A similar icon also appears in the Command+Tab application switcher. Clicking or selecting the icon opens Mail and displays a message that you were composing on your iPhone, with the insertion point blinking where you left off.

Here are a few things to know about Continuity and Handoff:

- Handoff works only when two devices are near each other. If you're composing an email on your iPhone in Hawaii, a Handoff icon won't appear on your office Mac in San Francisco. Devices discover each other by using Bluetooth Low Energy (BTLE), with a range of at most a few hundred feet.

- Handoff works between any combination of Macs and iOS devices (between two Macs, for example, or between an iPhone and an iPad) that are logged in to the same iCloud account.

- Applications must support Handoff explicitly.

- The two applications involved in a handoff don't have to be the same on both devices, but they must be from the same developer. Only apps sold through the App Store or signed with a registered Apple Developer ID can support Handoff. A single developer can create a suite of cooperating iOS and OS X applications.

- Handoff and Continuity work with Mail, Safari, Maps, Reminders, Calendar, Contacts, Notes, Keynote, Numbers, Pages, iPhone calls, Messages (SMS support), Personal Hotspot, and AirDrop. For an overview, see Apple's Continuity webpage at *apple.com/osx/continuity*.

- Handoff works between iOS apps and Safari on OS X. You can start an activity by using an app on your iPhone, for example, and then pick it up on the app's corresponding website in Safari on your Mac.

- You can pick up a phone call to your iPhone from your Mac, initiate a phone call from your Mac, or hand off an ongoing Mac phone call to your iPhone. When you make a phone call from your Mac, it's relayed through your iPhone using your existing phone number. You can dial a phone number anywhere that you see it on your Mac (Contacts, Calendar, Mail, Messages, Spotlight, Safari, or any document).

- To set up Continuity on your devices, read the Apple support article "Connect your iPhone, iPad, iPod touch, and Mac using Continuity" at *support.apple.com/HT204681*.

- To toggle Handoff on your Mac, choose > System Preferences > General, and then turn the Handoff option on or off. Handoff requires a recent Mac model (2012 or newer). Continuity's system requirements are listed in the Apple support article cited above.

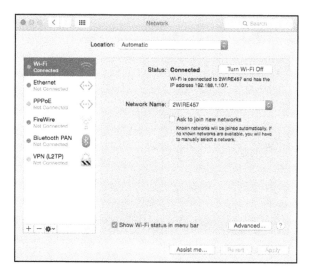

Online Connections

As an individual, you can't connect to the internet directly. You must pay a go-between **ISP (internet service provider)** and rely on it to provide setup instructions, turn on your service, equip and maintain dependable connections, and help you when things go wrong.

You can also connect to a computer or network remotely. You can, for example, connect from your laptop or home machine to an unattended, distant machine in your office or at school to access its files and resources.

If you upgraded from an earlier version of OS X, your existing connections were preserved and should work fine.

Connection Order

Connections are managed in the Network panel of System Preferences. The network connection services list shows the ways that your computer is set up to connect to the internet or other network (a remote office or school network, for example): Ethernet (wired), Wi-Fi (wireless), External Modem (dial-up), Bluetooth, FireWire, VPN, and so on. A colored dot shows each connection's status: green means turned on and connected to a network; yellow means working, but not connected; and red means the connection isn't set up yet.

The order of connections in the list is the sequence that OS X uses to go online when you open a browser or any program that needs internet or network access. OS X tries the first connection method; if that doesn't work, it tries the second, and so on. OS X can maintain multiple connections simultaneously—if a connection dies while you're using it, OS X switches automatically to the next. Laptop users usually sort the sequence by decreasing connection speed (or decreasing security): Ethernet, Wi-Fi, External Modem.

To set the order of connections: Choose > System Preferences > Network. Click ⚙▾ > Set Service Order. Drag the items up and down in the services list into priority order.

Broadband Connections

Broadband (DSL, cable, fiber, or office-network) connections are fast, always on, and easy to set up. Most broadband connections autoconfigure by using **DHCP** (Dynamic Host Configuration Protocol), so require no setup from you beyond plugging in an Ethernet cable or choosing a wireless network from the 🛜 menu (see also "Types of Networks" on page 144). For PPPoE connections, your ISP will give you an account name and password.

To create an Ethernet (wired) connection: Choose > System Preferences > Network. Click (+) and then choose and name a new Ethernet service.

To create a wireless (wi-fi) connection: Choose > System Preferences > Network. Click (+) and then choose and name a new Wi-Fi service.

To configure an Ethernet connection: Choose > System Preferences > Network. Click Ethernet in the services list. Select from the Configure pop-up menu and (if you're not using DHCP) type the IP addresses provided by your ISP or administrator. When you're done, click Apply in the Network panel. (Alternatively, you can set up a connection by stepping through a series of interview windows: click "Assist me" at the bottom of the Network panel.)

To configure a wireless connection: Choose > System Preferences > Network. Click Wi-Fi in the services list. Select a wireless network name, turn on the Wi-Fi menu 🛜, and set the other options. When you're done, click Apply in the Network panel. (Alternatively, you can set up a connection by stepping through a series of interview windows: click "Assist me" at the bottom of the Network panel.)

To configure a PPPoE connection: Choose > System Preferences > Network. Click Ethernet in the services list and then choose Create PPPoE Service from the Configure pop-up menu. Alternatively, click (+), choose and name a new PPPoE connection, and then click it in the services list to configure it.

To remove a broadband connection: Choose > System Preferences > Network. Click the target connection in the services list and then click (–).

To connect to a wireless network: Choose 🛜 > *network_name* (or choose from the Network Name pop-up menu in the Wi-Fi pane of Network preferences). If the network is secured (denoted by 🔒), type a password. To join a closed (hidden) network, choose Join Other Network and then type the network name.

Troubleshooting Wireless Connections

Common wireless connection problems include:

- A network's signal strength is strong enough to appear in the 🛜 menu but too weak to support an actual connection (move closer).

- A wireless router broadcasts its presence even when its internet connection is down.

- A network is restricted to only certain machines (by MAC address).

- A commercial network requires a credit-card payment.

To see wireless network diagnostics quickly: Hold down the Option key and click the 🛜 menu. Network diagnostics are shown in gray text under the name of the active network. The BSSID is the MAC (Media Access Control) address of the wireless access point. To see your Mac's MAC address ("Wi-Fi Address"), choose > System Preferences > Network > Wi-Fi > Advanced > Wi-Fi pane. Some administrators secure networks by restricting access to only certain MAC addresses.

To manage wireless networks: Choose > System Preferences > Network, click Wi-Fi in the services list, and then click Advanced > Wi-Fi pane.

Ad-hoc Networks

You can create a wireless **ad-hoc** ("computer-to-computer") network between two or more Wi-Fi-equipped computers without using a base station. This type of network lets you share files and play multiplayer network games. See also "AirDrop" on page 148.

To create an ad-hoc network: Choose 📶 > Create Network. Name the network and select a channel.

To join an ad-hoc network: Move within range of the host computer and then choose 📶 > *network_ name* (or choose from the Network Name pop-up menu in the Wi-Fi pane of Network preferences).

Dial-up Connections

Each time that you connect to the internet or a remote network via dial-up, your analog modem dials your ISP or network over a standard phone line. Dial-up connections are slow compared with broadband, but they're a good choice for frequent travelers, because big ISPs provide local access numbers over large geographic areas. In some areas, dial-up is your only choice. You need an analog Bluetooth or USB modem. OS X doesn't support Apple's (discontinued) USB modem, so you must use a non-Apple modem that supports OS X (try Zoom or USRobotics). The modem comes with its own software and instructions.

To create a dial-up connection: Connect the modem. Choose > System Preferences > Network. Click (+) and then choose and name a new External Modem service.

To configure a dial-up connection: Connect the modem. Choose > System Preferences > Network. Click External Modem in the services list. Type the local access number, user name, and password provided by your ISP or administrator. Turn on the modem menu 📞.

You can use the Configuration pop-up menu to add, rename, or delete multiple dial-up numbers. It's sensible to name a configuration after the ISP and access location ("AT&T San Francisco", for example).

You can prefix a number with dialing codes. Add a 9 to get an outside line, for example, or *70, to turn off call waiting (a comma pauses dialing for 2 seconds). Calling-card numbers are valid too.

Click Advanced to set other options. In the Modem pane, set model, dialing, and sound options. In the PPP pane, specify the idle-time before autodisconnect and the number of redials to a busy number. To autodial whenever you open your browser or email program, select "Connect automatically when needed" (otherwise, you must connect manually each time).

When you're done, click Apply in the External Modem pane of Network preferences.

(Alternatively, you can set up a connection by stepping through a series of interview windows: Click "Assist me" at the bottom of the Network panel.)

To remove a dial-up connection: Choose > System Preferences > Network. Click External Modem in the services list and then click (–).

To connect to a dial-up network: The modem will autoconnect if you turned on "Connect automatically when needed" when you configured the dial-up connection. To connect manually, choose a configuration in the 📞 menu, and then choose 📞 > Connect External Modem (or choose from the Configuration pop-up menu in the External Modem pane of Network preferences, and then click Connect).

To disconnect from a dial-up network: The modem will autodisconnect in some situations, depending on the options you chose in the PPP pane when you configured the dial-up connection. To disconnect manually, choose 📞 > Disconnect (or click Disconnect in the External Modem pane of Network preferences).

Network Locations

Network locations are for travelers who use different network settings in different places: Ethernet at work, wireless at home, dial-up when travelling, and so on. A "location" is actually a group of saved network settings that you can switch to easily.

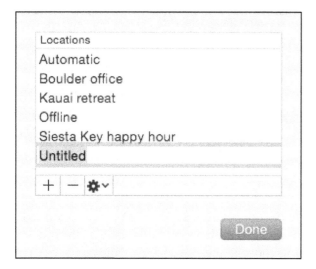

To set up a location: Choose > System Preferences > Network. Choose Edit Locations from the Location pop-up menu (near the top of the panel). Click (+), type a location name, and then click Done. You can click ⚙▾ to rename or duplicate an existing location, or (–) to delete one.

Back on the Network panel, click each network connection and then configure it (to disable it, click ⚙▾ > Make Service Inactive). Reorder the connections as needed (page 156).

To switch to a location: Choose > Location (this menu appears only after you set up more than one location), or choose > System Preferences > Network > Location pop-up menu.

Tip: If you have a laptop, create a location named Offline and make all its connections inactive. Choose this location when you're on an airplane or submarine or anywhere else where you don't want to go online.

Internet Sharing

To share one internet connection with every computer on a local network, you have two options:

Install a router

> A **router** is a small box with one jack that connects to a hub and another jack that connects to a DSL, cable, or dial-up modem. A **router/hub** doubles as a hub, sharing the modem's bandwidth among multiple Ethernet ports that the network computers connect to. A slightly more expensive **router/switch** is faster than a router/hub and should be used when you're passing lots of data around the network (when playing network games or sharing music, for example).

Use Internet Sharing

> Internet Sharing is a built-in OS X feature that acts like a software router. It's free but limited compared to a hardware router. You must designate one computer as the **host** (or **gateway**) through which all internet traffic passes. For broadband connections, the host must have two Ethernet adapters: one that connects to the DSL or cable modem and one that connects to a hub. Sharing also works with dial-up and Bluetooth cellphone connections. If the host is turned off, the other computers can't go online.

To share an internet connection: On the host, choose > System Preferences > Sharing and then clear the Internet Sharing checkbox (if it's not already cleared). Choose the source of the host's internet connection from the "Share your connection from" pop-up menu. In the "To computers using" list, select each port to indicate how the host will distribute the internet connection. Turn on the Internet Sharing checkbox. Turn off Firewall (page 162) for all but the host computer.

VPN Connections

A **virtual private network (VPN)** lets you connect from your computer to a network securely and privately by using the internet as a conduit. VPNs overcome direct dialing's twin evils: slow speeds and high costs.

To create a VPN connection: Choose > System Preferences > Network. Click (+) and then choose and name a new VPN service. Ask your network administrator which VPN Type (tunneling protocol) to choose.

To configure a VPN connection: Choose > System Preferences > Network. Click VPN in the services list. Type the server address and account name provided by your administrator. You can use the Configuration pop-up menu to add, rename, or delete multiple VPN connections. Turn on the VPN menu . Click Authentication Settings to specify security settings. Click Advanced to set other options. When you're done, click Apply in the Network panel.

To remove a VPN connection: Choose > System Preferences > Network. Click the target connection in the services list and then click (–).

To connect to a VPN: Choose a configuration in the menu, and then choose > Connect VPN (or choose from the Configuration pop-up menu in the VPN pane of Network preferences, and then click Connect).

To disconnect from a VPN: The VPN will autodisconnect in some situations, depending on the options you chose in the Advanced > Options pane when you configured the VPN connection. To disconnect manually, choose > Disconnect (or click Disconnect in the VPN pane of Network preferences).

Security & Privacy

OS X's security and privacy features include major tools like Firewall, FileVault, Keychain Access, and Parental Controls, and smaller ones like Password Assistant and secure virtual memory.

You can also use secure login options (page 12), secure-empty the Trash (page 92), secure-erase a drive (page 99), restrict program installations (page 102), and use Private Browsing mode in Safari. When you try to do something potentially dangerous (like run a program downloaded from the internet), OS X will warn you or prompt you for an administrator password.

Firewall

A **firewall** is a piece of software or hardware that helps screen out hackers and malware that try to reach your computer over the internet. It's the most important security component on your computer or network; if you don't have one, attackers can compromise your computer minutes after you go online. OS X provides Firewall for free, but consider using a router too.

A router is a small box that distributes the signal from your modem (DSL, cable, or dial-up) to the computers on your network. A router has a built-in firewall and appears to the outside world to be a computer without programs and hard drives to attack or infect; it's the safest type of firewall, because it protects your entire network and is always on. Even if you're not on a network, you can put a router between your computer and your modem. If you're on a network, a router won't protect you from *other* computers on the network if one of them becomes infected because someone downloaded a virus. For that kind of protection, you need OS X's software Firewall on your individual computer. See also "Types of Networks" on page 144.

To turn Firewall on or off: Choose ⌘ > System Preferences > Security & Privacy > Firewall pane > Turn On/Off Firewall (click 🔒 if the settings are dimmed). Turn off Firewall only if you're using a router, a different firewall, or someone's shared internet connection.

To configure Firewall: Choose ⌘ > System Preferences > Security & Privacy > Firewall pane > Firewall Options (click 🔒 if the settings are dimmed), and then set the following options:

Block all incoming connections
Blocks everything but a few crucial network services (secure but limiting).

[List of services and applications]
Blocks all incoming signals except those sent to programs that you've approved (the most flexible choice). In the list, OS X's sharing features appear automatically above the divider line. To add a program, click (+), choose the program, and then click ⇕ to set its limits. To delete a program, select it and then click (–).

Automatically allow signed software to receive incoming connections
Trusts well-known programs whose authenticity has been confirmed by a third-party certificate authority.

Enable stealth mode
Makes your Mac invisible to automated cracker programs trolling the internet. OS X won't respond to "pings" (including those from you when you're travelling).

Tip: To see the Firewall log, choose Applications > Utilities > Console > appfirewall.log.

FileVault

FileVault automatically encrypts and password-protects your entire drive (including external USB and FireWire drives). After you set up FileVault, it runs in the background. Everything works like before, with no noticeable performance hit, except now your data are secured against laptop thieves, drive thieves, cops, and customs agents at border crossings. Your files are readable by only you and anyone with a master recovery key. Any shared folders in your home folder become unreadable by others on the network when you're not logged in. Time Machine (page 172) can copy an encrypted home folder only when you're logged out. FileVault uses standard XTS-AES encryption with 128-bit keys; if you forget your password and the master recovery key, your data are lost forever.

Tip: To quickly encrypt a drive, right-click the drive icon in Finder or on the desktop and then choose Encrypt.

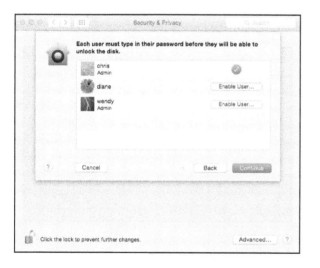

To set up FileVault: Choose > System Preferences > Security & Privacy > FileVault pane (click if the settings are dimmed). Click Turn On FileVault and then follow the onscreen instructions. During the process, an autogenerated key is added to the keychains (page 164) of assigned users, letting them unlock (decrypt) their FileVault-encrypted data by remembering only a login password. (Alternatively, you can use your iCloud password as the key.) You must give explicit permission to each user that you want to allow to log in to a FileVault-protected Mac. Any user with a passwordless account must set a password. Print, copy, or store the recovery key when it appears (in large type). The recovery key is a master password that lets an administrator access any account without knowing the account holder's password, or turn off FileVault for any account.

Tip: If FileVault is turned on, the Recovery HD partition (page 7) won't appear when you hold down the Option key during startup, but you can still hold down Command+R during startup to boot directly to it.

Keychain Access

Use Keychain Access to manage your passwords for secure websites, FTP sites, network servers, encrypted folders and volumes, and other secure items. OS X creates, maintains, and unlocks your default (login) keychain automatically, so passwords are available when they're needed to access secured items and locations. You can also store credit-card numbers, PINs, and other private data in secure notes on your keychain. Keychain Access remembers passwords only for programs that are keychain-aware. See also iCloud Keychain (page 70).

To open Keychain Access: Choose Applications > Utilities > Keychain Access.

To add a keychain item: Access a secure item or location normally and type your password when prompted. Select "Remember password in keychain" (you may have to click an Options button to see this checkbox). The password is added to your keychain and appears in Keychain Access.

To add a password item manually: In Keychain Access, click (+) or choose File > New Password Item (Command+N). Type a name or URL in the Keychain Item Name box. Type a user ID or account name or number in the Account Name box. Type the password in the Password box (select Show Typing to reveal your password as you type, or click 🔑 for password help). When you're done, click Add.

To add a secure note: In Keychain Access, choose File > New Secure Note Item (Shift+Command+N). Type a name for the note in the Keychain Item Name box. Type the note in the Note box. When you're done, click Add.

To delete a keychain item: In Keychain Access, select the target item and then choose Edit > Delete or press Delete.

To inspect or control access to a keychain item: In Keychain Access, double-click the item, or select it and then click i . To see the text of password or secure note, click the Attributes tab and then select "Show password" or "Show note".

To control access to the item, click the Access Control tab and then choose one of the following options:

Allow all applications to access this item
> Lets any program access the item, without showing a confirmation dialog box.

Confirm before allowing access
> Shows a confirmation dialog box for every program that tries to access the item. "Ask for Keychain password" determines whether the confirmation prompts for a password. Click (+) or (–) to add or delete programs that can access the item without triggering the confirmation.

Click Save Changes, type the keychain password in the dialog box that appears, and then click Allow.

To use a keychain item: Access a secure item or location normally. If Access Control permits access to the item without confirmation, the item opens without showing a confirmation dialog box; otherwise, click one of the following buttons in the confirmation dialog box:

Always Allow
> Lets the keychain open the item and adds the item to the Access Control list to suppress this dialog box in the future.

Deny
> Prevents use of the keychain item; type a password to access the secure item.

Allow
> Lets the keychain open the item this time.

To manage keychains: To create a new keychain, choose File > New Keychain (Option+Command+N). To view a different keychain, click ▣ to show the Keychains list and then click the keychain. To lock or unlock a keychain, select it and then click the lock at the top of the Keychain Access window. Keychains are stored as files in ~/Library/Keychains (~ denotes your home folder). You can copy these files to other Macs.

Parental Controls

Parental Controls lets you manage how your children (or anyone) can use the computer. You can set limits on programs run (including games played), web access, Mail and Messages communications, and login hours. You can also log a user's activities for later review. You, an Administrator, can apply these controls to only Standard user accounts, which then become Managed accounts in the Users & Groups panel.

To set up parental controls for an account: Choose > System Preferences > Parental Controls (click if the settings are dimmed). Select the account in the list and then click Enable Parental Controls. Set the desired restrictions in each pane (Apps, Web, and so on). To turn off all settings, click > Turn off Parental Controls.

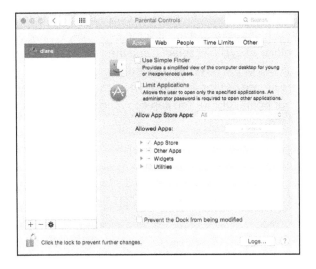

Remote Parental Controls

Parental Controls are useful in environments where multiple Macs on the same network are in use (in classrooms or crowded households, for example). You can adjust Parental Controls settings for Macs 1, 2, 3, and 4 while seated at Mac 5, for example. To do so, follow these steps:

1   Log in to the first remote Mac (not your Mac), choose > System Preferences > Parental Controls, click , enter your password, and then click the name of the account that you want to manage remotely.

2   Click > Allow Remote Setup.

3   Close System Preferences.

4   Repeat steps 1–3 for each account on each Mac on the network that you want to manage remotely.

5   Return to *your* Mac.

6   In Finder, choose Go > Connect to Server, and then click Browse.

    A list of the other Macs on the network appears.

7   Click one of the other Macs and then enter an administrator's name and password for that Mac.

8   Choose > System Preferences > Parental Controls, click , and then enter your password.

    A section named Other Computers appears in the Users & Groups list.

9   Click the account name (on the other Mac) whose Parental Controls settings you want to change remotely and then enter the administrator name and password of the remote computer.

10 Repeat steps 6–9 for the other Macs and accounts that you want to manage remotely.

Password Assistant

Password Assistant helps you avoid creating easily guessed passwords (names, birthdays, dictionary words, and so on). It can generate secure passwords or rate ones that you make up. To open Password Assistant, click 🔑 wherever you're supposed to create a password—in Users & Groups or Keychain Access, for example. To test your own password, type it in the Suggestion box; otherwise, use the Type pop-up menu and the Length slider to generate secure passwords. (FIPS-181 is a standard U.S. government password-generating algorithm.) The Quality bar shows password toughness.

Secure Virtual Memory

If you're running a lot of programs and hit the limits of physical memory (RAM), OS X claims drive space and creates a **swap file** to use as virtual memory. By default, OS X encrypts swap files so that thieves can't pluck data and passwords off your drive. (In old OS X versions, you had to turn on secure virtual memory manually.)

Privacy Settings

To set miscellaneous privacy-related options, choose ⌘ > System Preferences > Security & Privacy > Privacy pane (click 🔒 if the settings are dimmed).

Location Services

> Location Services lets apps and services use your physical whereabouts via the Mac's built-in positioning service, which determines your approximate location by using the data from nearby wireless hotspots. For example, Location Services lets your laptop determine its own time zone automatically, lets Maps determine your current location, and lets a weather website show your local weather the first time that you visit the site. The first time an app makes a request to use Location Services, OS X opens a location warning for that app, which you can allow or refuse. Your response sticks, and the request isn't shown again. You can turn off Location Services for some or for all apps and services.

Contacts, Calendars, Reminders

> Choose which apps and services can access your contacts, calendars, and reminders.

Twitter, Facebook, LinkedIn

> Choose which apps and services can access your social networking accounts (if you've created those accounts in ⌘ > System Preferences > Internet Accounts).

Accessibility

> Choose which apps and services can control your computer's Accessibility features (page 53).

Diagnostics & Usage

> If you select these checkboxes, your Mac will quietly and automatically send anonymous data to Apple and third-party developers (via Apple) about your crashes, freezes, programs, hardware, peripherals, and so on. Don't bother; save the bandwidth.

Maintenance & Backups

OS X includes tools to keep your system running smoothly.

Software Updates

Apple regularly releases updates for OS X system software and other Apple programs. These updates include bug fixes, new features, security patches, version upgrades, and other improvements. All Apple software updates are available from the Updates section of the Mac App Store (page 111).

Tip: Updates for third-party programs downloaded from the App Store are also available from the App Store. If you didn't get a program from the App Store, check the developer's website for updates or use the program's built-in updater. See also "Installing & Removing Programs" on page 102.

 By default, OS X automatically checks for updates every day, but you can check manually at any time. If any updates are available, App Store sends a notification and adds a numbered badge, denoting the number of updates, to the App Store's dock icon and menu entry.

To open App Store, choose > App Store. Available updates are listed in the Updates pane. To learn more about an update, click its icon or its *More* link. You can update any single item by clicking Update next to its name, or you can update everything by clicking Update All at the top of the window. You're also free to ignore updates.

Tip: If you're on a large network, your network administrator might distribute updates via network server.

To set up software updates: Choose > System Preferences > App Store.

Set the following options:

Automatically check for updates
    Check for updates automatically and periodically.

Download newly available updates in the background
    Download updates in the background without being asked. You'll still be notified before the updates are installed.

Install app updates
    Install downloaded app updates without asking you.

Install OS X updates
    Install downloaded OS X updates without asking you.

Install system data files and security updates
    Install downloaded critical system updates without asking you.

Automatically download apps purchased on other Macs
    Download apps (from the Mac App Store) that you bought on other Macs.

Show Updates
    Open the Mac App Store and see any available updates.

Check Now
    Check for updates manually.

Power Nap

While your Mac sleeps, Power Nap will automatically:

- Download software updates from the App Store.

- Get the latest mail, notes, reminders, messages, calendar events, contact information, Photo Stream photos, and other iCloud updates.

- Make periodic Time Machine backups.

- Synchronize iCloud documents.

To turn on Power Nap, choose > System Preferences > Energy Saver > Battery pane > "Enable Power Nap while on battery power". For plugged-in Macs, you can configure Power Nap independently in the Power Adapter pane.

Power Nap works only on Macs that have flash memory, including the MacBook Air (late 2010 or newer), MacBook (2015 or newer), MacBook Pro with Retina display, iMac (late 2012 or newer), and Mac Pro (late 2013 or newer). If you have a compatible Mac but don't see Power Nap settings, you may have to update your firmware (> App Store).

Power Nap works whether your Mac is plugged into a power outlet or is using battery power (draining little power). Power Nap refreshes the data on your Mac silently; no fans or lights come on and the display remains dark (but the drive, processor, and networking hardware are all active).

Time Machine

Time Machine

Eventually your drive will fail catastrophically, taking your data with it. Or you (or someone) will delete important files irretrievably. Time Machine protects your files by backing them up periodically and automatically to an external drive, a network drive, or another internal drive. (Apple also sells Time Capsule (*apple.com/timecapsule*), a wireless drive that works seamlessly with Time Machine.) Time Machine remembers past versions of your files that you can go "back in time" to recover. By default, Time Machine keeps hourly backups for the past 24 hours, daily backups for the past month, and weekly backups until your backup drive is full. You can back up multiple Macs onto the same backup drive; each Mac's backup is stored in a separate folder on that drive. You can't back up to a CD or the startup drive.

You can exclude unnecessary files and folders from Time Machine backups to reduce the space needed on the backup drive. To configure backups, you use the Time Machine preferences panel. To restore backups, you use the Time Machine application. You can optionally encrypt backups.

To set up Time Machine: Connect or mount the backup drive. Choose > System Preferences > Time Machine > Select Backup Disk. In the window listing available drives, select the drive that you want to use for backups, and then click Use Disk. If necessary, move the Time Machine slider to On. For security, select "Encrypt backups". For quick access to Time Machine, turn on the Time Machine menu 🕐.

Tip: You can designate multiple backup locations and then switch among them. This feature lets you make separate backups at, say, home and work.

To exclude items from backup: Choose ⬛ > System Preferences > Time Machine > Options. Click (+) or (–) to add or remove excluded items in the list. Choose whether to be warned when Time Machine starts replacing old backups with new ones because your backup drive is full.

To check the status of Time Machine backups: Choose ⬛ > System Preferences > Time Machine, or choose 🕐 > Open Time Machine Preferences. Backup status appears in the Time Machine panel (if a backup is in progress, a progress bar appears). The first backup takes a long time. After that, backups are fast because only the changes ("deltas") to the original backup are recorded.

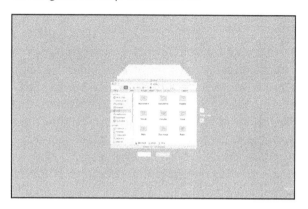

To restore a backed-up file: Open the drive or folder to restore. Choose Applications > Time Machine, or choose 🕐 > Enter Time Machine. The Time Machine interface replaces the desktop. To navigate to the past version of the file that you want to restore, click the backward or forward arrows; click along the timeline on the right edge of the screen; or click the title bar of the window version that you want to see. Select the item that you want to restore, and then click Restore. Time Machine restores backups to their original location in Finder. If you open Time Machine when a Spotlight search window is active, you can browse backward through the search results.

Target Disk Mode

Target disk mode turns one Mac (the target computer) into an external drive for another (the host computer). It's the fastest way to bulk-copy data and useful for transferring files from laptop to desktop or old Mac to new Mac. Each Mac must have a FireWire or Thunderbolt jack. You need a 6-pin FireWire 400 cable (older Macs), a 9-pin FireWire 800 cable, or a Thunderbolt cable (newer Macs).

To use target disk mode: Connect the target and host computers with a FireWire/Thunderbolt cable. On the target, choose > System Preferences > Startup Disk > Target Disk Mode, and then click Restart. After the target restarts, the target's drive will appear on the host's desktop, labeled with a FireWire icon or Thunderbolt icon . After you finish copying files from target to host, eject the target drive normally from the host desktop, and then restart the target.

To use target disk mode (the old way): Disconnect all FireWire devices from the target and host computers. Turn off the target computer (if it's a laptop, keep it plugged in). The host computer needn't be turned off. Connect the computers with a FireWire/Thunderbolt cable. Start the target computer and immediately press and hold down the T key until the FireWire icon or Thunderbolt icon appears. The target's drive will appear on the host's desktop. After you finish copying files from target to host, eject the target drive normally from the host desktop, and then restart the target. This method is quicker because you don't have to open System Preferences and works when the host Mac can't start on its own.

Switching from Windows

The following glossary lists Microsoft Windows terms and features and their OS X equivalents. Features with no OS X counterparts are marked N/A (Not Applicable).

Windows	OS X
About *Program* (Help menu)	About *Program* (Application menu)
Accessibility	Accessibility preferences
Accounts	Users & Groups preferences
Active Desktop	Dashboard
Add Hardware	N/A
Add or Remove Programs	Drag-and-drop installation
Address Book	Contacts
Administrative Tools	Utilities folder
Adobe Reader/Acrobat	Preview
Aero Peek	Exposé
Aero Snap	N/A
Aero Shake	N/A
All Programs	Applications folder
Alt key	Option key
Alt+Tab	Command+Tab

Windows	OS X
Automatic Updates	App Store
AutoPlay	CDs & DVDs preferences
Backspace key	Delete key
Backup and Restore	Time Machine
BIOS	Firmware
BitLocker	FileVault
Blue screen of death	Spinning beachball of death
Bluetooth Devices	Bluetooth preferences
Briefcase	N/A
Calculator	Calculator
Calendar	Calendar
Camera and Scanner Wizard	Photos and Image Capture
Character Map	Keyboard Viewer and Characters panel
Clipboard	Clipboard
Close	Close
Color Management	ColorSync Utility
Command Prompt	Terminal
Computer folder	Computer folder

Windows	OS X
Computer Management	Utilities folder
Contacts	Contacts
Context menu	Shortcut menu
Control Panel	System Preferences
Ctrl key	Command key, usually
Ctrl+Alt+Delete	Option+Command+Esc or Apple menu
Cut, copy, and paste	Cut, copy, and paste
Date and Time	Date & Time preferences
Default Programs	Open With
Delete key	Forward Delete key
Desktop	Desktop
Desktop Background	Desktop preferences
Desktop Gadgets	Widgets
Desktop Slideshow	Desktop preferences
Device Manager	System Information
Devices and Printers	Sidebar
Directories	Folders
Disk Defragmenter	N/A (automated)
Display	Displays preferences
DOS Prompt	Terminal
Drive letters	Drive names
Ease of Access Center	Accessibility preferences
Eject	Eject key ⏏
End Task	Force Quit
Exit	Quit
Explorer	Finder
Favorites	Sidebar
Fax/Fax and Scan	Fax
Firewall	Firewall

Windows	OS X
Folder Options	Finder > Preferences
Folders	Folders
Fonts	Font Book
FTP	Finder > Go > Connect to Server
Gadgets	Widgets
Games	Game Center
Getting Started	N/A
Help and Support	Finder > Help
Hibernate	Sleep
HomeGroup	Family Sharing
Indexing Options	Spotlight
Internet Explorer	Safari
Internet Options	Safari > Preferences
Jump lists	Dock Exposé and Stacks
Keyboard	Keyboard preferences
Libraries	Smart folders
Logon and logoff	Login and logout
Mail	Mail
Maps	Maps
Maximize	Zoom and Full-Screen Apps
Menu bars	Menu bar
Messenger/Messaging	Messages
Modern/Metro apps	Widgets
Microsoft ID	Apple ID
Microsoft Security Essentials	N/A
Microsoft OneDrive	iCloud or iCloud Drive
Minimize	Minimize
Mouse	Mouse preferences
Movie Maker	iMovie

Windows	OS X	Windows	OS X
MSN Messenger	Messages	Power Options	Energy Saver preferences
Music	iTunes		
"My" folders	Home folder	PowerShell	AppleScript
My Network Places	Sidebar	Previous versions	Auto Save and Versions
Network and Sharing Center	Network preferences	Print Screen	Grab
Network Connections	Network preferences	Printers and Faxes	Printers & Scanners
Network Neighborhood	Sidebar	Program	Application or app
		Program Files	Applications folder
Network Setup Wizard	Network preferences > "Assist me"	Programs and Features	Drag-and-drop installation
Notepad	TextEdit	Properties	Info
Notification area	Menu extras (status menus)	Reader	Preview
		Recycle Bin	Trash
OneDrive	iCloud or iCloud Drive	Region and Language	Language & Region preferences
Options	Preferences		
Outlook (calendar)	Calendar	Remote Assistance	Screen sharing
Outlook (email)	Mail	Remote Desktop	Apple Remote Desktop (sold separately)
Outlook Express	Mail		
Parental Controls	Parental Controls	Restore	Startup options
Path	Path	Ribbon	N/A
People	Mail	Right-click menu	Shortcut menu
Path separator: backslash (\)	Path separator: forward slash (/)	Run command	Terminal
		Safe mode	Startup options
Performance Rating	N/A	ScanDisk	Disk Utility
Personal folder	Home folder	Scanners and Cameras	Photos and Image Capture
Personalization	General and Desktop & Screen Saver preferences	Scheduled Tasks	Terminal `launchd` command
Phone and Modem	Network preferences (dial-up connections)	Scrap file	Scrap file
		Screen Saver	Desktop & Screen Saver
Photos/Photo Gallery	Photos and Image Capture		
		Search	Spotlight
Picture and Fax Viewer	Preview	Shadow copy	Auto Save and Versions

Windows	OS X	Windows	OS X
Shortcut menu	Shortcut menu	Video	iTunes
Shortcuts	Aliases	Weather	Widgets
Show Desktop	Exposé	Window Color	N/A
Sidebar	Dashboard	Windows Action Center	N/A
Skype	FaceTime and Messages	Windows Explorer	Finder
Snipping Tool	Grab	Windows Firewall	Firewall
Sound Recorder	GarageBand	Windows folder	System folder
Sounds	Sound preferences	Windows Live ID	Apple ID
Sounds and Audio Devices	Sound preferences	Windows Live Mail	Mail
Speech	Dictation & Speech preferences	Windows Live Messenger	Messages
Speech Recognition	Dictation & Speech preferences	Windows Live Movie Maker	iMovie
Stand By	Sleep	Windows Live Photo Gallery	Photos and Image Capture
Start menu or Start screen	Dock	Windows logo key	Command key
Startup folder	Login Items	Windows Mail	Mail
Sticky Notes	Stickies	Windows Media Center	Apple TV (sold separately)
Sync Center	iCloud	Windows Media Player	DVD Player, iTunes, and QuickTime Player
System	Apple menu , System Information, Sharing preferences, and App Store	Windows Messenger	Messages
		Windows Mobility Center	Accessibility preferences
System Information	System Information	Windows Photo Viewer	Preview
System Restore	Startup options		
System tray	Menu extras (status menus)	Windows Search	Spotlight
		Windows Security Center	N/A
Task Manager	Activity Monitor		
Taskbar	Dock	Windows Store	Mac App Store
Taskbar and Start Menu	Dock preferences	Windows Update	App Store
		WordPad	TextEdit
Trackpad	Trackpad preferences	ZIP files	ZIP files
User Accounts	Users & Groups preferences		

Keyboard Shortcuts

Keyboard shortcuts involve the modifier keys and other keys. On laptop keyboards, you may have to press the Fn key in combination with the function keys, depending on your setting for > System Preferences > Keyboard > Keyboard pane > "Use all F1, F2, etc. keys as standard function keys".

To change a modifier key: Choose > System Preferences > Keyboard > Keyboard pane > Modifier Keys. Choose an action from the popup menu next to the modifier key that you want to change. To return the keys to their original settings, click Restore Defaults. For a list of the symbols used for modifier and other keys, see "Menus" on page 22.

To change keyboard shortcuts: Choose > System Preferences > Keyboard > Shortcuts pane. Click a shortcut category in the list on the left. In the list on the right, use the checkboxes to toggle shortcuts. To assign or change keyboard shortcuts, click a shortcut's name and press Return (or double-click to the right of a shortcut's name), and then type the new keystroke (on laptop keyboards, you may have to hold down the Fn key when you assign the new shortcut). To add or remove custom shortcuts, click the App Shortcuts category, and then click (+) or (−). To return the shortcuts to their original settings, click Restore Defaults.

To see keyboard-shortcut conflicts: Choose > System Preferences > Keyboard > Shortcuts pane. A yellow warning triangle next to a shortcut category or a keyboard shortcut denotes a conflict.

Accessibility

To	Press
Show Accessibility controls	Option+Command+F5
Toggle zoom	Option+Command+8
Zoom in	Option+Command+=
Zoom out	Option+Command+-
Toggle smooth images	Option+Command+\
Toggle white-on-black (invert colors)	Ctrl+Option+Command+8
Increase contrast	Ctrl+Option+Command+.
Decrease contrast	Ctrl+Option+Command+,
Toggle Sticky Keys	Shift five times
Toggle Mouse Keys	Option five times
Toggle VoiceOver	Command+F5

Apple Menu

To	Press
Sleep	Option+Command+Eject ⏏
Restart	Ctrl+Command+Eject ⏏
Force-restart	Ctrl+Command+Power ⏻
Shut down	Ctrl+Option+Command+Eject ⏏
Open the Sleep/Restart/Shut Down dialog box	Ctrl+Eject ⏏
Log out after a cancelable delay	Shift+Command+Q
Log out immediately	Shift+Option+Command+Q
Change "About This Mac" to "System Information" and suppress cancelable delays	Hold down Option, and then click

Dashboard

To	Press
Toggle the dashboard	F12 (or F4 on older Macs)
Refresh the current widget	Command+R
Close or delete the current widget	Option

Dialog Boxes

To	Press
Move to the next/previous control	Tab/Shift+Tab
Move to the next control when a text field is selected	Ctrl+Tab
Move to the next item in a list, tab group, or menu	Arrow keys
Move sliders	Arrow keys
Move to a control next to the text field	Ctrl+arrow keys
Select the highlighted menu item	Spacebar
Click the default (highlighted) button	Return or Enter
Click "Don't Save"	Command+D
Click "Replace"	Command+R
Click the Cancel button	Esc or Command+dot (.)
Close a menu without choosing an item	Esc

Dock

To	Press
Toggle dock hiding	Option+Command+D
Activate the dock	Ctrl+F3 (press the arrow keys to select an icon, and then press Return to open it)
Resize the dock	Drag the divider
Reposition the dock	Shift-drag the divider
Open the dock shortcut menu	Right-click the divider
Open a dock icon's shortcut menu	Right-click the dock icon
See a program's open windows	Right-click (or click-and-hold) the program's dock icon
Add an open program to the dock	Right-click (or click-and-hold) the program's dock icon, and then choose Options > Keep In Dock
See an item in Finder	Command-click the item's dock icon
Switch to another program and hide the active one	Option-click the program's dock icon
Switch to another program and hide all other programs	Option-Command-click the program's dock icon
Quit a program	Right-click (or click-and-hold) the program's dock icon, and then choose Quit
Force-quit a program	Option-right-click (or Option-click-and-hold) the program's dock icon, and then choose Force Quit
Force-open a document in a program	Option-Command-drag the document's icon to the program's dock icon
To drag an actual item (rather than its dock alias)	Shift-drag its dock icon
To freeze dock icons while dragging an item to the dock	Command-drag

Finder

To	Press
Open Preferences window	Command+, (comma)
Hide Finder windows	Command+H
Hide other programs	Option+Command+H
Open a new Finder window	Command+N
Create a new folder	Shift+Command+N
Create a new smart folder	Option+Command+N

To	Press
Open a new tab	Command+T
Open the selected item(s)	Command+O
Change "Open With" to "Always Open With"	Option+File menu
Close the active Finder window	Shift+Command+W
Close all Finder windows	Option+Command+W
Close the active tab	Command+W
Open Info window	Command+I
Open Inspector window	Option+Command+I
Open Summary Info window	Ctrl+Command+I
Duplicate the selected item(s)	Command+D
Alias the selected item(s)	Command+L
Preview the selected item in Quick Look	Spacebar or Command+Y
Invoke full-screen Quick Look	Option+Spacebar or Option+Command+Y
Show a slideshow of the selected items	Option+Command+Y
Show the original of an alias	Command+R
Add the selected item(s) to the sidebar	Ctrl+Command+T
Toggle to the sidebar	Option+Command+S
Add the selected item(s) to Favorites	Shift+Command+T
Move the selected item to the Trash	Command+Delete
Eject a CD or DVD	Command+E
Find (Spotlight window)	Command+F
Find by name (Spotlight window)	Shift+Command+F
Undo	Command+Z
Cut/Copy/Paste	Command+X/C/V
Select All	Command+A
Deselect All	Option+Command+A
View as Icons/List/Columns/Cover Flow	Command+1/2/3/4
Change "Clean Up Selection" to "Clean Up" and "Arrange By" to "Sort By"	Option+View menu
Toggle the toolbar	Option+Command+T
Toggle the View Options panel	Command+J
Go back	Command+[
Go forward	Command+]

To	Press
Open the parent (enclosing) folder	Command+↑
Open the parent (enclosing) folder in a new window	Ctrl+Command+↑
Open the All My Files folder	Shift+Command+F
Open the Documents folder	Shift+Command+O
Open the Desktop folder	Shift+Command+D
Open the Downloads folder	Option+Command+L
Open the home folder	Shift+Command+H
Open the Library folder	Option+Window menu > Library
Open the Computer folder	Shift+Command+C
Open the AirDrop folder	Shift+Command+R
Open the Network folder	Shift+Command+K
Open the Applications folder	Shift+Command+A
Open the Utilities folder	Shift+Command+U
Open a specified folder by typing its path	Shift+Command+G
Connect to a server	Command+K
Minimize the active window	Command+M
Minimize all Finder windows	Option+Command+M
Change "Minimize" and "Zoom" to "Minimize All" and "Zoom All"	Option+Window menu
Cycle forward or backward through Finder windows	Command+` or Shift+Command+`
Cycle forward or backward through tabs	Ctrl+Tab or Shift+Ctrl+Tab
Toggle to tab bar	Shift+Command+T
Open the Help search box	Shift+Command+?

Folder Navigation & Icons

To	Press
Expand/collapse the selected folder (list view)	→/← or click ▶/▼
Expand/collapse the selected folder and its subfolders (list view)	Option+→/← or Option-click ▶/▼
Open a folder in a new window	Command-double-click

To	Press
Open a folder in a new window, closing the current window	Option-double-click
Open the parent folder	Command+↑
Open the parent folder in a new window, closing the current window	Option+Command+↑
Open the selected folder in a new window, closing the current window	Option+Command+↓
Activate the desktop	Shift+Command+↑
Go back/forward a folder	Command+[and Command+]
Align icons	Command-drag
Copy (instead of move) an item	Option-drag
Move (instead of copy) an item	Command-drag
Alias an item	Option-Command-drag
Copy an item	Select it, press Command+C, open the new location, and then press Command+V
Open the selected icon	Command+↓ or Command+O
Select the next icon	Arrow keys
Select an icon by name	The first letter of its name
Select the next/previous icon	Tab/Shift+Tab
Add to the selection (icon view)	Shift-click
Select adjacent icons (list view)	Shift-click
Select or deselect nonadjacent icons	Command-click
Select the icon's name (to rename)	Return
Preview the selected icon in Quick Look	Spacebar or Command+Y
Invoke full-screen Quick Look	Option+Spacebar or Option+Command+Y
Show a slideshow of the selected icons	Option+Command+Y
Open a spring-loaded folder immediately during a drag	Spacebar
Scroll in any direction (list or icon view)	Option-Command-drag
Move an item from or to the System folder	Command-drag

Frozen Programs

To	Press
Stop a process	Command+dot (.)
Force quit	Option+Command+Esc
Turn off your computer	Power button ⏻
Force shut down	Shift+Option+Command+Power ⏻
Force restart	Ctrl+Command+Power ⏻

Menus

To	Press
Activate the menu bar	Ctrl+F2
Activate menu extras (status menus) in the menu bar	Ctrl+F8
Rearrange or remove menu extras	Command-drag them
Reveal extra information or commands when you click a status menu	Option
Navigate to a menu command	Arrow keys (or type a command name in the selected menu)
Choose a menu command	Return
Close a menu without choosing a command	Esc

Mouse Keys

To	Press
Turn Mouse Keys on or off	Option five times
Move up	8 (8)
Move down	2 (K)
Move left	4 (U)
Move right	6 (O)
Move diagonally	1 (J), 3 (L), 7 (7), 9 (9)
Click the mouse button	5 (I)
Hold down the mouse button	0 (M)
Release the mouse button	Dot (.)

Programs, Exposé, Spaces & Launchpad

To	Press
Activate the next/previous program	Command+Tab/Shift+Command+Tab
Cycle forward/backward through windows of the active program	Command+~/Shift+Command+~
Hide a program	Command+H, or Command+Tab to the program and then press H
Hide other programs	Option+Command+H
Open program preferences	Command+, (comma)
Switch to new program and hide the active one	Option-click a dock icon
Show all windows (Exposé/Mission Control)	F3 or Control+↑
Show all open windows of the active program (Exposé/Mission Control)	Control+↓
Show the desktop (Exposé/Mission Control)	F11
Show all spaces (Spaces/Mission Control)	F3 or Control+↑
Switch to a space (Spaces)	Ctrl+1/2/3/4/… or Ctrl+←/→
Show Launchpad	F4 (on newer Macs)
Quit a program	Command+Q, or Command+Tab to the program and then press Q

Screenshots

To	Press
Capture the whole screen as a file	Shift+Command+3
Capture the whole screen to the clipboard	Ctrl+Shift+Command+3
Capture part of the screen as a file	Shift+Command+4, and then drag
Capture part of the screen to the clipboard	Ctrl+Shift+Command+4, and then drag
Capture a screen object	Shift+Command+4, and then press Spacebar

Spotlight

To	Press
Open the Spotlight window	Command+Spacebar
Open a search window in Finder	Option+Command+Spacebar
Open the selected item in the results list	Return
Open the top hit in the results list	Command+Return
Jump to the previous/next category in the results list	Command+↑/↓
Display the selected item in Finder	Command-double-click the item
Get information about the selected item in the results list	Command+I
Clear the search text	Esc (once)
Cancel the search	Esc (twice)

Startup

To	Press
Start normally	Power button ⏻
Start from a CD/DVD	Press and hold C
Start from the first drive/partition	Press and hold D
Reset the laptop display	Press and hold R
Start from a network server	Press and hold N
Start in target disk mode	Press and hold T
Start from an external drive/disc	Press and hold Shift+Option+Command+Delete
Start in 64-bit mode	Press and hold 6 and 4
Prevent automatic login	Press and hold Left-Shift when the spinning progress indicator appears
Suppress Login Items and Finder windows at login	Press and hold Shift after clicking the Log In button
Select a startup drive/partition	Press and hold Option
Force-boot OS X	Press and hold Command+X
Eject a CD/DVD at startup	Press and hold Left mouse button
Start in safe mode (safe boot)	Press and hold Shift at startup until the login screen indicates a safe boot

To	Press
Troubleshoot at startup	Press and hold Command+S (single-user command-line), Command+V (verbose Unix console), or Option+Command+P+R (reset NVRAM/Parameter RAM)
Reinstall (recover) OS X	Press and hold Command+R

Trash

To	Press
Move the selected item to the Trash	Command+Delete
Put back the selected item from the Trash	Command+Delete
Empty the Trash	Shift+Command+Delete
Empty the Trash without confirmation	Shift+Option+Command+Delete

Windows

To	Press
Activate the next/previous window	Ctrl+F4/Shift+Ctrl+F4
Activate window drawer	Option+Command+`
Cycle forward/backward through windows in the active program	Command+~/Shift+Command+~
Minimize the active window	Command+M or double-click the title bar
Minimize all windows	Option+Command+M
Move a window without activating it	Command-drag its title bar
Close/minimize/enlarge all windows in the active program	Option-click the close/minimize/zoom button
Scroll quickly	Click-and-hold in the scrollbar
Temporarily switch between "Scroll to here" and "Jump to page"	Option-click in the scrollbar
Activate the toolbar	Ctrl+F5
Rearrange toolbar controls	Command-drag
Activate a floating window	Ctrl+F6
Activate the sidebar or drawer	Option+Command+~
Jump to a folder in the folder path	Right-click (Command-click) the window title

Index

A

About This Mac 31
Accessibility preferences 53
accounts. *See also* OS X
  about 9
  Apple ID 10, 13
  creating 9
  deleting 11
  editing 11
  forgotten passwords 13
  guest 11
  logging in 12
  logging out 14
  login items 11
  master password 11
  names 10
  parental controls 166
  passwords 10, 167
  switching users 13
  types of 9
active window 26, 104
Activity Monitor 111
ad-hoc networks 158
AirDrop 148
AirPlay 153
AirPort Utility 111
aliases 88
Alt key 16
Aperture 3
Apple ID 10, 13
Apple menu 23
AppleScript 128
Apple TV 125, 153
application menus 23
applications (apps). *See* programs

Applications folder 76, 77, 111
App Store 102, 111, 170
Audio MIDI Setup 112
Automator 112
Auto Save 107

B

backups (Time Machine) 172
battery menu 65
Bluetooth
  about 54
  Bluetooth File Exchange 112
  Bluetooth Firmware Update 112
  pairing devices 54
  preferences 54
  sharing 151
Boot Camp Assistant 112

C

Calculator 113
Calendar 113
CDs & DVDs
  burning 98
  preferences 54
  sharing 151
Chess 114
clipboard 29
clock 55
colors
  calibrating display 63
  ColorSync Utility 114
  DigitalColor Meter 115
  OS X color scheme 67
ColorSync Utility 114
Command key 16
Console 114

Contacts 114
Continuity 154
Control key 16
copying content 29
cutting content 29

D

dashboard 42
Date & Time preferences 55
desktop
  about 33
  background (wallpaper) 56
Desktop & Screen Saver preferences 56
dialog boxes 28
dial-up connections 158
Dictation & Speech preferences 58
Dictionary 115
DigitalColor Meter 115
disk image (.dmg file) 102
Disk Utility 116
displays
  AirPlay mirroring 153
  color calibration 63
  configuring 62
  multiple 63
  resolution 62
  screen sharing 150
  screenshots 118
Displays preferences 62
dock 34
documents. *See* files
Documents & Data 69
drives 75, 99
  encrypting 163
Drop Box folder 146
DVD Player 116

E

eject key **16**
Energy Saver preferences **64**
escape key **16**
Ethernet networks **144, 157**
Exposé **38**
extensions, filename **109**
Extensions preferences **66**

F

Facebook **71, 153, 168**
FaceTime **116**
Family Sharing **68**
fast user switching **13**
faxing **139**
files. *See also* **Finder**; *See also* **folders**
　about **75**
　aliases **88**
　backups (Time Machine) **172**
　compressing (ZIP) **92**
　copying **86**
　deleting **92**
　disk image (.dmg file) **102**
　documents
　　about **101**
　　associating with programs **109**
　　auto-saving **107**
　　faxing **139**
　　opening **109**
　　previous versions **107**
　　printing **134, 136, 138**
　　saving **107**
　extensions, filename **109**
　Finder **78**
　moving **86**
　naming **86**
　paths **2, 81**
　proxy icon **81**
　searching for (Spotlight) **93**
　sharing **146**
　tags **89**
FileVault **163**
Finder. *See also* **files**; *See also* **folders**
　about **78**
　folder views **82**
　navigating in **81**
　path bar **81**
　preview pane **85**
　proxy icon **81**
　Quick Look **85**
　sidebar **80**
　status bar **81**
　tabs **78**
　toolbar **80**

Find My Mac **70**
firewall **162**
Firewall **162**
FireWire networks **145**
Fn key **16**
folders. *See also* **files**; *See also* **Finder**
　about **75**
　aliases **88**
　backups (Time Machine) **172**
　compressing (ZIP) **92**
　copying **86**
　creating **86**
　deleting **92**
　Finder **78**
　home **76**
　moving **86**
　naming **86**
　paths **2, 81**
　proxy icon **81**
　searching for (Spotlight) **93**
　sharing **146**
　smart **97**
　spring-loaded **88**
　system **76**
　tags **89**
　views **82**
Font Book **140**
fonts **140**
full-screen programs **44**
function keys **16**

G

Game Center **117**
GarageBand **118**
Gatekeeper **102**
General preferences **67**
Gmail accounts **71**
Grab **118**
Grapher **119**
guest account **11**

H

Handoff **154**
help, OS X **31**
hiding programs **46**
home folder **76**

I

iBooks **119**
iCloud **68**
iCloud Drive **68**
iCloud Keychain **70**
iCloud Photo Library **124**
iCloud Photo Sharing **124**

icons
　about **25**
　alert badge **34**
　folder views **82**
　organizing desktop **46**
Image Capture **120**
iMessage **122**
iMovie **120**
Info window **28**
installing OS X **7**
Internet Accounts preferences **71**
internet connection sharing **159**
iPhoto **3**
ISP (internet service provider) **155**
iTunes **120**

J

Java **106, 121**

K

keyboard
　about **16**
　configuring **17**
　international **18**
　shortcuts **16, 22, 179–190**
　special characters **19**
　types of keys **16**
keyboard shortcuts **16, 22, 179–190**
Keychain Access **164**

L

Language & Region preferences **72**
Launchpad **105**
Library folder **76**
Location Services **168**
locking **14**
login items **11**

M

Mac OS X. *See* **OS X**
Macs. *See also* **OS X**
　About This Mac **31**
　drives **75, 99**
　installing OS X **7**
　locating missing **70**
　locking **14**
　OS X system requirements **7**
　restarting **14**
　security and privacy **161–168**
　shutting down **14**
　sleeping **14, 64**
　starting (booting) OS X **8**
　startup drive **8, 99**
　system information **31**

transferring files and settings 123
Mail 121
malware 102
Maps 122
master password 11
menu bar 22
menu extras 23
menus
about 22
Apple menu 23
application menus 23
battery 65
choosing commands via keyboard 24
configuring 24
menu bar 22
menu extras 23
shortcut (right-click) menus 23
sound 73
Messages 122
metadata 29
Migration Assistant 123
Mission Control 45
modifier keys 16–32
mouse
about 19
configuring 20
gestures 19
scrolling 19
multitouch gestures 21
My Photo Stream 69

N

networks. *See also* **sharing**
about 143
backups over (Time Capsule) 172
connections
ad-hoc networks 158
broadband 157
Continuity and Handoff 154
dial-up 158
Ethernet 157
internet sharing 159
locations 159
order of 156
PPPoE 157
troubleshooting wireless 157
VPN 160
wireless 157
diagnostics 157
firewall 162
hub 144
router 144, 159
types of
Ethernet 144

FireWire 145
wireless 145
Network Utility 123
Notes 123
Notification Center 47

O

Open dialog box 109
OpenType fonts 140
Option key 16
OS X. *See also* **accounts;** *See also* **Macs**
about 1
About This Mac 31
backups (Time Machine) 172
color scheme 67
default settings 2
drives 75, 99
encryption 163
help 31
installing 7
keyboard shortcuts 16, 179–190
Location Services 168
logging in 12
logging out 14
new features 2
paths 2, 81
security and privacy 161–168
services 130
software updates 170
starting (booting) 8
startup drive 8, 99
switching from Windows 175–178
system
date and time 55
folders 76
information 31
preferences 51–74
requirements 7
transferring files and settings 123
virtual memory 167

P

Parental Controls 166
Password Assistant 167
passwords
account 10
forgotten 13
generating secure 167
pasting content 29
paths 2, 81
Photo Booth 124
Photos 124
pixels 62
PostScript fonts 140

Power Nap 64, 171
PPPoE connections 157
Preferences dialog box 32
Preview 125
printing
background 133
controlling printouts 138
CUPS system 137
documents 136
printers
drivers 134
setting up 134
sharing 139
print queue 138
print spooler 138
programs
about 101
active 104
App Store 102, 111, 170
associating documents with 109
disk image (.dmg file) 102
frozen (crashed) 104
full-screen 44
Gatekeeper 102
hiding 46
installing 102
Launchpad 105
malware 102
opening 104
quitting 104
removing (uninstalling) 102
resuming 106
running older 106
software updates 170
switching 104
proxy icon 81
Public folder 146

Q

Quick Look 85
QuickTime Player 126

R

RAID Utility 127
Reminders 127
restarting 14
Resume 106
right-click menus 23
root directory 2–32
router 144, 159

S

Safari 127
Save dialog box 107

screen saver 56
screen sharing 150
screenshots 118
Script Editor 128
scrolling 19, 27
Security & Privacy preferences 168
services 130
Shared Folder 149
share sheets 152
sharing. *See also* networks
    AirDrop 148
    any-folder sharing 146
    Bluetooth sharing 151
    CDs & DVDs 151
    Continuity 154
    Drop Box folder 146
    files and folders 146
    Handoff 154
    internet connections 159
    Public folder 146
    screen sharing 150
    Shared folder 149
    share sheets 152
    with Windows users 148
shortcut menus 23
shutting down 14
sidebar, Finder 80
sleeping 14, 64
smart folders 97
Sound preferences 73
spaces 40
Spotlight search 93
spring-loaded folders 88
stacks 37
status bar 81
Stickies 128
System folder 76
system folders 76
System Information 31
System Preferences 51

T

tags, file and folder 89
Target Disk Mode 174
Terminal 129
TextEdit 129
Time Machine 172
title bar 26
toolbars 24, 80
trackpad
    about 21
    common tasks 21

    configuring 22
    multitouch gestures 21
Trash 92
TrueType fonts 140
Twitter 71, 152, 168

U

updates, software 170
user accounts. *See* accounts
Users folder 76
Utilities folder 111

V

Versions 107
virtual memory 167
viruses 102
VoiceOver 53
volume 73
VPN connections 160

W

widgets 42
windows. *See also* Finder
    about 26
    activating 26
    closing 26
    dock 34
    Exposé 38
    Finder 78
    full screen 26, 44
    Info 28
    Mission Control 45
    moving 26
    resizing 26
    scrolling 27
    spaces 40
    stacks 37
    title bar 26
Windows, Microsoft
    Boot Camp Assistant 112
    sharing with 148
    switching to OS X from 175–178
wireless networks 145, 157

X

X11 106

Y

Yahoo accounts 71

Z

ZIP archives 92

www.ingramcontent.com/pod-product-compliance
Lightning Source LLC
Chambersburg PA
CBHW080411060326
40689CB00019B/4207